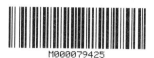

A Practical Approach to
CYBERPARENTING
and OPEN COMMUNICATION

Calm. Balance. Talk.

MANDY MAJORS

To
my husband, Matt,
my teenage daughter, and
my tween son

Always know I love you.
No matter what.

ISBN-13 978-0-692-83318-6

Italics in Scripture quotations reflect the author's added emphasis.

Details in some anecdotes and stories have been changed to protect the identities of the persons involved.

Editing and copyediting: Refiner's Touch Editorial Services
Interior design and typesetting: Finer Points Productions
Proofreading: Jeff Masching

Printed in the United States of America

2017—First Edition

21 20 19 18 17 / 5 4 3 2 1

CONTENTS

ACKNOWLEDGMENTS

To God, my foundation—this is Your book. You relentlessly spoke to my heart about writing it, even when I kept ignoring Your voice. Thank You for waking me up. If You hadn't opened my eyes, I'd still be a clueless, complacent mom. I'm grateful You called me to face my fears, get out of the boat, and walk on the water with You. Thank You for promising to be with me in every storm that lies ahead. Thank You for taking my mess of bad decisions and turning my life around. You've changed my curses into blessings. Thank You for the gift of open communication and Your Spirit to guide me on this parenting journey.

To my hubby and best friend, Matt—without your love and encouragement, I never would have finished this book! I know this season has been difficult for our family, and our schedule has been stretched to the limit. I recognize each and every sacrifice you've made and the amazing role you played from start to finish. Every time I wanted to quit, you pushed me toward the finish line. You made me tackle the overwhelming fear and kept me moving forward. You are the most humble and integrity-filled person I've ever known. Marrying you was the best decision I've ever made in my life (apart from deciding to follow Jesus). I love you so much!

To my daughter and son, who have been so patient during this crazy process. Thank you for allowing me to share some of our private conversations with other families. I cherish our talk time. You both teach me every day how to be a better mom and love me even when I don't get it right. I promise you won't have to eat cereal for dinner as much now. I'm ready for our regular bedtime talks and a lot of football playing in the front yard. I'm gonna be eatin' up the yards again. I love you!

To my mom—thank you for all the sacrifices you've made for me. Most important, you engrained in me the value of hard work. Often when I wanted to quit, I thought about you working three jobs to support me when I was a child. You'll never know how much I appreciate all you've done. I love you!

To my dad—I'm so happy and thankful for new beginnings, forgiveness, healing, and restoration. I love you!

To my grandma and grandpa—thank you for taking me to church when I was a child. Even though I didn't understand then about Jesus, I get it now. You set this path in motion.

To my mother-in-law and father-in-law—thank you for raising the most incredible man I've ever known on this earth. And for accepting me as your own from day one. I love you both!

Kim—I'm not sure how I've lived my whole life without you as a friend. You share truth directly and honestly, but it's wrapped in love and grace. You help keep me focused and grounded. Thank you for all the "difficult" conversations where you set me straight when I was being selfish. I love you dearly, sweet friend!

To the nextTalk team—Kim, Megan, Stacey, and Holly—God brought us together for such a time as this. I can't thank you enough for the countless hours you've spent volunteering, researching, praying, and working to launch this nonprofit. Each of you teaches me so much. I'm blessed to have a front-row seat to the many ways God is using your unique talents in our organization.

To my mentors, heads-up mamas, and others in my tribe—what would I do without you? You've helped me navigate some pretty tough storms. The wise advice you've given me is sprinkled throughout this book. Thank you for always remaining calm when I was a blubbering mess on the phone. I'm beyond blessed to learn from you and have you in my village.

To my publishing team—Jennifer, Angie, Chrissy, and Jeff—thank you for all your hard work, incredible skill, creativity, and expert guidance on this journey. Jennifer, thanks for the countless hours of editing and prayer you invested in this book. You made my message shine! You've taught this newbie author so much. Thank you for being patient with me and all my comma splices!

Introduction

You're Not Alone

Several years ago, my nine-year-old daughter asked a highly sexualized question that blindsided me. Another child had seen something pornographic online and shared the details with her. It went way beyond the birds and bees.

My daughter's innocent question turned my world upside down and opened my eyes to the far-reaching impact of the digital world. I suddenly realized how vulnerable my elementary-age child was to its lure. My girl, who didn't even have her own phone at the time, was learning about adult issues way too soon, and I was clueless, completely unaware of what she was being exposed to. Her question was a wake-up call for me. At that moment, all my naive beliefs about parenting changed forever. That's when this crazy cyberparenting journey began.

If you've picked up this book because your child found pornography online or heard about a sexual act, you're not alone. We're all struggling in this rapidly changing digital era. I like the word *cyberparenting* because so many of the issues we face today are the direct result of our kids' early online exposure. We're the first generation of parents whose elementary-age children can have unlimited access to all kinds of "screens," social media, apps, video games, and other digital media. Children between the ages of eight and twelve—*tweens*—are especially vulnerable.

We're in uncharted territory. The accelerated growth of technology has changed the entire landscape of parenting, and our kids are connecting to the world at younger ages than ever before. A shift has taken place that we must recognize. What our children are encountering digitally raises complicated questions at earlier ages, and many of us feel inadequate to address them. Pornography, cyberstrangers, pedophiles, sexuality, transgender, cyberbullying, terrorism, and live-streamed violence are just a few examples. There seems to be no end to the complex issues we have to figure out how to parent.

In the aftermath of that lightbulb moment with my daughter, I was overwhelmed with feelings of anger, bitterness, and fear. I was done. Exhausted. Defeated. SMH (shake my head). After tucking her in bed at night, I'd break down in tears because I saw her innocence slipping away. I felt helpless, crippled with fear over how to respond to the tough issues she was facing. I was desperate for answers but didn't know where to find them. I felt as if I'd been punched in the gut.

If you feel that way too, don't give up. Don't believe the lie that you're the only one who doesn't have this parenting thing figured out. No one has all the answers. In fact, I doubt that even the most experienced parenting expert could solve every issue we encounter in this complicated, screen-crazed world.

Let's be real. I'm no parenting expert. I'm just a mom like you. In. The. Trenches. Day. After. Day.

I've walked my daughter through the tween years into her teens, and my son is now a tween. I'm writing in real time. Along the way I've learned some valuable lessons, but I'm still struggling to figure out what parenting in this digital era is all about. Trust me, I don't always get it right. Like the time I told my son that a thong bikini was like dental floss for a butt. (Oh yes, I did!)

Even though I sometimes say the wrong things, at least I'm in the game now. I'm no longer parenting from the sidelines with my head in the sand. I'm awake and alert, and I'm even learning to laugh at myself.

The Discovery That Changed Everything

In the pages that follow, I'll share candid conversations I've had with my kids, and some of the cyberparenting lessons I've learned so far. I hope you'll find the insights encouraging and helpful for your own family.

First, we'll dive into the details of my story in part 1. I'll invite you along on my emotional roller-coaster ride when my daughter's question forced me to face the truth that I was a clueless and complacent parent. When I finally clued in, I didn't know where to turn for answers. In my search for solutions, I made so many mistakes. I felt like a failure. But that search eventually led to a deeper walk with God and an amazing discovery that transformed my life and my approach to parenting. What did I discover? Open communication. That's what this book is about.

If you're thinking about serious, sit-on-the-couch family meetings, you're in for a *big* surprise. Open communication isn't about family meetings or formal discussions; it's about creating a healthy, ongoing dialogue between you and your child. It's a practical, proactive, on-the-go approach to parenting.

What if you could have casual, spur-of-the-moment conversations with your kids about the real-life issues they're dealing with? Imagine talking about pornography in the car on the way home from school or the grocery store. Or discussing sex around your kitchen table while you and your kids are eating breakfast. No topic is off limits.

Here's another surprise for you: open communication isn't just for tweens and teens. It's essential for tackling the tough issues our children face *at any age*. We need to start building trust and open communication with them as early as possible so that when the tween years hit, we'll already be their safe place, their go-to source for information. I can't overemphasize how important this is.

I don't want to give you the wrong impression. Open communication isn't as simple as it may sound. It's a complicated process that takes time and hard work to achieve. When you adopt this approach to parenting, you'll encounter plenty of rough and stormy seas. But you're not alone. We're on this journey together!

In part 2, I'll unpack four key steps that will help you pave the path for open communication in your family:

1. Looking in the mirror
2. Strengthening communication in your marriage

3. Becoming your tween's safe place
4. Discovering the value of a tribe

These steps completely transformed how I communicate with my family, and I hope this will happen for you as well. In these chapters, we'll take off our masks and get real with ourselves and God. We'll also get real about the way we communicate in our marriages—patterns we often repeat with our kids. After working on our marriages, we'll explore how to build open communication with our children. In the process, we'll learn that cyberparenting is about relationship more than rules and restrictions. Finally, we'll talk about the value of an inner circle of friends to encourage us on this journey.

In part 3 we'll address some of the most difficult topics parents encounter today, and I'll share how I handle them with my own children. I'll also offer some ideas for conversation starters and taking things deeper after the discussion gets going. This is where we'll put the principles of open communication into practice. I designed the topic list for easy access so that when you're dealing with a specific issue and need a refresher, you can quickly flip to that chapter.

Here are some of the questions we'll be addressing:

- When should my tween get a phone?
- How am I going to monitor my kids' screen time and teach them about social media?
- How do I talk about sex with my tween?
- How do I address terrorism and mass shootings?
- What do I say to my children about homosexuality, bisexuality, and transgender?
- How and when should I warn my child about pornography?
- How do I even begin a conversation about masturbation with my tween?
- What should I say about suicide?
- How in the world do I talk about all these difficult topics with my kids without causing confusion or fear?

Do some of these issues scare you? They scare me, too. But you know what frightens me even more? Not being a safe place for my kids to openly discuss all the issues they're exposed to online. I'm not okay with that.

We can't afford to ignore or avoid these complicated topics. We have to face them head-on for the sake of our children, and open communication is the key.

Your Family, Your Choice

As we talk about how to address real-life issues with our children, we may not always see eye to eye. But we can still work together to find common ground. Please don't let disagreements over how you and I approach specific topics stop you from talking with your kids about them. They need a safe place to go with their questions, and I want it to be you, not a peer, an online search, or a stranger.

You'll hear me say "Your family, your choice" throughout the book. That's because I strongly believe that you're the expert on your child, and I respect your right to make decisions for your family. We can respect each other's opinions and beliefs, right? Our children need to see that even when we disagree, we can mutually respect one another. Let's be good role models.

Before we go any further, I need to lay all my cards on the table. My approach to parenting is guided by my faith in Jesus. The Bible is my moral compass for determining right and wrong, and I rely on the Holy Spirit to direct my parenting decisions. I can't separate my faith from my parenting because it's engrained in who I am. It's also reflected in this book.

If you believe in Jesus like I do, I pray this book will take your faith deeper. Before this journey, I knew Jesus. But now I know-know Him. My relationship with Him is built on open communication. He speaks to me through His Word, and I listen. He keeps me balanced and on point when I feel like going into crazy-mom mode or a judgmental frenzy. He's the key to my parenting approach, and I want to share that with you.

But please hear my heart on this: I didn't write this book exclusively for Jesus followers. Regardless of your faith background, I hope this book will help you build open communication with your family and find cyber-parenting solutions. We're all struggling with the shift that has taken place in parenting and how this digital world is influencing our children. I want to bring us all together for an open, honest dialogue about the issues we're facing as we raise the next generation.

If you've had a bad experience with the church or hypocritical Christians, I'd encourage you to stay open minded. Don't let the hypocrites drive you away from God. I know this story all too well. I left the church as a teen because of hurtful experiences and hypocrites. But that's not Jesus. I pray you meet the real Jesus and His radical love in the pages of this book—the same Jesus who called out the hypocritical religious people of His day.

No matter your views on the issues, you are welcome here. Cyberparenting is too hard to go it alone. To keep our kids safe, we need everyone at the table, engaged in the conversation.

That includes dads. Though I'm speaking primarily to moms in this book, dads are an indispensable part of the team. They can benefit from the information as well. I'd encourage you to discuss the topics in part 3 with your spouse and brainstorm ways to approach them with your kids. Work together to develop open communication in your family, and include your husband in the conversations you have with your children. Your partnership is an invaluable resource.

If you're divorced and your ex still plays an important role in your kids' lives, share with him the ideas in this book. If you're a single parent whose spouse is no longer in the picture, you need others to encourage you. I know the demands of single parenting are challenging enough without adding cyberparenting to the mix. I was raised by a single mom, so I know firsthand that single parents are the hardest-working people on the planet. Keep doing what you do!

Learning Together

When my daughter first asked me that sexualized question, I had no idea what to do or where to turn for advice. In sheer desperation, I started a moms' group in my Texas community because I craved support and encouragement. I needed to know I wasn't the only parent who had missed something.

And guess what? I discovered I wasn't alone.

Neither are you.

Approximately twenty moms, whose kids were six years of age or older, came to that first meeting. Since then our group has expanded at a blistering speed. We also started an online group that has rapidly grown to more than a thousand moms from all over the world. No advertisements. Just word of mouth.

As I write this, we're planning our fourth semester of meeting face-to-face. We're testing satellite groups in other states, and we've started a nonprofit organization called nextTalk to make our resources available to everyone (not just moms). We've even been featured on television and radio.

At nextTalk, we offer a supportive community where everyone can come together to encourage and equip one another. Our goal is to unite parents, grandparents, school officials, and community leaders so we can …

- share information on rapidly changing social media, apps, sex, and everything in between;
- effectively develop open communication in our families; and
- learn how to safely raise the next generation in this digital world.

We always want to prepare for the "next talk" with our children so we can answer any question they have. (I hope you'll join in the nextTalk conversation via Facebook, Twitter, and Instagram.)

As parents in this digital era, we're uniquely qualified to help one another navigate the stormy seas of cyberparenting. We don't need to face the storms alone. We're all in the same boat. On the same side. Each of us has valuable experiences and insights to contribute to the conversation. So let's get to it!

Can you tell we have a lot to talk about?

PART 1

My Cyberparenting Journey

1

The Question That Sent Me over the Edge

The alarm clock sounded again. I rolled over in bed to check the time, but our fluffy dog blocked my view. Half asleep, I sat up, realizing I had hit the snooze button too many times. My husband had left early for a meeting at work, and I was running late getting the kids ready for school.

I jumped out of bed and rushed down the hall to my daughter's room, almost tripping over my son's football.

Barely awake, I stood in her closet frantically rummaging through purple-and-teal hangers to find something clean for her to wear. At the same time I was thinking about the day's weather forecast. *Warm enough for shorts? Or maybe jeans?*

Then I heard a meek little voice. Still lying in bed, my sweet nine-year-old daughter asked a question I wasn't prepared for. I'm not going to share the exact question. The conversations I have with my children are private and confidential. But here's what she gave me permission to tell you: the question was about sex—and it was detailed.

It was the "Where do babies come from?" question *on steroids.*

I didn't even know "this sex thing" existed until my college years. Not kidding. I would've given anything at that moment for the "Where do babies come from?" question.

Did I mention we were already running late?

So there I was, standing in her closet. Speechless. Frozen, actually. At that point I didn't even care what she was wearing to school. She couldn't see my face, but I felt as if my heart had stopped. This was MY. BABY. GIRL.

My thoughts spiraled. *Why is my fourth grader asking questions about sex? How does she know something this detailed?*

I collected myself and took a deep breath, praying silently for God to give me the right words. Then I stepped out of her closet, kissed my daughter's forehead, and sat down next to her on the bed. I looked her in the eyes and calmly said, "Thank you so much for asking me. That's what I want you to do when you don't know what something means. But we're going to be late for school, so could we talk later?"

She yawned and stretched before softly replying, "Yeah, sure."

At least I had bought myself some time.

Racing to the kitchen, I frantically packed lunches and poured cereal for breakfast. My mind was frozen yet racing at the same time. I couldn't even speak.

After a quick breakfast, I herded the kids toward the door, grabbing backpacks, water bottles, and lunch boxes on the way.

The entire drive to school, my thoughts were spinning like a tornado. But I put on my "normal" face as we prayed for our day. (I like to call it the *parent filter*: calm on the outside; a mess on the inside.)

Every day on the way to school, we pray for four things:

1. Safety—*Lord, please protect my kids and bring us all home safe and sound.*
2. Health—*Thank You, Lord, for our health, and please keep us healthy.*
3. Light—*Help us be kind to everyone, Lord. Let them see You in us by the way we love.*
4. Others—*this prayer varies depending on the needs we know about.*

I prayed for my kids' safety and thanked God for our health. Then I prayed that my children would be a light in their school by being kind and loving to everyone—except that crazy kid who told my daughter about that sex thing. UGH! I was going to have to dig deep to practice loving others in this scenario.

I was praying in autopilot, but my mind was racing with questions. Isn't the sex talk supposed to happen when kids are actually old enough to have sex? Like late middle school? *Oh no,* I suddenly thought. *What has my daughter been exposed to?*

As my kids prayed for some of their friends to wrap up our prayer time, I was thankful they couldn't see my inner turmoil.

"She's Just a Baby!"

After I dropped my kids off at the school entrance, the meltdown began. Tears began streaming down my face the moment they got out of the car, and my vision blurred. My head ached as if I'd been hit with a baseball bat.

Next to the public elementary school in our town is a small community center, so I pulled into that parking lot and went into full-blown, adult-temper-tantrum mode, sobbing and pounding my fists against the steering wheel. Yes, I was being a little dramatic (in retrospect).

What had I missed?

Our family appeared to be picture perfect—at least on the outside. We went to church *every* weekend. We read Scripture together and prayed before *every* meal. We even prayed before bedtime *every* night as a family. My daughter hadn't missed more than five weekends of church in her entire life. She'd asked Jesus to live in her heart when she was seven and asked to be baptized at eight. What in the world could my husband and I have done differently?

When I finally arrived home, I decided to call a friend—a mentor, really—who is a retired middle-school assistant principal. I remembered that when my daughter was in third grade, this friend told me I should be talking with my child about sex. I actually laughed at her. I seriously thought she was hysterical. After all, my kid was just a baby.

When my friend answered the phone, I recounted the morning's events, and she gently replied, "Take a deep breath, Mandy. This is normal. Children talk about these things very early."

If I'd been her, I would've said, "I told you so." But she had way more grace and understanding than I would have. (That's the kind of friend you need mentoring you on this parenting journey. File that away for our talk about your tribe in chapter 7.)

When I picked up my kids from school, all I wanted to do was act as if the morning had never happened. I wanted to sweep my daughter's question under the rug. Life is easier living in denial, right?

But my wise friend had given me some solid advice, so I knew I needed to address the question instead of ignoring it. It would send my child an important message: *You're important to me, and your questions are important to me. It's okay to be curious and want information.*

When we got home, I decided to wait for the right moment to address the issue. We followed our typical afternoon routine and talked about normal stuff for a couple of hours. Then I saw an opening as I was making dinner.

While my daughter was doing homework at our kitchen island, I casually said, "Hey, you know that question you asked this morning? I've been thinking about it because it's important to me. I'm so glad you asked me, and I want to give you the information. When you hear a new word or phrase, will you always ask me first?"

"Sure," she replied. "But who else am I going to ask?"

"Well, lots of kids ask other kids. Or they search online. Sometimes kids don't realize they're giving out wrong information, and if you search online, you may see inappropriate pictures or videos. It's your job to protect your mind from bad things. Your mind and body are your responsibility because I won't always be there to help you make decisions."

"Yeah, I know."

"The question you asked was very specific. I'm hesitant to give you all the details right now because you might not be able to get them out of your mind, and I want to talk to you about some other things first. But I want this to be your decision. I can tell you right now exactly what it is. Or do you want to wait?" (Again, #parentfilter.)

There was a long pause. *Did she even hear me? Hello?*

Finally she said, "I don't think I'm ready. Let's wait, because I want to protect my mind from this."

"I think that's a very grown-up decision," I replied. "I'm proud of you. If kids start talking about this again, will you please tell me? When you're ready to know all the details, I'm here with the answers. I want to be your source of information."

As we continued our discussion, I began asking my daughter open-ended questions to find out what she knew and didn't know about this topic. I tried to ask one question at a time so she didn't feel like I was interrogating her.

"Tell me about the conversation you had with these kids," I ventured. "What did they say? How did they describe what you asked me about?"

It was my first attempt to have a difficult conversation about sex with my tween. It wasn't great, but it was a start. A little move in the right direction.

By asking those open-ended questions, I discovered that another child had watched an inappropriate video online. From the graphic nature of the discussion, I assumed it was porn.

I still don't know the child's name. At the time I was so overwhelmed by what was happening in my family and so focused on making sure I was parenting my own child right, I didn't have the energy to track down the other child and figure out that story. Besides, was it really any of my business?

A Flood of Toxic Emotions

I would love to tell y'all that I handled this situation with grace. You know, that I acted like a real parent, focused on identifying how this happened, and then came up with effective solutions.

The truth? For months I did so many things wrong, though I didn't realize it at the time. Now I can see my mistakes clearly.

I distinctly remember pulling the covers over my head like a two-year-old one night and agreeing to come out only if I could watch all the DVR recordings of *The Real Housewives*. I desperately needed an escape from reality. (Oh, the irony.)

My emotions were downright raw for several weeks. I became bitter and cried a lot. My husband and I would talk behind closed doors after the kids went to bed, and I'd find myself saying things like, "This whole world is going to hell. I hate everything and everyone. Do these crazy parents know what their kids are telling other kids? What is happening to our society?"

There was profanity. And a whole lot of anger.

My husband and I became bitter toward other parents. Bitter over the condition of our world. We wanted to blame everyone else instead of looking at ourselves in the mirror.

Ouch.

This was a red-flag moment for me. Bitterness is a slippery slope. If I wasn't careful, hate would follow. I wanted to point the finger at everyone else because it deflected from my own mistakes.

Looking back I see more clearly what was happening. But in the moment, my feelings were in control (and out of control).

Bitterness. Anger. Hatred. I was feeling it all. I had a right to feel this way, didn't I?

Jennifer Rothschild says, "Feelings are powerful, but they don't always represent truth."[1]

That's a life lesson right there. We can get in trouble when we let our feelings guide our decisions instead of truth.

I was in a dark place at the time. I'm not proud of my initial gut response. I was judgmental and jaded. I found myself arguing with people just to make a point.

My behavior wasn't acceptable to God. He wanted me to look deep within my own life and heart instead of pointing the finger and blaming others. Why was I hesitant to talk with my children about difficult topics? What had I done wrong as a parent? What could I do differently?

God didn't want me to be bitter toward anyone. He wanted me to listen and learn. He was trying to teach me, but I wasn't ready to listen.

Bubble-Wrapping My Kids

Once I worked through my bitterness, I began talking with other moms about what was happening. I shared with them how I thought I'd missed something as a parent. I felt especially clueless about technology and early online exposure to adult topics.

I think deep down I wanted other moms to tell me I was overreacting. The opposite happened. They started sharing their own scary stories with me.

I discovered I wasn't the only mom lost in this cyberparenting nightmare, becoming bitter toward the world instead of looking at myself in the mirror. I wasn't the only one living in fear and feeling defeated.

One day I got a call from a precious friend who was heartbroken to find porn on her eight-year-old's iPad. He had been introduced to it at a sleepover.

I heard from another mom who was frantic because the only way a boy would communicate with her teenage daughter was through Snapchat, where photos automatically disappear. Was he asking for nude pictures? Why the secrecy? (Side note: I learned that when kids exchange nude photos, they share them with one another. It's called *trading cards.*)

One mom told me she had learned how to use Instagram and Twitter but then discovered multiple accounts and inappropriate pictures her teenage son had posted. (He was impersonating others online.)

I even heard from a mom who said that a child had been exposed to porn from another boy's cell phone during a weekend kids' church service.

Then there were national news reports of cyberstrangers killing children they met through social media.

The calls and stories kept coming. God was trying to show me something, but I was paralyzed with fear. I let it creep into my heart instead of choosing a teachable path. I wanted to bubble-wrap my children and never let them leave our home. My husband, Matt, and I began discussing private-school and homeschooling options.

But guess what? As I talked to other moms, I realized that the online world is *everywhere.* And so is the danger. Private school, public school, homeschool, or any other kind of school—it makes no difference. In the end, Matt and I realized we were simply running from the problem.

At the time, though, we were in a panic over what we were hearing. In a knee-jerk response, we said no to all technology. I made my tween pull back from social situations and tried to control her every move. Because of my fear, a wall went up between us. Communication wasn't happening.

She began pushing back. Bubble-wrapping my child resulted in rebellion instead of relationship.

Fear had crippled me and was preventing me from doing the things I needed to do as a parent. I had let fear control my decisions. And in the process, I had damaged my relationship with my daughter.

Nothing was working.

I felt defeated.

Looking for Answers in All the Wrong Places

I so wished I could blame someone else for what happened to my child, but I finally realized that bitterness was the wrong response. I also realized that fear wasn't the answer, because it was creating more tension in our relationship.

So I did what any reasonable parent would do: I turned to social media for answers. (Insert sarcasm.) Immediately I was bombarded with all sorts of conflicting and ever-changing "expert" opinions on how to be the perfect parent:

- "Don't monitor your child too much, or you'll be labeled a helicopter parent." (You know, a parent who hovers around their kids and swoops in to protect or rescue them.)
- "You need to respect your child's privacy."
- "If you don't do anything, you're negligent."
- "Maybe you're a lawn-mower or snowplow parent. You mow over or snowplow all the obstacles in your child's way so that he or she doesn't have to face anything difficult."

As I was trying to process all these divergent opinions and was feeling pressured to pick a side, it dawned on me that my tween was experiencing the same thing. She was also being bombarded with online opinions about who she should be and what she should believe in. She was being pressured to pick a side too. If I was stressed trying to figure it all out, how was my tween processing these things?

On top of that, all the opinions made me feel judged. I was confused and exhausted. I couldn't sleep—and I *need* my sleep!

I was done. Ready to throw in the towel. Hands in the air. SMH.

I felt worthless. Like the worst parent in the world. Other parents seemed to have this thing figured out, but I still didn't have a clue.

Let me be real with you. There are days when my son plays Minecraft and Super Mario all day. And days when he eats cheese balls for breakfast. There are even days when my kids and I don't get out of our pajamas. (I used present tense because these things *still* happen.)

If you have days like this too, it's okay. You are *not* a failure. Don't believe the lie that you aren't a good parent. Or that everyone else has this parenting thing figured out except you. No! We are *not* going to feel defeated because our kids eat cheese balls for breakfast.

Give yourself a break. You're doing a great job. How do I know? Because you're so determined to find answers on this parenting journey, you picked up this book.

Welcome to a community of parents where you don't have to be perfect. In fact, in our nextTalk community, we love it when parents share stories of real-life struggles instead of putting on a mask of perfection. Perfection is overrated and fake. I know that whenever I try to make everything look perfect on the outside, it usually means I'm falling apart on the inside. I'm done. It's time to be real.

We're all struggling. We're tired. Beat down. We need sleep! The question is, will we admit it, or are we going to keep posting perfect little pictures on social media and pretending everything is fine?

Well, it ain't. Life is messy. Parenting stirs up all kinds of yuck, chaos, and tangled webs.

I know. You probably feel like Debbie Downer right now. Doom and gloom. But hang with me, sister. I can't wait to share the hope with you. I'm already praying you're going to be empowered and will go to bed saying, "Boom, I got this!"

2

What Did I Miss?

I slowly wrapped up my pity party and worked my way toward adulting again. I didn't want to, but kicking and screaming I went. It was time to grow up and face it. I decided I was no longer going to parent out of bitterness, fear, or feelings of defeat.

It was much easier to blame others for my child's exposure to sexually explicit online content. But I knew I had to move beyond blame and look to God for help. He was calling me to a deeper understanding of the situation. To find out what I had missed. But I had to know Him better to figure out my next step.

So I turned off social media and began searching the Bible for answers. If my tween asked, "Why do we believe that way, Mom?" I wanted my answer to reflect God's truth.

While I was immersing myself in Scripture, I also scoured parenting books for practical advice and encouragement. I found Dannah Gresh's books *Six Ways to Keep the "Little" in Your Girl* and *Six Ways to Keep the "Good" in Your Boy* incredibly helpful. Dannah explained that the most important time to instill foundational values in our kids is during their tween years (from eight through twelve years of age). Another lightbulb moment! I realized that instead of coasting, I should have been preparing my daughter for her teen years, which would officially begin at thirteen. But I'd been asleep at the wheel. It was crystal clear that I had a lot of catching up to do.

As I was digging for answers in the Bible and flipping through parenting books, I was also talking with other parents about what it meant to be in our children's online world. We were all struggling to understand the major paradigm shift that was taking place in this digital era. We were the first generation of parents who had elementary-age kids with the world in their pockets. Technology was changing so rapidly that one tidal wave after another washed over us before we could catch our breath.

I couldn't believe how much had changed since the first desktop computers appeared on store shelves. Here are just a handful of examples:

- Devices are much smaller now, which means that kids not only carry them in their pockets, but inappropriate content can easily be hidden. Bad images can pop up on the tiny screens without anyone else seeing them.
- Kids today not only have 24/7 online access, but social media and an endless assortment of apps connect them instantly to friends as well as strangers. Even elementary-age children have their own devices, with access to social media.
- With 24/7 online access, kids have a mountain of information at their fingertips, including content on adult topics like sexuality, pornography, and suicide. Even young children can access content that used to be "for adults only." This mature content leads them to ask parents very detailed questions or search for answers online.
- For kids today, the digital world isn't just about information; it's about relationships. They watch online videos or exchange comments with total strangers and immediately feel a deep emotional connection. Cyberstrangers pose unique dangers that parents are often unaware of. On a daily basis, children are exposed to sex traffickers, terrorist recruiters, pedophiles, and cyberbullies on social media. These strangers can gain access to our children's personal information and even determine their exact location if safeguards are turned off. They take advantage of quickly formed relationships to establish trust, influence our children's beliefs, and even groom them to meet in person.

The more I learned, the more I realized that parenting tech-savvy kids in the twenty-first century requires a different approach. Parents today have to deal with challenges our own parents never faced and wouldn't understand. I couldn't call my mom and ask her, "How did you handle Snapchat when I was a kid?" She wouldn't have had a clue.

I didn't have a clue either. I still didn't know what I had missed. But I realized I'd just have to blaze my own trail to find the answers. It was time to develop a new set of parenting skills to respond to these challenges. I didn't need to be afraid of technology or ban it; I needed to teach my kids how to use it safely and wisely. So I made a conscious decision to teach myself how to effectively parent it. I sensed that if I wanted to get this right, it would require more than just monitoring my kids' online activity, setting guidelines, and enforcing restrictions. I'd have to make relationship building my top priority.

The Perfect Storm

Without realizing it, I had become a cyberparent overnight. My baby girl was growing up faster than I realized, and I was clueless about the impact technology was having on her formative years—and on our relationship. She was being exposed to things I never dreamed she—or I—would have to deal with at such a young age.

All these changes were happening simultaneously, and somehow I had failed to see them. It was a perfect storm.

What was I doing wrong?

The answers slowly started coming as I continued reading my Bible and Dannah's books, met with other parents, and kept praying that God would reveal what I was missing so I could fix it.

One morning I was sitting on my back porch reading my Bible, praying, and listening to the birds chirping. Every day I read a proverb corresponding to the date, and the passage that morning—the first day of the month—was Proverbs 1.

When I came to verse 32, I automatically read it aloud: "Fools are destroyed by their own complacency." As soon as the words tumbled out of my mouth, I thought, *That's why I've been missing all the clues.*

I knew I was onto something. I dug a little deeper and found Proverbs

31:27 (NIV): "[A wife of noble character] watches over the affairs of her household and does not eat the bread of idleness."

That was it. I'd become idle. Lazy. Complacent.

I looked up the word *complacency* in the dictionary, and here's what it said:

> A feeling of being satisfied with how things are and not wanting to try to make them better: a complacent feeling or condition; self-satisfaction especially when accompanied by unawareness of actual dangers or deficiencies.[1]

The truth hit me like a bolt of lightning. I'd been clueless, completely unaware of the dangers surrounding my child and my deficiencies as a parent. It wasn't intentional. I didn't know what I was supposed to be doing during my daughter's elementary years.

Once my kids had reached the age where they could bathe themselves and brush their own teeth—let freedom ring!—I thought I'd finally entered the easiest stage of parenting where I got to sit back and coast. Take a breather before the teenage hormones kicked in.

Looking back now, I realize I should've been talking more with my tween, investing in our relationship, and building a safe place for her to ask questions. Why hadn't I spent those early elementary years developing good communication with her? Why hadn't I done a better job preparing myself and my child for the challenges that lay ahead? Well, for one thing, I didn't even realize I had a tween!

I thought about how intentional my husband and I had been in our relationship. After we married, we purposely waited five years to have our first child. We invested that time in our relationship so parenting wouldn't tear us apart. We poured ourselves into each other, talked about everything, and worked on our bucket list before diving into the deep waters of raising kids. We took time to prepare ourselves for parenting because we knew it would require a great sacrifice on both our parts.

We started off strong as parents, with all the best intentions for our family, but somewhere along the line, we veered off track. We didn't become complacent on purpose. It was an accident, an oversight. We were so worn out from the infant and preschool stages of parenting, we simply wanted to catch our breath. We were busy. Enticed by other things. Building careers. Moving cross-country. Saving for college. Giving our kids everything we didn't have.

I realize now that we were in survival mode, parenting on autopilot. Our priorities had been misplaced. Our kids didn't need more stuff or fancy vacations or a perfect house. They needed us! Our time and guidance. I should have been pouring myself into our relationships, not prioritizing other things.

A perfect storm had been brewing all these years, and I had been blissfully unaware of it. I'd missed important warning signs along the way, and now I was caught in the middle of a hurricane. The ingredients were staring me in the face:

A nine-year-old in need of an engaged parent
to instill values and prepare her for the teenage years.

\+

A screen-crazed world exposing this tween
to adult issues way too early.

\+

A complacent parent, totally clueless that her baby girl
was growing up way too fast and had lots of questions
her mom wasn't equipped to answer.

=

One big mess.

Parenting disasters don't just happen overnight. They evolve over time as we make daily choices to coast rather than engage. To ignore issues instead of facing them. To sidestep our children's questions rather than figure out how to answer them. All too often we settle for complacency instead of rolling up our sleeves and doing the hard work of preparing our kids for life.

The band Casting Crowns wrote a song called "Slow Fade" that sums it up nicely:

> It's a slow fade when you give yourself away
> It's a slow fade when black and white have turned to gray
> Thoughts invade, choices are made, a price will be paid
> When you give yourself away
> People never crumble in a day
> Daddies never crumble in a day
> Families never crumble in a day[2]

Slow fade = Complacency.

It's true! "Families never crumble in a day." It's a day-after-day choice to live in complacency. A day-after-day choice to sweep issues under the rug instead of facing them.

That one little question about sex? Just ignore it.

That one little cuss word in a text message? Ignore it.

I'm too tired to deal with the drama. I don't know how to address it anyway.

Ignore. Ignore. Ignore.

I became complacent, and things spiraled out of control before I realized it.

Can you relate?

I can see now that I'd been slowly fading as a parent. One bad decision led to another. Then I reached the point of feeling defeated. I blamed God and other people for what happened with my tween, but my choices were the actual reason we landed there in the first place. Yet somehow I couldn't own up to my mistakes.

I didn't become complacent on purpose. But little by little I chose it.

That morning on my back porch as I read Proverbs and listened to the birds chirping, the light finally dawned. I had fallen into a trap. *Lord,* I prayed, *let me never be complacent again. Let me never think I have it all figured out and don't need to keep learning and growing.*

Lessons in the Garden

Dannah Gresh says that "complacency led to the first sin [in the garden of Eden]."[3] As I dug into that concept, God began showing me how the Genesis story related to my complacency as a parent.

Adam and Eve had a perfect life in the garden. No sin. No evil. No violence or death. No need for clothes. It was naked bliss. Innocence, peace, love, happiness. God had given them everything they needed. What more could they want?

Eve was satisfied, complacent. She didn't realize that evil was lurking in the shadows, waiting for the right moment to tempt her. Remember that complacency is "self-satisfaction especially when accompanied by unawareness of actual dangers or deficiencies."[4]

I had fallen into the very same trap. My husband and I were plugging along just fine. Life was great. We were healthy. Financially secure. American dream = garden of Eden.

But like Eve, I was satisfied with the way things were. I was so complacent in my comfort zone that I didn't see the danger lurking in the shadows. Yet all the time, Satan was "[prowling] around like a roaring lion, looking for someone to devour" (1 Peter 5:8). The Enemy was looking for the perfect opportunity to "steal and kill and destroy" (John 10:10).

God told Adam and Eve that they could eat fruit from any tree in the garden *except one*. Only one tree was off limits. And that one forbidden tree with its forbidden fruit enticed them.

Temptation came by way of a serpent. He was waiting for just the right moment to slither out of the shadows and manipulate Eve. Her complacency and blissful unawareness made her vulnerable to Satan's lies.

I was vulnerable too. Like Eve, I had been complacent when I should have been alert. Without warning, Satan slithered into my life and whispered his sugary-sweet lies into my ears. He convinced me that my family was picture perfect. But it was only a mask. In reality, we were ignoring issues we needed to face.

Notice that the serpent didn't say to Eve, "Eat this fruit, and you'll win the lottery." That would've been too obvious, appealing to her selfish desires. Instead, he tempted her with something good: becoming like God.

When Eve said she wasn't allowed to eat from the forbidden tree, Satan responded, "You won't die! … God knows that your eyes will be opened as soon as you eat it, and *you will be like God*, knowing both good and evil" (Genesis 3:4–5).

The serpent twisted God's clear guideline and manipulated Eve into believing that it was okay to break the rules. "Eat this, and you'll be like God."

Eve was probably thinking, *God wouldn't punish me for wanting to be like Him. I mean, isn't it a good thing I want to be like God?*

Do you see how quickly the situation shifted from complacency to manipulation? Eve let her guard down, and the Enemy pounced like a lion, distorting her view of God and convincing her that her desire to be like Him was more important than His guideline.

I have sympathy for Eve. I want to be like God too. I probably would have twisted the truth as well, rationalizing the choice to eat the forbidden fruit if I thought it would make me more like Him.

We're all vulnerable to Satan's cunning attempts to distort our view of God and His guidelines. God's rules are simple and clear-cut. This is the restriction. This is the boundary. If we know His heart, we understand that He only wants to protect us from harm and consequences. He's not trying to deprive us of good things. But Satan manipulates us into believing that God is the bad guy, and we end up convincing ourselves that it's okay to cross the line. We want what we can't have. Forbidden fruit.

I love what God says in Isaiah 55:8: "My thoughts are nothing like your thoughts.… And my ways are far beyond anything you could imagine." That day in the garden, Eve definitely wasn't thinking like God. If she had truly known His heart, she would have seen through Satan's manipulative scheme. Life in the garden was about relationship. Really knowing God and His ways. Listening to Him.

The best way to protect ourselves from that manipulative serpent and his twisted lies is to draw close to God—to see His loving heart and know who He really is. Listening to Him keeps us from becoming complacent on this parenting journey and helps us stay alert and aware.

There's something else I want to share with you. Immediately after Adam and Eve ate the forbidden fruit, "their eyes were opened, and they suddenly felt shame at their nakedness" (Genesis 3:7).

Do you feel like this? You're happily sailing through life. You think everything is fine, but you're totally unaware of the danger lurking in the background.

Then you have a lightbulb moment.

Your child sees porn. Sends a nude photo to a friend. Becomes suicidal. Has sex.

Innocence is gone, and your eyes are opened.

That's what happened with my daughter's question. My eyes were opened. My nakedness (complacency) was completely exposed. Reality slapped me *in the face.*

Did I miss important clues along the way? Did you?

Yes. But in our defense, cyberparenting blindsided us.

Eve was blindsided too. She had no advance warning about that serpent in the garden. So let's give ourselves some grace. We're awake now, and we need to face down the Enemy who is seeking to destroy our children.

Mama bear is about to come out. No one messes with our babies and gets away with it!

3

Game Changer

Danger was lurking in the shadows, waiting for the right moment to pounce. But complacency had lulled me to sleep. I had missed important clues along the way that would have alerted me to what my child was being exposed to.

I was wide awake now, but I had no idea what I should do. More than ever, I needed practical solutions, so I dug even deeper into God's Word, continued asking questions, and kept learning from other parents. I soaked up information like a sponge. Most important, I kept asking God to clearly show me what to do.

One day as I was sitting in the carpool line, I prayed something like this:

> *Please, Lord, I need help over here in real life. I don't understand all the confusing details in the Bible. I don't need to read about animals being saved on an ark. I need practical solutions from Your Word. I need concrete information and simple answers to difficult questions. I need wisdom and clarity. I know the world doesn't have it, because I checked social media. You are the answer. But I need You to show me what to do.*

I know God had to be texting "SMH" to Jesus. Because, seriously, who prays like that?

Me.

Step by step God led me down a path of understanding. He didn't sugarcoat the facts. He spoke directly to my heart, wrapping the truth in His love and peace. I began to see exactly what I had missed in my daughter's life. It became so clear to me.

The solution was amazingly simple: open communication.

The Bible says,

> You must commit yourselves wholeheartedly to these commands that I am giving you today. Repeat them again and again to your children. Talk about them when you are at home and when you are on the road, when you are going to bed and when you are getting up. (Deuteronomy 6:6–7)

That's what I had failed to do: talk about God's character and His ways with my kids at home and on the road, first thing in the morning, throughout the day, and at bedtime.

Sure, we read Scripture as a family, but I wasn't showing my daughter how it related to her world. We weren't communicating about relevant real-world things. We weren't talking about how God's Word related to her everyday life—protecting her heart and mind from bad images, helping her deal with cyberbullying, showing her how to choose friends wisely, teaching her online integrity, and so much more. I wasn't connecting the dots for her. I needed to get my head out of the sand and stop living in denial.

I wasn't giving my daughter practical solutions from God's Word because I didn't have them myself. It all boiled down to this: I hadn't been seeking God or listening to Him. I mean truly seeking Him with my whole heart, not just wearing a Christian bracelet or reading quotes on a meme about having faith.

If I wasn't seeking Him, how could I teach my children to seek Him?

God says, "Those who search will surely find me" (Proverbs 8:17), and "If you look for me wholeheartedly, you will find me" (Jeremiah 29:13). So I started seeking God like never before. Seeking Him with my whole heart. And He did not disappoint. Scripture came alive in a completely new and fresh way. It was no longer just words on a page. It meant *so much more*. It was changing everything.

On the Road and at Bedtime

Little by little, my tween and I started talking about God's Word and how it related to her world. Some of our most in-depth conversations took place when we were driving somewhere in the car. (They still do.)

One night when we were driving home from church, we had a detailed sex talk. I gripped the steering wheel and looked straight ahead. I was sweating like a beast and screaming inside, but I tried to stay calm. Remember the parent filter—calm on the outside; a mess on the inside?

My daughter was in the backseat trying to process what I was telling her. She was grossed out and said I needed to pull over so she could throw up. She wasn't joking; she was totally serious at the time. But we look back at that conversation now and laugh hysterically.

Another time when I was having trouble getting my tween to open up, I remembered some simple advice a mentor gave me many years ago: talk at bedtime. That's what it said in Deuteronomy 6:7, so I gave it a try. I crawled into bed with my daughter one night, and after we prayed together, I started asking questions.

JACKPOT! I found out more in five minutes than she had told me in a month—who had crushes at school, who was arguing, which boys were cute, and who kept dropping f-bombs.

Y'all, that advice worked so well, I started scheduling bedtime talks on my calendar. Then I'd have caffeine later in the day so I'd be able to stay awake for our talk time.

God knew. God knows. His Word has the answers to some of the most complex questions parents will ever encounter. But are we listening?

Open communication was a game changer for me. We could have informal chats throughout the day about whatever my kids were dealing with, and I could take advantage of these laid-back teachable moments to build trust in our relationships. I didn't have to carve out time in my busy schedule for a formal family meeting, a special retreat, or a book study. I could simply talk with my kids while I cooked dinner or drove them to school. The possibilities were endless.

Conversations with my kids included showing them how God's ways were relevant to their issues. But I began to realize that this approach could work for other parents, regardless of their faith. The basic principles could be adapted to any situation.

Open Communication Turned the Tide

The next discovery I made was Deuteronomy 23:5—"[God] turned the intended curse into a blessing because the Lord your God loves you." I'll never forget the day a friend texted this to me. It has become one of my favorite verses in the Bible because it opened my eyes to God's amazing ability to use bad things for good.

A similar verse appears at the end of Genesis, where the story of Joseph is told. The downward spiral began for Joseph when his brothers betrayed him and sold him into slavery in Egypt. There, Joseph became the servant of Potiphar, one of Pharaoh's officials. Sometime later, his master's wife falsely accused Joseph of rape, and he was thrown into prison for years. But Joseph remained faithful to God. I mean totally sold out to Him. God protected Joseph through it all, and when Joseph finally met up with his brothers again (begging Joseph for food), what do you think happened?

Joseph said to them, "You intended to harm me [curse], but God intended it all for good [blessing].... Don't be afraid. I will ... take care of you and your children" (50:20–21).

There it is again: curse ➡ blessing.

I'm not sure I could forgive my family for selling me into slavery and causing so much trouble in my life, but Joseph did. He suffered greatly because of his brothers' choices, yet God turned the curse into a blessing.

All the questions my tween was asking me, all the issues she and I were forced to confront, felt like curses:

- Exposure to porn in elementary school. Curse.
- Detailed sex questions in fourth grade. Curse.
- Pressure to have her own phone. Curse.
- Pressure to attend sexually charged concerts. Curse.

She was nine when this journey started. I call her fourth-grade year my hell year. It was. Lots of tears and confusion. It was so difficult to realize that my daughter was no longer a baby. Innocence gone.

But guess what? God turned those curses into a beautiful blessing. As my tween and I continued talking more openly, trust developed, and she began asking more questions.

Echoing Hosea 2:15, Jennifer Rothschild says, "God promises to [turn your] valley of trouble into a door of hope."[1]

A door of hope slowly opened in our family.

The tide turned.

It was a new day in our home.

When I'd pick up my daughter and her brother from school, she'd be quiet on the drive home. But as soon as we walked in the house, she'd pull me into a bedroom, shut the door, and say, "Mom, I heard a new word at school today. What does ______ mean?"

Then I'd calmly respond.

Open communication didn't happen overnight; it was a process. I had to prove that I was trustworthy. A safe place for her to ask tough questions.

One day she said, "I heard the f-word today. What does it mean?"

She didn't get in trouble for saying it, and I didn't freak out. I actually thanked her for asking and said it was exactly what I wanted her to do.

Then I replied, "It means 'forget you' or 'screw you' if someone gives you the middle finger. It's also a worldly, disrespectful, negative way to say the word *sex*. The world has taken a beautiful thing God intended for marriage and turned it into something dirty. It's a really bad word we don't use in our family."

Complete honesty with no anger, yelling, or shocked reactions changed the whole dynamic of our relationship. That's when an amazing relationship with my tween started to develop. Instead of being bitter toward others for exposing my child to sexual content, I was using it to build open communication. Rather than going to bed in tears, I'd think, *We totally rocked that today. What are you going to throw at us next, Satan? We're ready. We'll tackle it head-on.*

Today my daughter sees me as her safe place. She knows I won't yell no matter what she asks me. She knows she'll get the truth, and I won't broadcast our conversations on social media or tell others about them, except my husband. She understands that Mom and Dad have no secrets.

When I speak on stage in front of other parents, I ask her permission before I share a story about her. If she isn't comfortable with it, I don't share it outside the walls of our home. (That's why I also asked her permission before sharing any of our personal conversations in this book.)

With my son, confidentiality isn't an issue. He says, "Share everything. I want to be famous." Because he's so into popularity and being known, we continually talk about what's *really* important in life (and popularity isn't it).

It's all about building trust.

I'm no longer living in bitterness and fear, feeling like a defeated parent in a world full of change and uncertainty. I'm empowered and strong. I actually go to bed with courage and confidence. Good sleep is back!

I don't worry anymore about my daughter being exposed to something dangerous or inappropriate online and losing her innocence, because we talk about everything now, and I know she's hearing truth. Before I discovered open communication, I thought that by bubble-wrapping her, I could protect her from the world and safeguard her innocence. But that slimy serpent in the garden manipulated my thinking.

God finally showed me that facing the issues head-on and openly discussing them with my kids is the best way to protect their innocence.

I know from experience that God can turn every curse in my life into a blessing if I'm willing to seek Him and listen. He's taken all my parenting mistakes and the things I've missed as a mom, and He's using them for good. The fear is gone. I'm wide awake and on the lookout for that sly, manipulative serpent lurking in the darkness. The light is shining now. He may try to pounce on my family, but I know where to turn for help.

Game changer. Take that, Satan!

Since I started sharing my story with others, I've been receiving "blessing" calls on the phone. I still get calls from struggling parents who have just discovered our nextTalk community and are learning for the first time about open communication. But I also hear from parents who have been using open communication with their kids, and they tell me it's changing their whole family dynamic. Bitterness, fear, and anxiety are gone because they're facing issues head-on.

What are you dealing with right now? Have you found porn on your child's phone? Sext messages? Inappropriate pictures of your tween or a friend from your child's school? Have you discovered that your tween is the victim of cyberbullying—or even the bully?

Don't make the same mistakes I did and fall into a trap of bitterness, fear, and feelings of defeat. Breathe. Stay calm. Seek God with your whole heart. Psalm 34:18 says, "If your heart is broken, you'll find God right there; if you're kicked in the gut, he'll help you catch your breath" (MSG).

Dig into God's Word for the answers and listen to Him. Talk with your kids and teach them how God's ways relate to their world. It takes stepping out of your comfort zone, but He'll bless your obedience. He can open a door of hope for you and your children. He wants to turn curses into blessings and empower you to answer the tough questions your tweens are struggling with.

Are you ready to take the first step toward open communication?

PART 2

Paving the Path for Open Communication

4

Looking in the Mirror

The first step on the path to open communication is getting real with ourselves. Before we can talk openly and honestly with our children, we need to search deep within our hearts and examine our own faults and failures. Caution: it may sting.

Looking in the mirror instead of blaming the world requires courage. You may discover some uncomfortable truths about yourself in the process. But trust me, it's worth it. So buckle up, girl. Let's get to work.

So many times we share the beginning and the end of our stories but skip the gut-wrenching struggles. The daily grind. The place where perseverance resides. The arrow in the curse ➡ blessing diagram that represents grit and hard work.

The arrow is where we *face it*.

Remember when I talked about how Scripture became real for me and started jumping off the page? It was a breakthrough in my life. I want to share what I discovered so you can apply it to your own unique journey.

The curses in my life didn't transform into blessings overnight. It took a lot of prayer and hard work on my part (and still does). God didn't turn around our whole family dynamic without requiring me to change.

My inner journey (my arrow) included three important steps:

1. Face it.
2. Know God.
3. Listen to God.

As I worked through these steps, I became a better person. Peace filled. More stable and grounded. The journey has been far from easy. I'm still learning and growing. I've been stretched and tested, and you will be too. You may want to quit like I have. But you can't. Your kids' lives depend on it.

Face It

Social media and phone cameras weren't around when I was in high school and college. But if they had been, the shameful mistakes I worked so hard to hide from everyone would have been digitally engraved in stone. Please tell me I'm not alone.

As a college student, I carried around a lot of baggage and didn't make the best choices. On the outside I appeared to have it all together, but on the inside I was dying. The inner turmoil didn't match the picture I had painted for the world. It was a harmful pattern I repeated in my marriage and my approach to parenting.

Years ago in a sermon, my pastor defined *baggage* as

1. the pain we cause ourselves through our own choices;
2. the pain we suffer because of others' choices; and
3. the pain that's unexplainable and tragic (such as cancer and natural disasters).

Most of my pain fell into category 1 because of the choices I made. But some of that baggage came from my parents' divorce.

I was three when my parents separated, an only child. My single mom raised me and worked hard to provide, sometimes juggling three jobs. Because of her work schedule, communication wasn't high on the priority list. There wasn't enough time to address issues or have in-depth talks. We lived in survival mode. Money was a real issue, so we never had a stable home. We'd rent mobile homes, trailers, duplexes, and apartments, and we moved often (at least once a year; sometimes more).

My childhood might not have been perfect, but I knew I was loved. My mom and I have a special bond today because for years it was just the two of us.

My grandparents took me to church every weekend when I was a child, and I was baptized at the age of eight, though I didn't quite know what it meant. As I grew older, I started craving attention from guys. I left the church, and one bad decision led to another. Eventually I was filled with a lot of guilt and shame. As my choices spiraled into a mess, I felt defeated and hopeless.

I was the first in my family to attend and graduate college. But guess what? I was a runner. I basically went to college to escape the mess I created. I didn't want to face it. I wanted to start over.

But the new chapter didn't last long. Eventually I fell back into the same old patterns. Attention from guys. Lots of parties. Why couldn't I get it together?

Proverbs 14:12–13 says, "There's a way of life that looks harmless enough; look again—it leads straight to hell. Sure, those people appear to be having a good time, but all that laughter will end in heartbreak" (MSG).

Truth. One bad choice started a downward spiral, and a "slow fade" began to erode my hopeful new beginning. Pretty soon I could no longer recognize myself in the mirror.

It hurts to reflect on my past. But I've met a lot of women on this journey, and I know that many of you can relate. So many of us are walking around with baggage from our past. We have scars and bruises, but we hide them because we're ashamed. That shame prevents us from talking to our kids about important issues.

We know deep down that once we open up the conversation, our children may ask us difficult and uncomfortable questions like …

- "Did you ever do drugs or get drunk?"
- "Did you wait to have sex until you were married?"
- "Did you ever have an abortion?"
- "Did you ever have an eating disorder?"
- "Did you ever think about suicide?"

What is your dreaded "Did you …" question? (Perhaps like me, you have more than one.) When our children ask those questions, we really want to tell them, "I never did that." We want to be shining examples for them. But for most of us, that would be a lie.

What is the deepest, darkest secret you never want your children or anyone else to find out? Perhaps you think, *If my husband or kids knew this, they'd look at me differently. I couldn't bear the shame.* Or, *If my friends knew, they'd reject me.*

That's what you need to face, my friend. That's your personal demon. We all have them. Jesus said, "You will know the truth, and the truth will set you free" (John 8:32). But you can't be set free from the past unless you face your demons. Breaking the cycle starts right here, right now. (I'm sorry. I warned you it would sting.)

You may pray, *Lord, please don't let my kids make the same mistakes I did.* But guess what? If you don't talk to your kids about your past (and present) mistakes, it's likely they'll repeat the same pattern. If you want them to be honest with you about their mistakes, you have to own up to yours.

Open communication can't happen unless we're willing to look at ourselves in the mirror and *face it.* When I say "face it," that doesn't necessarily mean rushing off and telling your spouse and kids all your deepest, darkest secrets. It's a process. First you need to be real with yourself and God. (We'll dive into that later when we talk about what it means to know God.) Then after you've worked through some things, He'll reveal when and how much to share with your family.

So often we remain trapped in shame over the past because we don't want to face the truth. Instead of being honest, we hide behind a mask. Proverbs 28:13 (NIV) says, "Whoever conceals their sins does not prosper, but the one who confesses and renounces them finds mercy." Confessing and renouncing the mistakes of the past takes courage. It's messy. Yet if we want to find mercy and forgiveness, we have to take off our masks and be real. It's the only path to true open communication.

Mark 4:22 says that "everything that is hidden will eventually be brought into the open, and every secret will be brought to light." Isn't it time to bring your secrets out of the darkness into the light of God's mercy and forgiveness? Healing comes when we "confess our sins to [God]" (1 John 1:9).

Satan wants to keep you feeling defeated, believing that if your dark secrets ever came out, you'd lose everything. He wants to use the baggage from your past to extinguish the light Jesus wants to shine in your life. To convince you that you're unworthy. Stop buying into the Enemy's lies!

I'm not asking you to do anything I haven't already done. The first time

I was brutally honest with myself about my mistakes and choices, I woke up with puffy eyes. I was about to graduate from college and was newly engaged to an incredible man. But Satan kept whispering in my ear that I wasn't good enough. I felt unworthy. Dirty.

What happened?

The real Jesus walked into my life and began to change me. I finally recognized the difference between religion and actually knowing God.

Know God

Grab a cup of coffee or a Diet Coke, because we're about to go deeper into the arrow.

When I finally faced my mistakes, it hurt. REALLY hurt. My soul was searching for answers. I needed peace. Forgiveness. Healing.

That's what happens when you face your baggage. When you're in a deep spiral, and you don't have a clue how to stop the madness, you either continue the spiral or begin searching for answers.

During that season, I discovered an eye-opening truth. For a long time I thought Jesus and my church experience were the same. That knowing God better meant going to church more.

I'm not saying we shouldn't go to church more. But here's my point: A lot of folks attend church, yet they don't know God. They may know about Him and observe all sorts of religious rules and traditions, but they don't *really* know Him. Going to church isn't the same thing as having a personal relationship with God. Jesus had something to say about this.

Calling Out the Hypocrites

In Jesus's day, the religious leaders (the Pharisees) made a big show of being holier-than-thou. They loved telling others how to follow God. But more than once, Jesus called them out for pretending to be religious. His words cut straight to the heart: "Hypocrites! ... Outwardly you look like righteous people, but inwardly your hearts are filled with hypocrisy and lawlessness" (Matthew 23:27, 28). No political correctness there.

Satan uses modern-day Pharisees to convince the world that Jesus is about rules, hatred, and close-minded bigotry. But that's a flat-out lie from the Enemy. Another of his manipulative schemes. Why is this important to point out? Because we don't want to be Pharisee parents. We want to be Jesus parents, raising kids who have God's heart on the inside instead of just looking religious on the outside.

Jesus was known for His ground-breaking, life-altering love. He liked to hang out with the "less than" crowd—the people society viewed as sinners. His love extended to prostitutes, adulterers, tax collectors, murderers, drunkards, and other reprobates. No one had seen a love like this before.

The religious leaders couldn't believe Jesus would associate with such people. The Bible tells us that "Matthew invited Jesus and his disciples to his home as dinner guests, along with many tax collectors and other disreputable sinners. But when the Pharisees saw this, they asked his disciples, 'Why does your teacher eat with such scum?'" (Matthew 9:10–11).

On hearing this, Jesus said, "Healthy people don't need a doctor—sick people do.... For I have come to call not those who think they are righteous, but those who know they are sinners" (verses 12–13).

Jesus even invites a messed-up baggage girl like me to the party. Now that's good news!

Meeting God in the Middle of Our Baggage

Because of my parents' divorce, I had never been able to let my guard down with anyone. But as Jesus and I formed a deeper bond over time, I began to trust Him and submit to Him in ways I never imagined. As I dug deeper into the Bible, God showed me His heart and His purposes for my life. I started to understand that His guidelines were for my protection and peace.

I also prayed more. Some people think prayer is a cop-out, but we should never underestimate its power. Prayer is open communication with God. The key to peace, understanding, and wisdom. Next to the Bible, it's one of the best ways we can get to know God on a personal level.

Here's one of my favorite prayer stories: After two decades of marriage, the husband of one of my close friends left her to marry her best friend. My friend struggled through all the stages of grief. She felt rejected, angry, depressed, betrayed, and alone.

Years later she began to pray for her ex-husband and her former best friend. She gave all her baggage to God, and eventually she noticed a shift in her thoughts. Understanding replaced bitterness. Peace replaced anger. Over time God revealed to her that she and her husband hadn't made time for their marriage because they'd always put their kids first. Prayer opened the door for God to change her perspective and heal her broken heart.

When you pray, talk to God as if you're talking to your best friend. Don't worry about sounding eloquent or right. Talk normal. You don't need to use big words or babble (see Matthew 6:7). Just keep it simple. Pour out your heart to God. Remember my crazy prayer in chapter 3? It wasn't crazy to God. He hears our hearts. Ask Him for wisdom to cultivate open communication with your kids. Listen to His voice. Get to know Him.

Read God's Word—all of it—so you can see God's heart more fully. Let Him use Scripture to teach you. Mold you. Show you His ways and His truth.

One day as I was praying and reading the Word, I found the story of a woman who had baggage from the past. She avoided crowds because she had a "reputation." She was an outcast. She had made mistakes.

I could relate. I instantly felt like we could be BFFs.

The woman was a Samaritan. Because Samaritans were a mixed race and only half Jewish, the Jews and Samaritans didn't get along *at all.* In fact, it was socially unacceptable for a Jewish man to speak to a Samaritan woman. But Jesus did. One day as He was traveling through Samaria, He sat down near a well and asked this woman for water. He broke all the man-made, religious rules and societal taboos. He wasn't afraid of what others would think of Him.

Jesus met the woman at the well around noon. Given the fact that women usually went to the well in the morning or evening, this woman was probably in avoidance mode. Shame likely caused her to sweep her past (and present) under the rug.

Stating the obvious, she said to Jesus, "You are a Jew and I am a Samaritan woman. How can you ask me for a drink?" (John 4:9, NIV). She had no idea she was talking to God in the flesh.

The conversation started with well water, but Jesus suddenly took it deeper. He replied, "Those who drink the water I give will never be thirsty again. It becomes a fresh, bubbling spring within them, giving them eternal life" (verses 13–14).

Jesus offered the Samaritan woman living water. Then He candidly pointed out that she'd had five husbands and was now shacking up with a new man.

Jesus knew her past. All her deepest, darkest secrets. And yet He was offering her a fresh start. A new life. Hope. Peace. Everything she had been searching for but couldn't quite find on her own. He didn't ignore or overlook her baggage. He called it out because she needed to face it. Because He loved her.

The Samaritan woman had an encounter with the living God that changed her life forever. And Jesus even used her to lead others to Him.

What happened in the arrow phase of this woman's life to turn the curse into a blessing?

Jesus.

I am the Samaritan woman. You are the Samaritan woman. We're walking around with shame and guilt from past baggage. We avoid our personal demons and our kids' dreaded "Did you" questions.

Listen. Jesus knows all your past mistakes, every single personal demon you want to bury forever. And. He. Still. Loves. You.

Like the Samaritan woman, each of us needs a life-changing, personal encounter with Jesus. He's the real deal. We need to experience His love and forgiveness. We need His healing. And His wisdom for this messy thing called parenthood.

Have you encountered the real Jesus? Not religion, but Jesus? Romans 10:9 says, "If you openly declare that Jesus is Lord and believe in your heart that God raised him from the dead, you will be saved."

There's no script or formula. It's as simple as asking Jesus into your heart. If you're not sure what to pray, say something like this: *Lord, I need You. I need Your peace and forgiveness for all my mistakes. Thank You for dying on the cross for me. Come into my heart. Give me wisdom through Your Word. Teach me how to follow You. In Jesus's name I pray, amen.*

God knows your heart and hears your prayer. He'll give you the living water you're thirsting for. Knowing Jesus is the key to becoming not only a better person but a better parent. God's Word says that "anyone who belongs to Christ has become a new person. The old life is gone; a new life has begun!" (2 Corinthians 5:17). Your past mistakes no longer define you. Your identity is wrapped up in Christ *alone*, not in your kids and their success. When they make mistakes or bad choices, you don't need to feel like a failure anymore. You'll be able to love them unconditionally when they mess up because Jesus has loved you and forgiven all your messy mistakes. It's a beautiful cycle of forgiveness.

Listen to God

Now that we understand the difference between religion and a relationship with Jesus, let's talk about another important distinction. Knowing God will get you to heaven, but listening to Him changes every facet of our earthly lives. That's the difference between knowing Him on a surface level and developing an intimate bond with Him.

Think about your spouse. If you're not continually connecting and communicating with him, you'll grow apart even though your marriage certificate says you're married. It's the same with Jesus (except He'll never leave you).

Listening to God is about pursuing a deeper relationship with Him. It's a moment-by-moment choice. Listening prepares us to face the things He might want us to deal with, but our human flesh is telling us to hide from or ignore. So often, instead of listening to God, we tune Him out.

My daughter does this. I'll ask her to get her laundry basket. But she tunes me out so she doesn't have to follow through. By saying she didn't hear me, she thinks it will get her off the hook.

Oh, I do it too. Please tell me I'm not the only one who ignores God because I want to avoid hard work.

Before I started writing this book, God would wake me up in the middle of the night with chapter titles and quotes. I'd also get calls from moms

I didn't know who were struggling with how to handle what their children were being exposed to online. But I kept tuning it all out. The thought of writing a book was too intimidating.

Sometime later I was on a radio panel with a state senator I had never met. During a commercial break, he leaned over and said, "You should write a book." My husband was in the audience, and when he overheard the comment, he sent me a text message: "That is more confirmation. Write it."

But I kept ignoring these prompts for several months, tuning them out so I didn't have to respond. I wanted to stay in my comfort zone. Complacency again.

One Thursday evening, during a dinner date with my husband, I blurted out, "I know I'm supposed to write this book, but I don't want to. I want to quit teaching the classes. I want to stop all the work on the nonprofit. I'm done. It's too much hard work."

He replied, "I hear a lot of 'I's' in there. Sure doesn't sound like the woman I married. This is not about you."

Ouch.

Even after everything God was showing me, I wanted to revert to my cushy, little, complacent life. Satan was manipulating my feelings, convincing me this path was easier. But it really wasn't. You see, had I chosen to ignore God, my kids would probably be spiraling out of control at this moment because I wouldn't be addressing the tough issues head-on.

Many of us (me! me! me!) avoid listening to God because we simply don't want to do what He asks. But when we tune Him out and settle for a shallow relationship, we miss out on all the character growth and blessings He wants to give us.

Or we avoid listening because we don't like His rules. Oh, shoot. I'm guilty of this, too. (Read on, and you'll see how much I struggle with this.) Again, Satan manipulates us into believing that God gave us restrictions to make us miserable. But the truth is, He does it because He loves us and wants to protect us from harm. Isn't that why we don't allow our children to have a certain app or social-media platform? We do it not to be mean but to protect them. Because we love them.

Even if we're not intentionally ignoring God, the noise and frenzied pace of our screen-crazed world can drown out His voice. It's hard to still the motion of our lives long enough to hear what He's whispering to our hearts. We hit the ground running in the morning and don't stop till we collapse into bed at night. We'd like to sit quietly at His feet like Mary instead of rushing around like Martha, but we don't know how. (Check out the story in Luke 10:38–42.) We keep hoping that someday we'll be able to slow down enough to listen, but right now life is just too hectic. It never occurs to us that we can still listen to God on the go.

The problem is, when we don't listen to Him, everything begins to spiral downward, and we end up creating messes. We need Him if we're going to get this parenting thing right. He's the only one who can supply the wisdom, understanding, and patience we need for the journey.

Cyberparenting has forced me to go deeper in my faith and listen to God like never before. I look at these kids He's given me, and I'm overwhelmed with the responsibility of molding their little souls. I've got to get it right. The stakes are too high.

You may be thinking, *Okay, I'm sold on the idea that I need to listen to God. But how do I actually do it?*

Here are some practical guidelines:

➡ Read the Bible. Memorize it. Dig deep and hide it in your heart.

➡ Submit to God's truth. (Even if you struggle with submission, keep seeking God and the wisdom in His Word.)

➡ Talk with God (pray). Ask Him to correct you, mold you, change you, and guide you (and let Him do it).

➡ Surround yourself with a Jesus-loving tribe (we'll cover this later).

➡ Let the Holy Spirit (your secret weapon) guide you.

God has given us all the tools we need to listen to Him. In fact, the Bible teaches us that everyone who believes in Jesus is given "the gift of the Holy Spirit" (Acts 2:38). Jesus said that the "Holy Spirit … will teach you everything and will remind you of everything I have told you" (John 14:26). He lives in our hearts as our teacher and guide.

This may sound weird if you're not a Jesus follower, but the Holy Spirit, living in my heart, guides my conversations and fills me with His love and peace. He tells me when I need to be stern with my kids and when I need to show grace. He tells me when to zip my lips or bare my soul. He calms me when I feel overwhelmed.

Before my daughter asked that question about sex, I wasn't in tune with the Holy Spirit. I knew God and believed in Jesus. But reading the Bible and praying were just items on a religious checklist instead of relationship-building activities. Complacency in my relationship with God created an opening for Satan to slither in and wreak havoc in my life. I spiraled out of control and missed important clues I should have noticed as a parent. I turned to social media and people for the answers when I should have been listening to God.

Open communication works best in our families when we listen to the Holy Spirit and allow Him to guide every word and decision. He is our secret weapon. We learn to hear His voice by immersing ourselves in prayer and God's Word and inviting Him into each moment of our lives.

The Holy Spirit keeps us from swinging to extremes in our parenting. At times our emotions may swing toward crazy-mom mode, but if we step back and listen to His voice, He'll keep us centered and on point.

Overreacting doesn't work (I'm speaking from experience), and neither does underreacting. Parenting is about *balance*. And balance is necessary for open communication with our kids.

The Holy Spirit is available 24/7 to guide us, but we have to listen to Him. Just because He is living in our hearts doesn't mean we can't go into a spiral and make a mess of things.

Check out what Scripture has to say about this:

> Those who live according to the flesh have their minds set on what the flesh desires; but those who live in accordance with the Spirit have their minds set on what the Spirit desires. The mind governed by the flesh is death, but the mind governed by the Spirit is life and peace. (Romans 8:5–6, NIV)

When the Spirit is in control, we have "life and peace." Isn't that what we want for our families? But for that to happen, we need to listen to God with open ears and hearts instead of tuning Him out. Then we have to be willing to do what He asks. Submitting or surrendering to the Spirit is a moment-by-moment choice that takes practice. We have to learn to do it.

Just because we're listening to God today doesn't mean we will tomorrow. We may rely on Him when we face some difficult issues but ignore Him and try to handle other problems on our own. The result? One big mess!

Years ago I learned a painful lesson about ignoring problems and not listening to God. When I was pregnant with my son, I was ill. I didn't want to appear weak, so I ignored the warning signs. Eventually things got so bad, I went to the doctor and was diagnosed with severe prepartum depression, which happens *before* the baby comes. The doctor immediately started me on antidepressants, and I began seeing two counselors. I'd love to tell you I felt better the following week, but it took time. Those were some of the darkest months of my life.

I allowed things to get worse because I was in denial. I chose not to listen even though I had a relationship with God and knew He was there. He carried me through, but I ignored Him. I should've gone to my doctor at the first onset of symptoms, but I let things spiral out of control. Ignoring the problem only made it worse. The entire time God was calling out to me, *Let Me heal you. I'll work through medicine, doctors, counselors, friends, prayer. I want to help you. But you have to let Me.*

Proverbs 3:5–6 says, "Trust in the LORD with all your heart; do not depend on your own understanding. Seek his will in all you do, and he will show you which path to take."

In hindsight, I know what got me in trouble during my pregnancy. I chose to ignore my depression and tried to handle things on my own instead of listening to God. If I'd only listened and trusted Him, I would have spared myself a lot of grief.

Looking in the mirror stings, doesn't it? It forces us to admit our mistakes and face our problems. But being real with ourselves can also open the door to a deeper relationship with the God of the universe, who knows all about our darkest secrets and loves us in spite of them. As we seek to know His heart and listen to Him, He'll help us pave the way for open communication one step at a time.

5

Strengthening Communication in Your Marriage

Now that we've honestly looked at ourselves in the mirror, I'm about to get even more up in your business. The next step on the path to open communication is taking an honest look at our marriages. (This will sting too. Sorry.)

Have you noticed that the way you communicate with your children is a reflection of how you communicate in your marriage? It's true. The patterns we develop with our spouses often get repeated with our kids. And so do our mistakes.

If we don't model open, honest conversation with our spouses, our children won't learn the value and importance of it. That's why it's so essential to pave the path for open communication in our marriages.

When Love Fades

The way my husband, Matt, and I met is a cheesy story, but I can't resist telling it. During college, I had sworn off guys and was trying to start a new chapter in my life. But then Matt showed up one summer at a grocery store where I worked as a checkout girl. He was Keebler Boy, the guy who restocked cookies, and he came through my line to buy a Snickers bar. Totally not the way I dreamed I would meet my husband. But God obviously has a sense of humor.

When Matt and I started dating, it was a new kind of relationship for me. Healthy, not physical. We talked a lot, and eventually I felt safe enough to tell him about my past mistakes. I actually expected him to break up with me because he was looking to marry a sweet, pure Christian girl. And there I was. Baggage girl.

One night I told him about all the horrible mistakes I'd made in my life. We were sitting on an ugly blue couch in his tiny apartment, with his huge orange cat sleeping between us. I cried. He listened. I didn't sugarcoat anything. It was the first time I'd ever shared all that stuff with anyone.

When I finished, he calmly said, "You're human, Mandy. We all make mistakes. God still loves you."

I was stunned. Matt accepted me, the real me, all of me. After that I understood God's grace a little better. I really was forgiven. I didn't have to live with all that guilt. The truth set me free. The Bible was right again.

Even after hearing all my baggage, Matt didn't treat me differently. If anything, he showed more respect because of my honesty. This was new to me. Genuine.

We've now been married seventeen years, and he has never brought up my past mistakes or thrown them in my face. Not even when I'm being unreasonable or we're in the heat of an argument. Not once.

When I started speaking to audiences, I asked him, "Are you okay with me sharing my personal story publicly?"

You know what his response was?

"If you think it will help people. But remember, you're not that person. You're new and different and forgiven."

Then he reminded me of 2 Corinthians 5:17: "Anyone who belongs to Christ has become a new person. The old life is gone; a new life has begun!"

Matt is my PC. Prince. Charming. Yes, all kinds of cheesy.

Picture-perfect love story, right? No. Nothing is perfect.

My husband is wonderful, but he isn't a saint. (Neither am I, by the way.) The man has some faults that really get on my nerves. His loud burps, for instance. They're like an alarm clock going off in my head. (I'm totally not kidding.) But because I don't believe in husband bashing, I'm going to zip it right there. See how this works? Walking with balance in the Spirit.

On a serious note, we've had some tough times. We moved from Indiana to Texas when our daughter was one, and it took years to get adjusted.

New friends, new house, new schools, new church. It was a process. Then I had an unexpected miscarriage, followed by a complicated pregnancy with my son (and the diagnosis of prepartum depression).

After our healthy boy arrived, we were consumed with late-night feedings, lack of sleep, Matt's long work hours and job change, roof leaks, house repairs, and so on. You know. Life.

We were in survival mode, and I struggled just to get through the day. The moment my husband walked in the door, I'd go upstairs for a quiet shower while the kids tackled him like a jungle gym. By bedtime, Matt and I were exhausted. A kiss on the cheek, an "I love you," and then we'd go to sleep. Repeat the next day.

We were living on autopilot.

We weathered the storms and remained faithful to each other. We prayed. Read the Bible. Attended church every weekend. But we weren't actually talking. (A pattern I repeated with my daughter.) We'd put our marriage on the back burner, and now we were drifting apart. Complacency.

One night God prompted me to share a friend's story with my husband (the same friend I mentioned earlier). You see, she'd been married twenty-five years and had raised two awesome kids. They seemed like the perfect churchgoing family on the outside. Then they divorced. I'll never forget what she said to me: "When the kids grew up, we looked at each other and realized we were strangers. We put everything into our kids and forgot about our marriage."

Matt and I were headed down the same path. Picture perfect on the outside. A growing communication gap on the inside. It's not that we didn't love each other. It's not that we weren't committed to our marriage. We were just so dang exhausted from the demands of life.

After I shared her story, Matt responded, "I can totally understand how that can happen. Kids require so much."

That opened up a new line of communication in our relationship. Over the next several weeks, we had many deep, honest conversations and made some changes. I also made a detailed mental list of why I married my husband. I went back to that day in the grocery store when Keebler Boy first came through my checkout line and bought a Snickers bar.

The C-Word Again

Remember when we talked about complacency in our parenting and our relationships with God? What about complacency in our marriages? Like ...

- Putting the kids first and not making time for each other.
- Having a huge fight and then sweeping it under the rug for months because it's too hard to work through.
- Spending too much money at the mall or on a hobby and not telling your spouse.
- Receiving a friend request on social media from an ex and failing to mention it to your spouse.
- Disregarding your husband's opinion and throwing a party even though he says he's too tired.

Complacency.

We can't ignore the "little" things anymore. One little thing can start a downward spiral in our marriages. A little white lie is a BIG problem. Remember, Satan is lurking in the shadows just like he did in the garden, waiting for an opportunity to destroy your marriage. First, he creates a tiny wedge between you and your spouse. And as the wedge sinks deeper, it forms a crack in the family foundation. Pretty soon the foundation is crumbling.

Like a knitted sweater that starts unraveling when one little thread is pulled out of place, if we ignore little problems in our marriages, we'll eventually end up with a gaping hole.

One choice to settle for complacency sets off a chain reaction. Communication slowly dwindles and dies. Then one day we wake up and realize we're married to a stranger.

Reciprocal Honesty

To prevent this scenario from unfolding, we need to get real about what's happening in our marriages. Remember, how you communicate with your spouse will impact the way you communicate with your kids.

Are you open and honest with your spouse? Is it a two-way street—reciprocal honesty? By reciprocal, I mean 100 percent truth in both directions. Let me give you an example.

Sometimes my husband will tell me about a situation at work, and I let him know I totally disagree with how he handled it. I'm not mean or disrespectful. But I'm never a silent partner. We speak our minds. I often say, "I know I may not see the whole picture, but I don't think you should've said that. I think you owe that person an apology."

That's what open communication looks like. The truth, even when it hurts.

My husband does the same with me. One morning my tween son was eating breakfast before school. I yelled at him for spilling milk, and he got upset. Seriously, I'm a slow learner.

After I dropped my kids off at school, I got a call from Matt.

He said, "You are an amazing mom and do almost everything right. But today you messed up. Honey, you're not yelling when they show you porn, but you're yelling over spilled milk? Think about that. You really owe him an apology."

Ugh. That hurt. But he was so right.

Matt and I are honest not to hurt each other but to help each other. To develop each other's character and integrity. We're sharpening each other "as iron sharpens iron" (Proverbs 27:17, NIV).

Your marriage needs to be a place where you and your spouse can tell each other the truth. The tough things. It's about reciprocal honesty. "The truth will set you free" (John 8:32).

The truth is often difficult to hear. Can your husband tell you sensitive things without offending you or putting you on the defensive? Things like …

- "Honey, you're hot, but those jeans don't look right on you."
- "Did you notice so-and-so at the party? When she leaned over, I saw her bra and boobs."
- "I was scrolling through your Facebook feed and couldn't help but notice all the bikini pictures that so-and-so keeps posting."

These are honest statements. Guys are visual—as Matt is constantly reminding me—and they need to process what they see. They need to move those visuals from the emotional part of their brains to the thinking part (more on this in chapter 11).[1]

Being honest with me allows my husband to deal with emotionally based sexual temptations in a healthy way so his mind doesn't wander down a trail of inappropriate thoughts. He's honest, but he's never disrespectful. He would never tell me another woman is hot or that I'm not attractive enough. That wouldn't be okay. There's a difference between processing and being disrespectful.

It doesn't bother me if Matt notices a beautiful woman or sees boobs when a lady bends over. He notices them and then looks away. But he shouldn't stare. He shouldn't lust or fantasize. End of story. (By the way, I notice the same things!)

I love how one of my pastors addresses this issue. He tells husbands they have three seconds to look at a beautiful woman and determine whether she needs assistance. After that, they should look away. He calls it the *three-second rule*.

In defense of husbands everywhere, large racks of boobs are plastered all over the place. Stuck in eight lanes of traffic on the highway? Look up and you'll see a billboard of boobs. Even my tween son notices them and asks about them. (Side note: Matt says it's either "rack" or "boobs," but not both. I don't care. I'm leaving it because I like how it sounds.)

I'm Matt's best friend, his safe place. I'm the place where he can process his thoughts. We don't walk on eggshells around each other. He's my best friend too, the person I share my deepest, darkest secrets with. It's a two-way street. My village and inner circle of friends play a significant role in my life, but it's not the same as my relationship with Matt. He is my safe place.

Are there times when I zip my lips? Absolutely. I have to strike a balance. Walking in the Spirit.

The Elephant in the Room

Before we dive any deeper into marriage, we need to address the elephant in the room. You know, the whole "submission" thing.

Let me be real honest: I hate the word *submission*. Absolutely hate it. The first time Matt tried to open the car door for me, I put my hand on my hip with lots of sass and said, "Really? I've never needed anyone to open the door for me. I've managed just fine opening my own doors, thank you. I'm strong and independent. I'm not a delicate flower who needs to be taken care of."

He smiled.

Submission. I've asked God a million times why He needed to use that word. It used to send me into a tailspin of emotions. My "strong, independent woman" speech would play in my head again and again. I'd get mad at God and wouldn't want to dive any deeper into His Word. Because I didn't agree with it. *God is sexist, and I'm done,* I concluded.

Here's the scripture I'm talking about: "Wives, *submit* yourselves to your own husbands as you do to the Lord. For the husband is the head of the wife as Christ is the head of the church, his body, of which he is the Savior. Now as the church *submits* to Christ, so also wives should *submit* to their husbands in everything" (Ephesians 5:22–24, NIV).

When I was engrossed in religion, that's where I stopped. I judged God and decided the whole Christian thing wasn't for me. I didn't like His rules. But in college when I began to realize that Jesus wasn't the same as religion, I wanted to dig deeper into the Word. I read Ephesians 5:25–29 and saw it in a whole new light:

> Husbands, … love your wives, just as Christ loved the church. He gave up his life for her.… In the same way, husbands ought to love their wives as they love their own bodies. For a man who loves his wife actually shows love for himself. No one hates his own body but feeds and cares for it, just as Christ cares for the church.

God calls husbands to a *much* higher standard in the way they treat their wives. The husband must love his wife as he loves himself. He has to give himself up for her the way Jesus gave His life for us. Wow! How had I missed that? Satan.

The Enemy had manipulated me into thinking that submission was bad. Just as he manipulated Eve in the garden. He wanted me to believe that if I submitted in my marriage, my husband would order me around and try to control me. That's a lie straight from the mouth of that slimy serpent.

I realized that God established guidelines like submission not to make my life miserable but to protect me. Submission became beautiful to me. And amazing. And life changing. It didn't feel like rules and regulations anymore. It was freeing and healthy.

Both my husband and I submit to God (see James 4:7), and we mutually submit to each other (see Ephesians 5:21). I feel safe submitting to Matt because he submits to God and loves me as much as he loves himself. That's God's blueprint for marriage. When it's working the way it was designed to work, it's beautiful.

What does submission look like in our daily lives? If Matt and I have a big decision to make, and he is on one side and I'm on the other, we pray that God will balance things out. If God doesn't move one of us from the other side, Matt will say, "We can't make this decision unless we're on the same page. I can't go against what you're thinking." So we wait.

Mutual submission. See how this works?

Lessons in Open Communication

Now that we've dealt with the elephant in the room, let's focus on practical ways to build open, honest communication in our marriages. I've discovered four guidelines that help me communicate with my man:

1. Respond calmly.
2. Don't pick fights.
3. Choose the right time.
4. Make your marriage a priority.

1. Respond Calmly

Here's the thing. Many times when our husbands make comments (like seeing racks of boobs all over the place), we get emotional. We fly off the handle and take things personally. We cry or yell (or we go into silent-treatment mode).

I speak from experience. But guess what happens if I lose my mind over something my husband says? He stops talking. My angry reaction drives a wedge between us, a barrier to open communication, and he can't tell me his true struggles or thoughts.

Reacting with anger or other negative emotions won't solve the problem. It makes things worse. We need to create a safe zone so our husbands can be honest with us about any issue. When your husband shares something that raises a red flag, STOP before you fly off the handle. Take a deep breath. Ask God to calm you and guide your words. "Speak the truth in love" (Ephesians 4:15). If you need time alone to regroup, say so. But do it with respect.

Let me give you another example. I have a friend whose smile literally lights up a room. She's gorgeous, but she doesn't know it. And that makes her even more gorgeous. Several years ago her husband confessed that he struggled with pornography. She felt betrayed, hurt, and angry that he even told her. She *really* didn't want to know. Her gut reaction was denial. Like Eve in the garden, she wanted to live in blissful unawareness. It was an incredibly long and tough journey, but she looked to God's Word for answers, and her faith pulled her through.

Now her husband texts her a certain emoji when he's struggling with a desire to look at pornography, and she stops to pray for him. He has online filters to keep him accountable, and she has the passwords. Instead of reacting in hurt and anger, she stays calm and supportive. She's a safe place for him to be honest about his struggles.

They recently celebrated their eleventh anniversary, and for every year of their marriage, he wrote something he treasures about her and placed it in a rose. How sweet is that?

Was it a process? Yes. Was it painful? Absolutely. But their relationship is stronger because they faced their issues head-on. Their marriage is a beautiful testament to open communication and allowing God to turn curses into blessings.

2. Don't Pick Fights

You know what else raises a barrier to open communication? A ready-to-rumble spouse. (Oh, shoot. I'm guilty.) This is going to sting again, but if it doesn't hurt a little, we're probably not facing the truth, right?

The book of Proverbs has a few things to say about fight pickers:

> A quarrelsome wife is as annoying as constant dripping. (19:13)
>
> It's better to live alone in the desert than with a quarrelsome, complaining wife. (21:19)
>
> A quarrelsome wife is as annoying as constant dripping on a rainy day. (27:15)

Can you imagine what it would be like to have a spouse who is constantly picking fights and tearing you down? You'd feel trapped in your marriage, unable to get away from the criticism and conflict. Nightmare on your street!

Being ready to rumble means we're poised for battle, determined to get in the first and last words—and anything in between. We're all about arguing, not listening. (I know.) Nothing shuts down open communication faster than a ready-to-rumble spouse. Our verbal grenades drive our spouses into hiding when our words should be creating a safe space for honest sharing.

When our house was being built, I wrote the words of Proverbs 19:13 on the studs behind my bathroom sink to remind me that a ready-to-rumble spouse is like a dripping, leaky faucet. I can't tell you how many times I've been standing at the sink brushing my teeth when my husband says something that makes me want to pick a fight.

Oh, God knew.

I think about that verse in Proverbs. Literally picture it on the stud right behind the wall. And I consider what God is trying to tell me. I bite my lip and regroup.

It goes back to walking with balance in the Spirit. We need an attitude adjustment. We also need to discern when to lay the truth out there and when to zip it. Instead of picking fights, we need to close our mouths and tune our ears to the Spirit. The Holy Spirit is all about peace, not combat. If we listen to Him first and accept His correction, it will be easier to listen to our spouses without swinging the pendulum to crazy-wife mode.

It's a constant, moment-by-moment walk, and we won't always get it right. God knows we've made mistakes (and will keep on making them), and He still loves us.

3. Choose the Right Time

I suck at this too. Actually, I wonder how my marriage has survived, because I stink at all of these guidelines. Wait. I know the answer. I have an Ephesians 5 husband who loves me as he loves himself. Submission really is a beautiful thing. So when I mess up, Matt shows me grace and forgiveness.

Okay, back to timing. Let me give you a typical example: My husband called on the way home from work one evening and told me he'd had a bad day. He wanted to go to bed early because he was stressed and had to get up early the next morning for a meeting. I could tell he was depleted. I needed to listen to him—and the Spirit. Here's how the scene played out: We got the kids to bed and prayed together as a family. Then my husband and I crawled into bed. But instead of remembering he'd had a stressful day and comforting him, I launched into a forty-five-minute account of some drama happening in my friend group. Hello? All. About. Me.

Matt had already warned me that he was exhausted. He needed sleep. And here I was piling on more crap. He didn't want to be rude, but he was upset because I hadn't listened.

Timing!

My husband wants to hear about my day and know everything that's going on in my world. But the timing has to be right.

There will be nights when all you want to do is tell your husband about the sex conversation you had with your son, but he's too tired or stressed to listen at that moment. Don't get mad at him. Walk with balance in the Spirit and listen for prompts from Him.

Timing shouldn't be used as an excuse not to talk to your husband about something important. Work on finding the right time to talk with him. It will look different for each of us.

Here's what I've learned to say on nights like that: "Hey, I had a very important convo with our son today and want to tell you about it, but I know you're exhausted. Let me know when it's a good time to talk."

When Matt starts snoring five minutes later, I've learned not to believe the Enemy's lie that he doesn't care. He's just tired. Normally he'll call on the drive to work the next morning. He's refreshed and eager to listen by then. He wants to know. When the timing is right, the conversation is better and more productive.

I'll end this topic on a note husbands will like. If he's flirting with you and wants some action, don't launch into all your problems and stresses of the day. Shut it off and have sex with your husband. Then maybe you can talk afterward. Or maybe not. But enjoy the sex.

During a prayer time with our nextTalk leaders, one of them said, "Lord Jesus, I pray for good sex for all the marriages represented here." Amen to that. We all need some good sex to get us through the crazy.

4. Make Your Marriage a Priority

Okay, I hear your thoughts right now. *Do you know how much I juggle? My husband has got to grow up and be an adult, because I don't have time to baby him. I don't need another child.*

I get it. Those are my thoughts 99 percent of the time too. But they aren't necessarily truth. Satan might just be trying to drive a wedge between you and your spouse.

We need to give our husbands credit for all they do. My own hubby juggles a lot, between a demanding job, commuting two hours a day, finishing his master's degree, and helping me transport kids to and from activities.

He often says to me, "I know I'm doing my job if everyone under this roof is happy and healthy, but I'm exhausted."

He carries all that weight on his shoulders day after day. In fact, we were tossing around names for a nextTalk dads' group, and he suggested "Tired Dads." Ha!

We're all busy and tired. All of us. We need to consciously make time for our spouses so they know they're a priority. What does that look like?

- *Keep dating.* We all *need* this as a stress reliever. Matt and I have a date weekend once a month when our parents take both kids on Saturday night and all day Sunday. No matter what your date looks like, create the space for it. If you don't have family in town, trade off with friends and take turns babysitting.
- *Use your time wisely.* Be intentional with your time management. We use Matt's commuting time to talk through parenting stuff, financial issues, and life decisions we need to make.
- *Turn off the screens.* If you're in bed with your spouse, and you're both on your phones, *turn them off.* Connect with your spouse. Have lots of good sex. Talk. Vent. Laugh. Pour into your relationship to keep it growing.

I'm bad about the phone thing. Matt thinks I'm on my phone way too much and feels it's more important to me than he is. One time when we were in bed together, he actually texted me a message: "I exist."

I immediately went into defensive mode. I thought, *Do you know I'm writing a book? And launching a nonprofit organization at the same time? You don't have any idea what my stress is like.*

But instead of saying those things, I stopped and asked the Holy Spirit to calm me down and help me respond with grace.

It wasn't about defending myself; it was about *listening* to my spouse. He needed to be heard. So after I regrouped, I assured him he's much more important than this book or the nonprofit organization. He and my kids are my top priority. But I had to follow up my words with actions.

Now I'm trying to implement a cell-phone-free zone every evening from five thirty to nine. I put my phone on the bench in our mudroom and leave it alone. It hasn't been easy. But I have so much more time to pour into my family when I'm not checking it constantly.

You better believe Matt hears from me when he checks work e-mails late at night. (Voicing my opinion has never been a problem for me.) This accountability thing is a two-way street, after all.

I think most of us believe our spouses are a priority. Of course we do. But do our actions match our beliefs (and words)?

How much time are you pouring into your spouse? If you don't have any time for him, pinpoint why. Are you too busy?

I ask because I'm guilty.

The Bible says, "A wise woman builds her home, but a foolish woman tears it down with her own hands" (Proverbs 14:1). One way I tear down my house is when I overschedule myself. Then there's no time for meaningful conversations because I'm too tired to listen to my husband. I miss out. I run the kids everywhere, and there's nothing left for my marriage—no energy, time, thought, space.

We all tear down our houses in different ways. How do you do it?

- Yelling or speaking instead of just listening?
- Being the volunteer queen and saying yes to everything?
- Letting anxiety and fear control you so you spend all your free time worrying?
- Connecting to social media instead of talking to your family?
- Spending too much money and seeking happiness in material things instead of relationships?

Identify the ways you tear down your house and get to work fixing it. Then you'll have more time to pour into making your marriage a priority.

If the foundation of your marriage has cracked and everything has spiraled out of control, there's still hope. It will take some time and effort, and each of you has to accept responsibility for your part. But God is able to turn the curses into blessings in your marriage.

Open communication won't happen overnight. It's a process. If you need help, please see a family counselor. Talk to your family doctor or pastor and get a recommendation.

Fight for your marriage. Get involved in a couples' support group. (A number of Bible-believing Christian churches offer them.) Work through the tough issues with *grit*. (Remember the arrow?)

Don't let the Enemy manipulate you into believing that everyone *but you* has a perfect marriage. Social media may give that impression, but it's a lie! There is *no* perfect marriage. We all struggle. We argue with our spouses.

We don't see eye to eye sometimes. We get frustrated with each other.

The key to a strong marriage, however, is always talking things through. Open, honest communication day after day.

Open communication isn't a destination to aim for so you can coast through the rest of your marriage. It's an ongoing, moment-by-moment choice to continue working on your relationship. To keep listening and talking to your man. Just like you do in your relationship with God.

Becoming Your Tween's Safe Place

As we learned earlier, open, honest communication is much easier if we start laying the groundwork *before* the tween years. Becoming a safe place for our kids takes time. Trust doesn't develop overnight. The sooner we begin paving the path for open communication, the better.

If you respond in an affirming way to your children's questions when they're young, their natural instinct will be to run to their safe place (you) with tougher issues when they're tweens or teens. Instead of being afraid to tell you what's happening in their lives, they won't think twice about putting it all out there, because they'll feel secure and accepted.

I started authentic, open communication with my daughter when she was nine. With my son, we started at six. Starting early made a huge difference. Night and day!

Now I know you may be thinking, *My kids are already tweens (or teens), and I didn't pave the path for open communication when they were younger. I blew it.*

Hear me on this: It is *never* too late to improve communication with your kids. Sure, it's easier if you start early, but our God is a BIG God. "Nothing ... is impossible with [Him]" (Luke 1:37, MSG).

Even if you and your child have zero trust or communication right now, God can turn this curse into a blessing. Don't give up. He's got this. Seek His wisdom. Listen to Him.

You're not alone in this cyberparenting chaos. We're all learning together. We've all missed things. But we're facing them now, right?

"I'm Your Safe Place"

The most important thing we can do to pave the path for open communication with our children is to become their safe place. (It needs to be you, not their peers or the online world.) They need to know they can trust us with their problems and questions, and that we'll keep their confidences.

Tell your child continually, "I'm your safe place. Your secrets are safe with me. You can ask me embarrassing questions, and I'll never repeat them or share them." Just make sure your actions match your words.

I don't share my tween's stories on social media. EVER. In fact, since my daughter hit middle school, I've posted nothing on social media about her unless I have her permission (not even a bragging post about grades).

I'm serious. Sharing things online without your kids' permission can damage the trust and open communication you've worked so hard to build. Whatever they share with you should be kept in strictest confidence—questions, discussions, feelings, reactions, *everything*. Keep your promises not to share what they tell you. Prove you can be trusted.

Being a safe place for our kids also requires applying the parent filter I talked about earlier. You know, calm on the outside; a mess on the inside. Always, always remain calm whenever your children confide in you. No matter what they tell you, don't fly into a tirade (crazy-mom mode). By remaining calm, you'll build trust and encourage them to be real and honest with you about everything.

For example, when my friend's son was in kindergarten, he told her, "Mom, when one of the ladies at my school leaned over today, I could see down her shirt. I saw her bra and part of her boobies."

My friend remained calm. She didn't yell or have a crazy-mom moment. She didn't shame the lady. She simply said, "Oh, I'm really glad you told me this. I don't think she actually meant for that to happen. It happens to me sometimes too, and I don't realize it. I'm so proud of you for telling me your thoughts. It's your job to look away after you notice. I'm your safe place to talk about things like this."

This was a great teachable moment, and it built trust in their relationship. This is the kind of practice we need to prepare our kids for the tween years. We want them to feel safe being completely honest with us.

Here are some other key pointers for becoming a safe place for your child:

- *Find out when your tween likes to talk and capitalize on it.* Is it on the way to school in the morning? After school? At bedtime? It may not always be the best time for you, but do it anyway. You just might be amazed at what your child tells you.
- *Listen to what your child is telling you. Really* listen. Not just to the words but to the emotions and beliefs behind the words. When your child begins to talk, zip it and listen. Make listening your top priority.
- *Take a deep breath before you respond.* If you need time to process, let your child know you'll follow up later. But make sure you do.
- *Pray.* Search the Bible for answers. Listen to God. Ask the Holy Spirit to guide your words and the conversation. This will help you stay balanced.
- *Practice what you preach.* It sets apart a hypocritical Pharisee parent from a Jesus parent.

When your tween is being completely honest with you, how do you tend to react? Do you scream, shout, cry, or give your child the silent treatment? Do you go into crazy-mom mode? Negative emotional reactions like these create barriers to open communication, and our kids quickly learn they can't tell us anything. It's tough, especially when they tell us things we'd rather not hear. But we need to face it.

Becoming your child's safe place will take time and patience. Every teachable moment is an opportunity to lay one more paving stone on the path to open communication. You'll be tempted to become complacent and settle for the status quo. Don't! Your efforts will pay off big-time if you stick with it. Trust me on this.

Learning to Listen

I want to camp on listening for a moment because it's vital if we want to create a safe place for our kids. Before we shift into motormouth mode and spout unsolicited advice, we need to stop and listen to what they're saying to us.

James 1:19 says, "You must all be quick to listen, slow to speak, and slow to get angry." What a great theme verse for building open communication with our children.

I want to be honest. Listening isn't my strong point. I'm getting better at listening to Jesus and my husband, but it's harder to get it right with my kids.

Here's an example: One evening last year, both kids were sitting at our kitchen island doing homework. I was unloading the dishwasher and talking through homework problems with them. The kitchen was a mess, with dirty dishes piled in the sink and clean dishes needing to be put away. In the middle of the mess, I was getting several important texts, and my son kept asking me how to spell words for a book report. I tried to help him sound out letters while I was typing replies.

I could feel irritation creeping up my neck. I didn't yell, but my tone was rude: "Bubba," I replied, "I've helped you sound out that word like five times. *Please* give me a minute."

After that little exchange, my son got moody and started moping. I can't take whining. Um, no.

I asked him, "What's wrong? Why the attitude? Are you feeling okay?"

Nothing. Silence.

Fifteen minutes later, he was upset and telling me he just wanted help with his homework. He said, "I'm sorry if I was bugging you, Mom."

Punched in the gut.

Suddenly a voice in my head whispered, *Yeah, and you're the leader of nextTalk. What a Pharisee mom!*

I was tempted to make excuses for myself, but I zipped it and took the dogs for a walk. As I cried and prayed (and got my legs caught between two dog leashes), God spoke to my heart: *I love you, Mandy, but you messed this one up. Ask him to forgive you and move on.*

That night I told my son, "Bubba, today was not your fault. I was trying to do too many things at once, and the number-one priority was helping you with your homework. So I'm implementing a new guideline. Whenever we're doing homework, my phone will not be in the room, and you'll have my undivided attention. I'm sorry for messing up."

His reply? "It's okay, Mom. We're all still learning. I love you."

My son was echoing what I'm always telling him. It was a beautiful cycle of forgiveness.

Communication is a powerful thing, my friend. By being good listeners, we set an example and show our tweens that what they say is important to us.

Make it your top priority to be fully present with your children. When they confide in you, don't jump right in and start giving advice. Proverbs 18:13 says, "Answering before listening is both stupid and rude" (MSG). Resist the urge to interrupt. This is the time to listen to the whole enchilada. Let the Spirit guide you.

If your kids aren't talking to you or sharing things that really matter, focus on building trust and open communication. Be patient.

When my daughter entered fourth grade, I wasn't prepared for the challenges of cyberparenting because I hadn't paved the path for open communication. It took two years of hard work to develop honesty and trust in our relationship. You know how I started talking to her?

One night as I tucked her into bed, I asked, "What can I do better as a mom?"

She gave a brutally honest reply: "You're not a good listener, Mom. Many times when I'm talking, you're on your phone, unloading the dishwasher, or cooking dinner. It makes me very angry when I have to repeat my story because you weren't listening."

(I told you. Listening isn't my strong point.)

Her response hurt me to the core. Feeling defensive, I thought, *Do you realize what I have to deal with every day? You have no clue how much I do.*

Yada. Yada. Yada. All about me.

Thankfully I resisted the urge to come back with excuses. Because if I had, my tween would have shut down instead of giving me honest feedback.

She needed to be heard, and I needed to look in the mirror. Yep, it stung.

Ever since our talk, I follow up every few months and ask her how I'm doing. One time she even gave me a report card. It became our joke. I'm always saying to her, "Well, you know I'm not perfect. I'm still learning too."

Asking for my children's feedback holds me accountable to become a better person. It's all about character development. And it shows them that their input matters to me.

We need to welcome real, honest feedback from our kids. It may hurt, but if we allow their words to penetrate our hearts, shape our character, and improve our communication skills, it might just transform our parenting.

Cultivating Open Communication

As we become our tweens' safe place, we earn the right to speak truth into their lives. Trust is essential. Without it, our truth talk will fall on deaf ears.

Work on cultivating open communication as you do life together. Take advantage of teachable moments to instill foundational truths in your kids' lives. When my children were younger, I used the following one-liners in conversations to teach key truths Matt and I wanted them to learn. I still pull out these comments when my kids need a reminder. They apply at any age.

1. *"Not everything you hear or read is true, so when you hear a new word or phrase, ask me about it."* Preschool or kindergarten is the perfect age to prepare our children for encountering new words and phrases. As soon as they begin spending time away from us and can communicate their emotions, we need to pull out this one-liner during teachable moments.

For example, I'd tell my preschooler, "Sometimes kids say things but don't really know what they mean. I want you to know that you can always ask me what something means, and I'll be 100 percent honest. I'll never get mad at you for bringing it up. I'll be so proud of you for telling me. So whenever you hear a new word or phrase, will you ask me?"

If you say you're going to be 100 percent honest, be honest. Always. When you're not sure how to respond, you could say, "Your question is really important to me, and I want to give you the best information. Can I think about it and get back with you?"

My personal rule is to follow up within twenty-four hours. This shows my children that their questions are important to me. By following up, you become a trustworthy, reliable resource. If you fail to follow up, it will destroy your credibility.

Younger children sometimes ask about words they've heard that aren't age appropriate to discuss in detail. If your young elementary-age child asks about oral sex, for example, remain calm, ask open-ended questions, and try to determine where he or she heard about it. It's okay to say, "I want to be honest with you, but this is difficult to describe at your age. And I want to cover other information with you first. Would that be okay?"

Since apps and social media have wide-open boundaries, kids see all kinds of inappropriate content online. We should be their go-to source when they want to know what something means. It's also important they understand that the information they discover online doesn't always represent truth.

When my kids were little, we had a family guideline that they weren't allowed to search online (or within an app) without a parent present. I told them, "The online world doesn't always represent truth. Bad pictures and images often pop up during searches. So ask me. If I don't know what it is, I'll research it for you."

As our daughter has gotten older, Matt and I have allowed her more freedom with online searches because she's proved herself trustworthy by reporting to us what she sees. We're building trust. She's still required to stay in an open area of the house (nothing behind closed doors), but she doesn't need a parent by her side.

One of my former pastors used a kite string to illustrate trust. The more we trust our children, the more string we can let out so they can fly higher. If they mess up or stumble, we reel them in to correct and teach them. When they demonstrate growth, we give them more string (freedom) again. I love that analogy.

2. *"The Bible is our moral compass for determining right and wrong."* We all need a moral compass, even if it isn't the Bible. Your family, your choice. What's the moral compass for your family? What helps you determine right from wrong?

One time my daughter came home from school upset. Her friend told her about a crush she had on someone and cautioned her not to tell anyone. My daughter was panicked and said, "What should I do if someone asks me? Do I lie? Is it okay to lie so I don't break the promise to my friend?"

"That's a good question," I replied. "Let's go to the Bible and see what God says."

While she looked up *lying* in her Bible's concordance, I Googled "lying verses in the Bible." The first verse that popped up was Colossians 3:9: "Don't lie to each other."

After we did our research, she said, "Lying isn't okay. So what do I do?"

"Well," I suggested, "what if you said, 'This isn't really a question for me. I think you need to ask her'? That way you remove yourself from a sticky situation, and you don't have to lie."

Teachable moments like this show our children that we have a moral compass and value what God has to say about *everything* in our lives. When we seek truth together in the Bible, it can open up conversations and teachable moments we never dreamed were possible. Another paver on the path. That's how God works.

3. *"God tells us to guard our hearts and minds."* I say this often to my kids—almost weekly—and I've been amazed at the impact it's had on them.

When my daughter (now a teen) tells me about finding something questionable online, she'll add, "But I protected my mind and heart and didn't search it because I didn't want to see the pictures." Then she'll ask me what it is, and I'll Google it so I can explain it to her. We're a team.

Our children need to learn as early as possible that they're ultimately responsible for what they allow to enter their hearts and minds. They need to understand the importance of protecting themselves from harmful influences. We can protect them from some things, but we aren't with them 24/7. And phone restrictions and parental controls don't block everything that could tempt them or lead them in the wrong direction.

That's why they need to develop integrity and learn to seek God on their own. They need to know they're responsible to Him for what they look at, listen to, think about, download, search for, comment on, and participate in.

One of the most important lessons I've learned on this journey is that it's not about dictating rules to our kids and giving them a gold star when they obey. It's about helping them know God on a heart level and seek Him in their everyday lives. We need to teach them how God's Word is relevant to their world. The best way to do this is to model what it means to seek Him in our own lives. As they watch us trusting God and turning to Him for answers, they'll learn to do the same.

Real growth takes place in the chaotic messes of life. The arrow where life happens (curse ➡ blessing). That's where our kids need to seek God most and discover that He is their ultimate go-to source.

For example, when my daughter started middle school, she'd come home from school and say, "Mom, I hear the f-word a million times every day. It's getting engrained in my head, and sometimes I almost slip and say it. How do I protect my heart and mind from this?"

I wasn't disappointed in her. I listened. And understood. I also praised her for being honest with me. I wanted her to know that I was her safe place.

Recognizing this was a teachable moment for her, I replied, "Let me think about your struggle and get back to you with some ideas on how to handle it. I'm so proud of you for telling me."

Then I jumped into action:

- ➡ I searched God's Word for answers. I Googled "Bible verses on peer pressure" and found Luke 6:26: "Your task is to be true, not popular" (MSG).
- ➡ I spent time in prayer, asking God to guide my words and give me wisdom.
- ➡ I called one of my mentors, who reminded me that Jesus dined with sinners. Then she said, "If you tell your daughter to leave every time someone is sinning, she'll leave every situation and won't have any friends. She has to be in the world, but she doesn't have to participate. Her goal isn't to separate herself from everyone but to be a light and let Jesus shine through her." Invaluable advice!

The next day I went back to my daughter and said, "Okay, let's talk about the cussing struggle."

First, I told her about Jesus dining with sinners, and then I said, "Sometimes when you're sitting in the midst of all that bad language, it's okay to stay but not participate. Jesus did that. He hung out with sinners, He was a light. You don't have to shame kids or call them out. By not using those words, you automatically set an example, and others will notice. But there may be times when you feel prompted to speak up in a respectful way. And there will be times when you feel like you're getting sucked into whatever others are doing. That's when you need to politely excuse yourself from the situation. You should always leave if they're doing something illegal."

I ended with these Spirit-guided words: "Only you will know when to stay, when to leave, or when to speak. You have Jesus in your heart. He's your inner compass. He's the one who can point your heart in the right direction and help you make the right decisions."

Teachable moments are excellent opportunities to help our kids learn how to walk in the Spirit and seek God for themselves. Whenever something bad is happening, a red-flag alert should automatically go off in their heads, and they should take immediate action to protect their hearts and minds. If they don't, they've already fallen into the trap of complacency.

Here are some relevant Bible verses you can share with your tween:

> I will walk within my house in the integrity of my heart. I will set no worthless thing before my eyes.... A perverse heart shall depart from me; I will know no evil. (Psalm 101:2–3, 4, NASB)

> Guard your heart above all else, for it determines the course of your life. (Proverbs 4:23)

> My child, listen and be wise: Keep your heart on the right course. (23:19)

> From the heart come evil thoughts, murder, adultery, all sexual immorality, theft, lying, and slander. (Matthew 15:19)

> Temptation comes from our own desires, which entice us and drag

us away. These desires give birth to sinful actions. And when sin is allowed to grow, it gives birth to death. (James 1:14–15)

Choices begin with thoughts, and bad thoughts lead to bad choices. Pretty soon our lives start unraveling like a knitted sweater. If our children learn how to guard their hearts and minds when they're young, they'll do it instinctively as tweens and teens whenever they encounter harmful influences.

4. *"We don't take or send pictures of people without clothes on."* Sending nudes (aka "trading cards") is an epidemic among tweens and teens today. According to a recent survey, "66% of teens and young adults … have received a sexually explicit image [via sexting] and 41% have sent one."[1] Does that shock you?

Start the conversation about picture taking with your child as early as you can. Establish ground rules prohibiting devices in bedrooms, bathrooms, dressing rooms, or locker rooms. Explain that it's never okay to take or share a picture of someone without clothes.

That guideline goes for parents, too. If we expect our children to abide by our rules, we must practice what we preach. Our actions must match our words. For example, the other day my nine-year-old was taking a bubble bath and looked so adorable completely covered in bubbles that I grabbed the phone and snapped a picture.

He said, "Mom, you're breaking our rule of no phones in the bathroom."

"You aren't naked. You're completely covered with bubbles," I replied. "But you know what? You're absolutely right. I broke the rule, and that was a big mistake on my part. See, I'm learning too."

Even preschoolers can walk into the bathroom carrying an iPad. If that happens, there's no need to yell. Just enforce the family guideline by calmly explaining that it's not allowed because a picture could accidentally be taken. I've said to my kids, "What happens if you're taking a picture of something innocent but don't realize that it's picking up someone in the mirror changing clothes?"

Set guidelines regarding the kinds of pictures your kids can take, and explain the rules clearly. For example, one of our family guidelines is that parental approval must be given before photos can be taken of anyone in a bathing suit, pajamas, or less. If a photo has already been taken, our kids know they should report it to my husband or me so we can look at it with them. We always remind them it's important to protect their hearts and minds.

If you've started this conversation early, your children will already know what's unacceptable in your family by the time they enter middle school. But it's important to keep having this conversation because kids often feel like everyone else is taking nude pictures, and their peers pressure them to join in.

If your tween tells you that someone has asked for a nude photo, remain calm and thank him or her for telling you about it. Help your child process any thoughts or feelings and role-play how to say no.

Even if a photo is sent over Snapchat or another app that claims photos "disappear," anything can be screenshot and circulated online. So I always tell my daughter, "If you wouldn't want your principal or me to see it, then you shouldn't take the picture in the first place."

Sharing nude photos on social media from school locker rooms is a serious problem. No child should experience the shame and humiliation of discovering that a classmate Snapchatted an image in a locker room and then circulated it online. We need to teach our children online integrity and hold them accountable for the photos they take. Period. (Clear guidelines on the use of devices should also be established and enforced in our schools.)

5. *"None of us are perfect. Mistakes will happen, but we have to learn from them. We're all still learning."* Okay, so this foundational truth isn't exactly a one-liner, but it's essential to instill in our children when they're young. Too many kids grow up terrified of making mistakes because they somehow got the impression they should be perfect. When they mess up, they feel a deep sense of shame. We need to teach them that mistakes are a normal part of life, not something to fear or feel ashamed of.

Our kids need to understand that we aren't perfect either, and we don't expect them to be. When we mess up as parents, we should apologize. Sharing mistakes from our past can also lead to teachable moments. My children love to hear about the mistakes I made growing up. Love it! It always opens up a whole new dialogue.

Being transparent with our kids about our mistakes (past or present) isn't easy. In fact, it can make us downright uncomfortable. If your children are older, you may need to be even more transparent. It's important for them to know that once a mistake is made, it can't be erased. Talk about the painful consequences you've experienced. The agonizing nights you broke down in tears because you wanted to turn back the clock and undo your mistakes. But all you could do was ask God and others to forgive you and then try not to make the same mistake again. Make sure to remind your kids that no mistake is ever so big that God won't forgive them if they ask Him.

When someone is mean to my children or does something wrong, I say, "Well, we're all still learning." I use this phrase a lot because I don't want to shame others or raise judgmental hypocrites (Pharisees).

If my daughter says, "Did you see what so-and-so posted on Instagram today? So inappropriate," my response is, "Well, we're all still learning. But I'm glad you recognized that kind of post could offend someone."

With my kids, I try to avoid using the phrase "I'm so disappointed in you." I'm not disappointed in them when they mess up; I'm disappointed in their behavior and choices.

Last year my daughter failed to turn in an assignment at school. She's normally a responsible student, so it was completely out of character. When she asked if I would e-mail her teacher to apologize, I refused. I told her that she was in middle school, and it was her responsibility to communicate with her teacher. She did, and they had a great face-to-face conversation.

We need to teach our kids that learning from mistakes is the way we grow and develop character. If they understand what they did wrong the first time and are forced to face it, they're less likely to repeat the same mistake again. It can also serve as a valuable life lesson about personal responsibility and consequences.

When my kids make a mistake, I say, "Well, you messed up. Let's learn from this and not let it happen again. If it does, there will be a consequence, like losing phone privileges at home or being grounded."

When my daughter failed to turn in that school assignment, I didn't discipline her. Instead, I said, "Okay. This happened once, and you learned from it. If it happens again, you'll hand over your phone every day after school for three days."

My husband took advantage of this teachable moment to drive home the importance of personal responsibility. He told her, "If I fail to turn in a report at work, I could lose my job. Then we can't go to the grocery store or Starbucks. Do you see why it's important that you learn personal responsibility now? It will save you a lot of heartache in the future."

Talking through mistakes not only teaches our children practical life lessons; it's also a great way to build trust as we learn and grow together.

Now that we've laid the groundwork for open communication with our kids, let's talk about the importance of having a tribe we can turn to for encouragement on this journey.

7

Discovering the Value of a Tribe

When my daughter started fourth grade, I didn't really have a close inner circle to turn to for support or advice during this stage of parenting. But as I began paving the path for open communication with my family and learning from other moms in my group, a support system started to form organically.

Over the years this community has become a huge asset for me as I've navigated the challenges of cyberparenting. These moms guide me, encourage me, and pray for me. We walk through difficult issues together and share information about new and evolving social-media platforms and apps. God knew exactly what I needed.

A support system is vital for parenting tweens. We can't afford to go it alone. It's too hard. Even Jesus had an inner circle on Earth. He had a tribe of twelve disciples and an inner circle of His closest confidants within that tribe. They were with Him during the toughest moments of His life. (Okay, so they fell asleep in the garden and scattered when He was arrested, but Jesus still valued their friendship and support. The disciples were learning too!)

God created us for relationship, and He knows the value of community. We all need a tribe we can count on when the parenting journey gets rough.

If you're an introvert and think this whole inner-circle thing isn't for you, please give it a chance. Believe me, I know I'm asking a lot. I'm an introvert too. Community doesn't come natural to me either, and sharing the innermost details of my life with a group of women makes me uncomfortable. I'm in my late thirties, and I'm only now beginning to be real in front of my friends. Sad that I didn't learn this earlier in life.

I thought I'd conquered Mount Everest when I started opening up with my husband and children. But being transparent with other parents seemed like Mount Everest on steroids. So imagine my relief when I discovered that talking with other parents isn't the same as sharing deeply personal things with my family. For one thing, I'd never share my story in depth with a group the way I share it with my husband and children. And no matter how much I value my village, it will never replace my family. They will always come before my tribe.

But we shouldn't underestimate the value of an inner circle on this journey. We need other parents with us in the trenches. We're all struggling to survive in this "brave new world" of cyberparenting. All of our kids are being exposed to potentially harmful things online, and each of us has valuable information and experiences to share, so why not pull together, share our resources, and help one another?

The People We Count on When Life Happens

As I've worked with other moms to launch our nonprofit group nextTalk, I've learned the importance of community. Our mission is to create more open communication in our families on issues like sex, cyberparenting, social media, apps, and everything in between. Nothing is off limits. We often use the hashtag #LearningTogether because that's exactly what our group is about. None of us have all the answers.

Looking back now, I can see that God wanted me to pave the path for open communication in my family before He brought these precious women into my life. God knew. He had a plan (see Jeremiah 29:11).

I can't even begin to express how much I value these dear friends and all the wisdom and encouragement they've shared with me. They're completely honest and real. They often give me constructive, hard-to-hear criticism, but it's wrapped in love and grace. Their leadership and motherly advice is priceless. They've truly helped me become a better person.

While writing this book, I had a meltdown over a new washer my husband and I bought. In the first three weeks after it was delivered, we had more than eight service calls, and the technician flooded my house because he failed to reconnect the drain hose. So then I had to wait for insurance adjusters to come and give damage estimates.

End of my rope! I mean I had an adult-temper-tantrum breakdown. I was on my laundry-room floor crying real tears. It was ugly. I sent my next-Talk leaders a text laced with profanity and all kinds of selfish complaints. "Does anyone understand I have a book deadline in twenty-one days? I just need my washer to work correctly!" I sounded like a brat. (I know because I reread the message the next morning.)

The grace-filled text they sent back went something like this: "Step away from the washer. Go somewhere else to write. Go buy new underwear and forget about it. We're praying for you. This is not about the washer; Satan is trying to mess with you."

No condemnation or judgment, which would've been rightfully earned in light of my emotion-driven, self-absorbed tirade. Just grace and good advice.

When a friend finally got me on the phone, I was bawling like a two-year-old whose lollipop had just been ripped away by another child on the playground. Snot everywhere. I told her, "I can't do the book. It's just too much."

She calmly but firmly replied, "Mandy Majors, stop right now. Stop. When I gave birth to my firstborn without pain meds, I remember my coach telling me that right before I made the final push for that beautiful baby, I'd want to die. I'd want to give up. I'd be selfish and consumed with my own pain. It might be the worst moment of my life. But I'd push through because I'd be birthing my baby. All this work is for something amazing, Mandy. You are birthing this book. People need to hear your story. You are going to push through. You are at this selfish place where you want to quit because it's difficult. Quitting is not an option. No ma'am."

(Everyone in my village calls this friend our "No ma'am girl.")

See how blessed I am? My tribe brings me back to reality when my feelings push me to the edge of the cliff. They talk me back to normalcy and steer me in the right direction when I begin to spiral. They keep me centered and focused and call me out when I'm being selfish.

Oh, what a gift!

Building Your Inner Circle

If you don't have a close inner circle and feel the void, you're not alone. Before I developed a more intimate group of friends, I felt a void too. I used to scroll through Facebook and see all these happy, cool mom squads. I'd literally ache for these types of friendships. I had good friends, including hundreds and hundreds of Facebook "friends," and yet I didn't have an inner circle I could call at 2:00 a.m. in an emergency.

But guess what? As I prayed and trusted God, He brought together exactly the kind of tribe I needed. I know He can do the same for you. (By the way, having an inner circle is important for our husbands, too. But like many men, my husband cringes at the idea. It's not his thing. However, he does have one or two godly male friends who are husbands and fathers. They're his go-to friends for advice, but it's totally not cool to call them his inner circle. His tribe looks different from mine, and that's okay.)

So how do you build an inner circle if you don't already have one? Here are three initial steps to take:

1. Reach out to us at nextTalk. (You can find us on Facebook, Twitter, and Instagram.) We may know of a group that meets near you. If not, we can connect you with an online community in the interim. Remember, you're not alone. We're in this together.
2. Pray for God to send you good, wise, reliable, honest, and trustworthy friends. Ask Him to put together your inner circle. He knows the kind of support system you need most.
3. Reach out to people you'd like to be part of your tribe. But keep in mind that building your inner circle is a process—like developing open communication with your child. It takes time. Don't expect trust and close friendships to happen overnight. As you do your part, God will bring your inner circle together in His time and way.

There is no cookie-cutter tribe. Each tribe is different and has its own unique qualities and characteristics. But I think every great village has one thing in common: at least one mentor and a "heads-up mama." Let me explain.

Several of the women I rely on are older, wiser friends who have been in my life for years. One of them is the retired assistant middle-school principal I mentioned earlier who has shared a wealth of information with me about public-school culture. One of her kids is a college professor, and the other is a teacher. Education is in their blood and their hearts.

Another mentor is a dear friend with two beautiful, vibrant, Christ-centered daughters who recently graduated from college. One of the daughters is in ministry and is a gifted writer. It's an honor to know her before she becomes a best-selling author. The other daughter recently graduated with a master's degree and works in a psychiatric facility. It's beautiful to see each of them serving others in different ways.

These two older mentors come from very different backgrounds. One is divorced, and the other has been married for more than thirty years. They aren't close friends with each other, but together they've been the perfect mentors for me. They are truly amazing.

For me, it's especially important to have mentors with solid biblical understanding. These are my go-to people when I need to know "What does the Bible say about this?" or "Why do we believe this?" They give me sound biblical advice on putting my family first, keeping us grounded in God's truth, and choosing friends wisely.

As much as I treasure these mentors, they weren't able to give me the cyberparenting advice I needed. They never had to deal with social media or a screen-crazed, digital world when their kids were in elementary school. So when I asked God to meet this need, He blessed me with two special friendships. These cybermoms have children who are slightly older than my own kids, and let me tell you, their advice has been invaluable. I call them my *heads-up mamas*.

When my daughter was exposed to porn in fourth grade, I contacted these women. They knew exactly what I needed to do and gave me great advice. They kept me calm and pointed me to God's Word so I didn't go into crazy-mom mode.

My heads-up mamas know social media inside out, so they're able to keep me informed about new developments. They don't have tech degrees, but they have high school kids. They're in their teens' online world, and their kids teach them the ins and outs of social media and apps. My heads-up mamas are my tech guides, walking a few steps ahead of me and giving me a heads-up so I can prepare for what's coming.

Before my daughter started middle school, both of them said, "Get ready. This social-media platform is popular!" So I learned how to use that particular app. I wanted to know it thoroughly before I let my daughter download it.

We all need a tribe, but we need to be careful about the types of people we invite into our inner circles. They can either help or hinder our journeys. The Bible actually has something to say about this:

> The godly give advice to their friends; the wicked lead them astray. (Proverbs 12:26)

> Walk with the wise and become wise; associate with fools and get in trouble. (13:20)

These verses are not only good reminders for us, but they're great to share with our kids as they're developing their tribes. Again, walk the talk. Be the model.

If our choice of friends matters to God, it should matter to us as well. The women we invite into our inner circles will have a significant impact on our lives and our parenting. This isn't the time to settle for just anyone. We need to ask God for discernment and even be a little picky about our choices. It's that important.

Let's review seven important guidelines for building our inner circles:

1. *Aim for different ages and stages.* As I discussed earlier, we need godly, older mentors who can give us sound biblical advice, but we also need heads-up mamas with children a few years older than our own who can give us essential cyberparenting advice. I recommend including at least one of each in your inner circle. Pray that God will clearly lead you to moms in

later stages of parenting who will give you the right advice. Other moms with kids of various ages can offer love and support as well as different perspectives and fresh insight. You're in the trenches together trying to figure it all out.

2. *Keep your inner circle small.* Again, there is no cookie-cutter tribe, but I recommend keeping your tribe small. My inner circle is composed of nine women. They're not all from the same circle of friends, however. That's okay. I suggest no more than twelve members in your inner circle, modeled after Jesus and His tribe. Too many opinions will make it confusing, but a handful of differing perspectives is good.

3. *Seek out moms who share your values.* Shared values are important and can have a significant impact on your parenting. So look for women who share the values that are most important to you. What is their moral compass? Where do they get their truth? All of the members of my inner circle share a deep love for Jesus and believe the Bible is our moral compass for determining right and wrong. That's essential for me. We don't have everything figured out. We wrestle with verses we don't like. Sometimes we even interpret Scripture differently, but that's okay because it challenges and encourages us to grow. However, we do agree that the Bible is where we get our answers.

4. *Character matters.* Genuine, integrity-filled character can be hard to find. The moms you include in your inner circle should exhibit good character. Their actions should match their words. They shouldn't gossip about others. No one's perfect, but if their walk consistently doesn't reflect their talk, something's wrong. Ask God to lead you to people with strong character and integrity who practice what they preach. It's not about perfection; it's about character. Just as Jesus's disciples didn't always get things right, your tribe won't either. My village isn't perfect. Remember, the only one who will never let you down is God.

5. *Family values are essential.* Apart from God, family comes first. The members of your tribe should value family, promote it, and defend it when necessary. When you call your friend complaining about your spouse, you need someone who won't put your husband down but will help you see him with fresh eyes. Instead of joining in the husband bashing, she'll fight for

your marriage and remind you of the reasons you married him in the first place.

If one of my friends thinks my husband is at fault, she'll say, "This issue could create a huge wedge in your marriage. Let's pray about it and dig into Scripture." In the past I had friends who joined me in attacking my husband. But that just made me angrier with him. By the time he walked in the door after work, I was ready to rumble. We know that's not good!

Members of your inner circle should be peacemakers. Sure, friends let friends vent, but they should also help you regain perspective so you can calmly talk things out with your husband. Your inner circle should hold you accountable and speak the truth even when it's hard to hear. Good friends will call you out when venting crosses the line into trash talking.

6. *Steer clear of judgmental people.* Again, none of us have all the answers. We're all learning as we go. Your inner circle should be a safe place where everyone can share their stories, fears, and struggles about parenting in this digital world. You should respect each other's opinions. Every parent-child relationship is unique. Each of you has the right to decide how to parent your children and handle specific problems. Every family determines their own guidelines. Your family, your choice.

We give advice in my tribe, but we don't get upset if others don't take it. We may disagree, but we don't criticize or judge those who choose to do things differently. Cyberparenting is hard enough without being judged. We're free to share our opinions and openly discuss controversial issues so we can each come up with a plan that works for our individual families.

We regularly discuss complicated topics in my inner circle. Tough, tough stuff. Nobody's got time for fluff or gossip. Open communication is gut-wrenching, middle-of-the-arrow work. Grit. It's about digging deep within our souls to discover what we really believe and how we're going to answer the questions our children throw at us. My tribe tackles life head-on, even when it's difficult. We don't walk around defeated in darkness. We bring problems into the light and figure out how to handle them *together*.

An inner circle should be a community that encourages, supports, and empowers one another. We're tattered, stressed-out, busy, frazzled moms who need each other. What we *don't* need is comparing and judging. The members of your tribe should love and accept one another, faults and all. And with God at the center, your inner circle can be a beautiful place of friendship and one of your most valuable parenting resources.

No one in my inner circle or my nextTalk group knows everything or has it all together. Porn has hit our families too. Confusion and turmoil knock us off balance. Social media and its effects have caused our lives to spiral out of control. We all make mistakes, but together we're learning what parenting means in today's world.

Your inner circle should be a community of grace. Resist the urge to say "I told you so" when a friend calls you and says, "Oh my gosh, I totally missed this. A complete stranger just contacted my daughter on Instagram. Your warnings were right on target. I thought you were crazy, but I was so wrong." Extend grace and understanding. Each of us is at a different place on this journey, and we need friends who will love us and walk with us through the hard times. That's what community is about, right?

7. *Everyone in your tribe should be trustworthy.* You must be able to trust your inner circle. No one should share confidences with anyone outside the group without permission. Our goal as parents is to create a safe place for our children to openly communicate with us, so we want to avoid the following scenario.

Let's say my friend's daughter Ashley is struggling because all her friends are taking nude photos (trading cards) and sending them to boys. Ashley and her mom have a good relationship, so Ashley tells her mom about it. Ashley's mom is trying to process the information and determine next steps, so she asks her inner circle for advice. A mom in the tribe goes home and says to her daughter Eva, "Did you know Ashley's friends are taking nude photos?" Ashley and Eva happen to go to the same school, and Eva broadcasts the news on social media. She also starts calling Ashley's friends "sluts."

Now Ashley's mom is in deep trouble. Ashley told her about the nude photos in confidence. But when Ashley sees Eva's post, do you think she'll ever share anything with her mom again?

Confidentiality is no laughing matter in your inner circle. A breach can destroy the trust and open communication you're trying to build with your children. That's why it's so important to make sure the members of your inner circle are trustworthy and take confidentiality seriously.

Your tribe should also establish clear guidelines so that everyone knows what's acceptable to share outside your inner circle with permission and what isn't. When everyone agrees on specific ground rules for confidentiality and sharing, the scenario I just described will be less likely to play out.

Here are two confidentiality guidelines I've implemented in my own life:

1. If I share a story from my inner circle (or from our nextTalk group), I do so anonymously. I never share the names of people or schools.
2. I don't text my friends about my kids' secrets. If your tween son tells you about the girl he's crushing on, don't run and group-text your inner circle. What happens if he picks up your phone and sees you just blabbed that secret to your friends? He'll instantly think, *My mom just told my biggest secret to her friends. They're more important to her than keeping my confidences.* This is why I say your family always comes before your inner circle.

The only exception to the second guideline is when someone's safety is at risk. In that case, protecting a child's life takes priority. Even then, no posts on social media. You should text only the tribe members you trust wholeheartedly.

Let's say your tween just told you a big secret about a friend at school talking to a stranger online. Based on the details, you're fairly certain the stranger is a pedophile. He's older, lives out of state, and is asking personal questions like the girl's age, address, and school. In this situation I'd be thinking, *What do I need to do to protect this child? What if she's abducted, and I knew about it but failed to report it?*

I would send a text to my heads-up mamas, supplying generic information (no names) and seeking their advice. I already know what they'd say: "Contact the school counselor or the police if you don't know the parents personally." We have a responsibility to speak up when a child may be in danger.

If I need to break my own guidelines and text my friends about a situation, I normally give my kids a heads-up like this: "I'll always keep your secrets, but this is something I need to report. We'd both feel terrible if something happened to your friend. So I'm going to ask my heads-up mamas for advice to figure this out. But I won't tell them your friend's name."

Deciding what to do in these kinds of situations requires prayer and discernment, as well as sound advice from trustworthy friends. Above all, we need to rely on the Holy Spirit to keep us balanced and show us what to do. He's the key to figuring it all out. Our secret weapon.

Now that we've laid the foundation for open communication, are you ready to tackle some issues head-on? You've been brutally honest with yourself, worked on strengthening your marriage, created a safe space for your children, and started building your inner circle.

Now it's time to apply what you've learned to real-life topics. Don't worry. I've got your back!

PART 3

Real Talk

8

Facing the Storms Head-On

If you're committed to honest, open communication with your kids, buckle up. Fierce storms are ahead. They won't be run-of-the-mill thunderstorms either. I'm talking category-5 hurricanes.

When your tween starts telling you everything that's happening in his or her world, you're going to experience the downside of open communication. I want you to be prepared. You're likely to get some crazy, left-field, jaw-dropping questions.

You aren't going to just *think* you know about your child's culture, you're going to *know*. You're going to know which kids are straight-up lying to their parents. You're going to know about the straight and gay porn videos online. You're going to know which kids are cutting and which are sharing nudes. Even among the "religious" kids. Yep, I just said that.

It's downright scary.

Is your tween asking hard questions or talking about difficult things with you? If not, you'll need to work on open communication and becoming a safe place, because you may not be getting the full story. I know it may hurt to hear this, but I don't want you to make the same mistakes I did. Iron sharpens iron, right?

Believe me, tweens are seeing and hearing it ALL. So if your child isn't confiding in you, that doesn't necessarily mean everything is fine. It typically means you're out of the loop. I'm sorry. I know it stings.

The flip side is when our kids tell us everything they're seeing and hearing, but we're not really sure we want to know. Fear may tempt us to plug our ears and ignore what they're saying. It's a natural response, but Satan can use it as a manipulative tool to keep us from doing what needs to be done. We can't allow fear to overwhelm us and send us into hiding. That's complacency. We can't give up on open communication because we're afraid. No! We're alert and awake now. No quitting or letting things slide. This is too important.

I'm not being a drama mama. As I was writing this chapter, I received another notification that a middle schooler who was being bullied just committed suicide, and a teen girl went missing with an older man she met online. We're fighting for our kids' lives. Literally. Our babies are being groomed online for the sex-slave industry. The stakes are too high to give up because of fear.

Think of how much territory we've already covered. We've faced our baggage, learned the importance of strengthening our marriages and creating a safe place for our kids, and recognized the value of a tribe. We've also discovered a powerful secret weapon: the Holy Spirit.

God is showing us things. He's empowering us and building a community that will help us tackle our fears together.

Courage to Face the Storms

What calms my fears when the storms hit? Let me tell you a Bible story that my tribe talks about often.

One day Jesus's disciples were in a boat in the middle of a lake. A storm was brewing. The winds were howling around them, and waves were splashing against the boat.

The storm represents what happens when our kids are exposed to things online and then ask us honest questions about complicated issues. When our children feel safe with us, storms will hit more often. Fierce, turbulent storms. Howling winds and towering waves. When we make a choice to live in the real world and face issues head-on, we become aware of what's happening in our tweens' culture and see the storms creating chaos and confusion in their lives.

Our gut reaction is to deny or ignore what's actually happening. It seems so much easier to camp out in the boat (our comfort zone) and let the storm do its thing. But "feelings don't always equal truth."[1]

While the disciples were watching a storm brew all around them, Jesus appeared, walking toward them on the water. They were terrified because they thought He was a ghost. But He told them, "Don't be afraid.... Take courage. I am here!" (Matthew 14:27).

Jesus speaks the same words to our fearful hearts when the storms of parenthood strike.

When Peter realized it was Jesus, not a ghost, he called out, "Lord, if it's really you, tell me to come to you ... on the water."

And Jesus replied, "Come" (verses 28–29).

Peter didn't think twice. He climbed out of that boat and set off across the lake, his eyes fixed on Jesus. He was actually walking on water!

Suddenly the wind and waves filled Peter with fear. He took his eyes off Jesus and began to sink.

Isn't that what we all do? We climb out of the boat, intent on addressing an issue. We start out strong with our eyes on Jesus. Our problems seem smaller and more manageable when He's in control. We're walking in the Spirit. Then all of a sudden, a wave slams into us, and we lose our focus on Jesus. Our eyes are on the storm. We cower in fear and begin to sink.

At least Peter had the sense to cry out, "Save me, Lord!" (verse 30).

And guess what happened? Jesus immediately reached out His hand, grabbed hold of Peter, and saved him.

Immediately! Don't miss this.

When we're sinking and cry out to Him, Jesus is instantly there to help us. He doesn't fold His arms and say, "I'm a little irritated because you haven't been listening to Me lately, so I'm going to let you drown."

No. He *immediately* reaches out to save us. That doesn't mean He'll instantly resolve our problems. He may require us to wait for an answer or make some changes in our lives. But we can trust Him to hear our cries and respond when we call to Him for help.

After Jesus rescued His water-logged disciple, He said, "You have so little faith.... Why did you doubt me?" (verse 31).

Notice that Jesus didn't just save Peter; He also confronted Peter's lack of faith. It's the same with us. God rescues us, but He holds us accountable in His loving, fatherly way so we can learn from our mistakes.

The lessons Peter learned that day are relevant for us as we navigate the stormy seas of parenthood. God is the only one who can pull us out of deep waters and fix our messes. He is bigger than any storm we'll ever face.

Let's say you find some inappropriate DMs (direct messages) between your tween and his girlfriend in his social-media app. You really don't want to address this. You're frustrated and don't even know where to start.

God wants you to get out of the boat and trust Him. You need to acknowledge the problem. Tackle it. Bring it into the light. But it feels safer in the boat. It's your comfy place. So you ignore the problem. Denial is so much easier. Instead of facing your fears and inadequacies, you'd rather sweep it all under the rug.

Here's the thing. Do you actually think the problem will go away if you ignore it? That things won't get worse, and your son won't continue to spiral down?

Don't be manipulated into believing that this problem will solve itself.

You need the courage to face this storm head-on and get out of the boat, relying on Jesus to help you discuss the issue with your son in a calm, logical manner. Trust me. God can turn this curse into a blessing. It's a beautiful thing when He transforms a situation and creates open communication in a relationship.

Listen, girl. You *cannot* live in denial. You can't. You know what needs to be done. Jesus wants you to trust Him enough to leave the safety of your boat. He wants to calm the raging storm and take away your fear so you can help your child.

Remember the arrow we talked about earlier? It represents grit and hard work. Being willing to get out of the boat and walk with Jesus on the water.

Only one disciple was willing to take that step of obedience: Peter. All the other disciples stayed in the boat—their safe place. But Peter wanted to go much deeper in his relationship with Jesus. To reach way beyond his comfort zone. So he got out of the boat.

The other disciples missed out on a faith-stretching experience with Jesus because they didn't step out and take the risk.

To experience Jesus, we have to get our butts out of the boat and be willing to venture into uncharted territory. We have to brave the storm that is swirling around us, fix our eyes on Him, and trust Him to help us.

The Choice: Live in Denial or Face the Storms

As I'm writing this, my eyes are puffy because my daughter and I were in tears last night. Really serious, tough stuff happens in middle school. Our kids are struggling to figure out who they are and how they're supposed to act. Online exposure takes it to a whole new level in today's digital world.

Middle-school culture is filled with judgment and stereotypes and labels. Cutting and self-harm are real. FaceTiming with strangers is no biggie. Asking for nudes is a thing. Eleven-year-olds are walking around casually announcing to the world that they're bi (you know, bisexual). Tweens think it's cool.

Guys, I'm not making this up. Why is no one talking about it? No more denial! I can't imagine the pressure and confusion our tweens are experiencing. They need us to wake up and get out of the boat RIGHT NOW.

As we take that first step toward open communication, we begin to enter their day-to-day world. We walk in their shoes. We hear the real stuff. And it stinks.

Don't get me wrong. I'm *so* thankful my kids are talking to me. So very thankful. But every time they share more stories with me, I feel like I've been punched in the gut.

Last night after both of my kids were asleep, I told my husband, "I just want to live in denial. I don't want to know any more. Ignorance is bliss."

He replied, "That's a lie. Living in denial isn't an option. Face it and conquer it."

He's so right. We have a choice to make every day: Will we live in denial or face the parenting storms that come our way? Remember what we learned about listening to God? It's a moment-by-moment choice. We have to continually face the storms, or we'll end up sliding back into complacency and cluelessness. We'll miss the life lessons Jesus wants to teach us. We'll miss the character building and seeing how God can turn our curses into blessings.

If I'm not struggling as a parent, I know I'm probably missing something. Or I'm complacent. We don't grow by taking the easy way. Growth happens in the middle of the storm—when we rely on God's strength, not our own.

We can't let our tweens face the storms alone. They need us to enter their world and confront their reality so we can help them navigate through it. Will we want to quit sometimes? Yes. I want to quit almost every time a new issue comes up. Will fear overwhelm us at times? Absolutely. Satan loves to use our feelings against us.

But we're *not* alone in the storm. Jesus is with us. Philippians 4:13 says, "I can do everything through Christ, who gives me strength."

We can do this, Mama.

Navigating through the Storms of Life

In the following chapters, we'll be wrestling with the issues parents ask me about most often. Some questions will have clear-cut, black-and-white answers in the Bible. Others won't. When we encounter gray areas where there are no right or wrong answers—like "When should my tween get a phone?"—I'll share how my husband and I (or my heads-up mamas) made decisions and discussed the issues with our kids.

I realize you may not always agree with how I've handled a certain issue. That's okay. I respect your right to make different choices. Your family, your choice. Only you can decide what's best for your family. Remember, I'm not an expert. I'm just a mom like you, figuring things out one step at a time and sharing with you as I learn. In real time.

I want you to pull up a chair and join our family at our kitchen island. Drive along with us in the car. Listen in on our conversations. Think about how you might approach the issues with your kids, because there isn't a script to follow. Each child is different. Each parent-child relationship is dynamic.

As we've already discovered, so much information is just one click away. Our children are asking tough questions in elementary school and middle school that previous generations didn't ask until high school or beyond. We're in uncharted territory, and our tweens need help to safely navigate the complex issues they face.

Now is the time to apply what you've learned about open communication to the real-life situations your children encounter every day: stay calm, listen, pray, be a safe place for your tween, use your parent filter.

My goal for this section is simple: I want to open up the discussion so we can figure out together how to communicate with our kids about specific issues and not be paralyzed with fear. We have to break the silence.

The topics we'll be covering aren't exhaustive. I've limited the discussion to issues that come up most often in my own family, at speaking events, and in meetings with other parents. As we walk through each topic, we'll discuss ways we might address it and explain it to our kids. I'll include some helpful statistics as well, but keep in mind that the digital world is changing so rapidly, research on tech-related topics is often outdated.

I'll also share examples of real conversations my kids and I have had and suggest some ideas and questions you can use to jump-start conversations in your family. The examples I share offer a glimpse of the struggles our family faced to be honest and real with one another. Sometimes we discussed topics before our kids encountered them, and at other times, we had to address them on the fly. These examples aren't cookie-cutter templates that will work for everyone. You'll need to determine what will be most helpful for your children and modify your approach to fit your situation.

I haven't directly encountered some issues as a parent, so I can't share from personal experience how I walked my children through them. For example, my kids haven't questioned their sexuality or gender identity, and they've never been suicidal. So if your child is dealing with issues like these, I'd encourage you to seek out the advice of a medical expert (your family doctor, a counselor, etc.). What I can offer in addition to the conversations I've had about these issues with my own children are some of the steps my husband and I have taken to *prepare* them for what they may encounter.

The tween years are prime time to instill values and pour a solid foundation they can build on.

No matter what your kids are walking through, *love them*. Unconditionally. Remember, their mistakes don't define your identity. Your identity is in Jesus alone.

If your children are younger, I recommend reading this book and then working on paving the path for open communication with your kids. Discuss the topics in this section with your husband to see where you both stand. (Don't try to cover everything in one night. You can do this over the course of several months.) Figure out your cyberparenting plan together. I wouldn't discuss any of these topics with your preschool or elementary-age children unless they come up in conversation. You're in information-gathering mode right now. Way to go for being so proactive. You figured it out way before I did!

If your children are older and are already engulfed in social media, you'll need to jump in with both feet. Don't buy Satan's lie that it's too late to build trust and open communication with your kids. Anything is possible with God. But before you talk with them, try to get on the same page with your spouse regarding how to approach the situation.

Again, walking with balance in the Spirit is essential for open communication. If God opens a door and your child asks a question about a specific topic you're ready to tackle, follow the Spirit's lead and dive into that conversation.

As we encounter the storms ahead, this is my heart's prayer for each of us:

Lord Jesus, help us keep our eyes on You, not the storms. Help us look to You for the courage and wisdom we need to get out of the boat and face the wind and waves head-on. Give us open ears and sensitive hearts that seek to listen to Your voice. Teach us how to effectively listen to our husbands and kids. Really hear them. May we become a safe place for them. Show us what we need to improve as parents. Help us stay balanced and on point. Create a new dynamic in our families that is real, honest, and open. Teach us how to communicate with one another in a way that will deepen our relationships. Father, bring into the light the issues our children are struggling with so that we can work through them together. I pray that You would use the curses in our lives for good and turn them into the blessing of more open communication. Most of all, give us hearts that truly seek You and trust You on this parenting journey. I ask this in Your name. Amen.

9

Phones and Contracts

Technology Guidelines, Social Media and Apps, Monitoring Products and Filters

One of the questions parents ask me the most is "When should I allow my child to have his or her own phone?"

If you're wondering the same thing, you may be disappointed to hear that there are no cut-and-dried answers to this question. You know your children better than anyone, so only you can make that decision. Since each child is unique, you may decide to allow your kids to have a phone at different ages based on specific factors, such as maturity level. Your family, your choice.

But don't worry. I'm not going to end the conversation there and leave you hanging. We have a lot to talk about!

Throughout this chapter, I'll share the three-step approach we implemented in our home. One of the benefits of this approach is that we were able to gradually transition our daughter into having her own phone. Before moving on to the next step in the process, Matt and I made sure she demonstrated the skills and responsibility we expected.

As we unpack these steps, we'll discuss questions to ask yourself to determine when each of your kids is ready for a phone. (Note: when I use the word *phone*, I'm referring to a smartphone with online features.) We'll also talk about establishing phone guidelines and a written contract so your child understands your expectations and family ground rules. By the end of our conversation, we'll see once again that even though rules and restrictions are good and necessary, it's all about relationship.

Before we dive in, though, let's take a quick look at some big-picture statistics. According to a Pew Research survey,

- Only 12 percent of teens between the ages of thirteen and seventeen reported having no phone.
- Ninety-one percent of teens "go online from mobile devices at least occasionally," and of that group, 94 percent "go online daily or more often."
- Seventy-one percent of teens "use more than one social-network site."[1]

Some parents ask me why I don't discuss whether kids should have phones in the first place. For them, it's about morality more than timing. Here's the thing: right or wrong, like it or not, phones and other digital devices are part of our world. My husband and I have chosen to accept that reality. Of course, my job as a cyberparent would be way easier if kids didn't have phones at all. But they do. Only 12 percent don't.

Matt and I decided that our daughter was ready to have her own phone in fifth grade. Since then we've had more input, not less, about what she looks at. When she didn't have her own phone, she was exposed to pictures, videos, and other inappropriate content kids were showing her. So instead of saying no to a phone, Matt and I made a conscious decision to teach ourselves how to effectively parent it.

Over the past few years, we've learned to manage the technology and teach our daughter how to safely use it. We walk hand in hand with her as we learn how to navigate this digital world together.

I will say this: delay giving your tween a phone as long as you can. (My tween son doesn't have a phone, but he's already asking for one. I'm saying no for now and telling him there are too many naked pictures online.) Please don't take this decision lightly. It's a *huge* responsibility that will require a lot of work on your part.

Don't make the same mistakes I did. This isn't about getting your tween a phone, checking it off your cyberparenting to-do list, and then coasting.

It's about talking through phone-related issues with your child on a daily basis. Open communication. This is an important distinction we can't afford to miss.

Step by Step

If you're willing to accept the extra parental responsibility of monitoring your child's phone use, then you need to decide whether your tween is ready to have his or her own phone. Notice I said tween. No matter how responsible or mature your child is, I don't recommend giving a phone to a child under eight years of age.

Once a child enters the tween years, there are still many factors to consider before deciding whether he or she is actually ready for a phone. Like open communication, it's a process. This brings us to the first step in our three-step approach.

Step 1: Prep and Practice

Before we gave our daughter her own phone, I let her practice on mine. During this stage, I continued building open communication and trust with her. We talked about expectations and family guidelines for using the phone. I explained how she should handle inappropriate content and made sure she was consistently reporting it to me. I also began asking myself some key questions to determine if I thought she was ready for her own phone.

I'd recommend asking yourself the same questions:

1. Does my tween know how to operate a phone and regularly use one to communicate with friends?
2. When my child sees bad words or pictures on any digital device, does he or she tell me?
3. Does my tween abide by our family technology guidelines (such as no online searching without a parent)? Or have I caught him or her disregarding the rules?
4. Why does my child need a phone?

Let's tackle these questions one at a time.

1. *Does my tween know how to operate a phone and regularly use one to communicate with friends?* For years before my daughter got her own phone, she would text and play games on my phone. It was great practice for both of us. I easily monitored her content, and she learned how to communicate with friends via text messages. Breaking news: tweens text more emojis in their messages than actual words!

Toward the end of fourth grade, my daughter started asking for her own phone. That's not when we let her have one, but my husband and I started thinking about it. We didn't just say no. We actually told her, "We're thinking and praying about it, but our main goal is to keep you safe. There are inappropriate photos and videos online, as well as strangers who will message you and want to talk. We don't want you to be in an awkward situation and not know how to respond. We trust you; it's the other people we don't trust."

We almost always explain to our children the reasoning behind our decisions and try to refrain from using the phrase "Because I said so." This helps build an open, honest relationship. Remember, the goal is to be our kids' safe place.

2. *When my child sees bad words or pictures on any digital device, does he or she tell me?* Several years ago we were eating dinner with friends in a Mexican restaurant, and my daughter (a fourth grader at the time) was using an app on my phone that was recommended for kids four years of age or older. She built her own avatar, picking hair color, clothes, accessories, and other features to mirror her own appearance. Then she texted the cartoon-like character to her friends. She and her three closest friends shared their cute little avatars via group text.

As we were sitting there, she came over to me and whispered, "There's something bad on this app."

I looked at it. One of the shirts said, "F*** You." The entire cuss word was spelled out, and I almost spit the queso right out of my mouth! It was rated 4-plus! However, I didn't announce it to everyone at the table or show them the app, because I didn't want to embarrass my tween. Remember, I don't tell her secrets or broadcast the info she gives me.

Instead, I stayed calm and whispered to her that I was so thankful she showed me. Remember, the parent filter.

That night I told my husband, "I think we can trust her. She's really learning how to use a phone and report things to me."

Even then we decided to wait a little longer before giving her a phone and kept observing her screen-behavior patterns.

If your child regularly uses your phone and hasn't shown you anything inappropriate, make sure your technology guidelines are clear. What do you expect your tween to report to you? Bad words? Pictures? Kids are likely to see something inappropriate online, so if your tween hasn't reported anything to you, he or she may not understand the family guidelines. (Or, as I've already mentioned, your tween may not be telling you about it. If that's the case, you'll need to spend more time working on open communication.)

In our family, the guideline is that bad words and any picture of someone in a bathing suit or less should be reported. That doesn't mean I think all bathing-suit pictures are bad. That's just our threshold so I can make sure our kids are reporting things to Matt or me.

3. *Does my tween abide by our family technology guidelines (such as no online searching without a parent)? Or have I caught him or her disregarding the rules?* This is pretty self-explanatory. If your tween disregards simple tech guidelines regarding the family iPad or your phone, he or she isn't ready for more freedom. Hold off for now. (Remember the kite-string illustration?) Extend more freedom only if your tween proves to be trustworthy (positive reinforcement). And when you do, make sure you explain how your child earned it.

When Matt and I finally decided to give my daughter a phone, one of the first things we said to her was, "Showing us the avatar with the cuss word proved to us that we could trust you. We need you to keep reporting those things to us. The more open and honest you are with us, the more freedom you'll earn."

4. *Why does my child need a phone?* Of course, every tween wants a phone to communicate with friends, but what are the actual benefits of having one? Your child may need it for time away from home or after-school activities or for a variety of other good reasons. It's going to require more work on your part, so let's make sure your tween really needs a phone.

When my daughter was a fifth grader in elementary school, I learned that the following year in middle school, she would be allowed to use a phone without restrictions during lunchtime. Phone use before and after school and in some classes, with teacher approval, would also be permitted. This was a big deal for me as a parent.

So my question for you is, what are your school-district rules regarding student phone use? This may impact your decision about when to get your tween a phone.

I knew my daughter would be exposed to lots of additional online content in middle school—some appropriate, some not so much. (I knew this because it was already happening in elementary school on more than one occasion.) I was also concerned that other kids would take pictures of her and post them on social media. As a parent, I knew I needed to be in her online world, and I realized I'd have more input if she had her own device, because I'd be able to set guidelines and discuss expectations with her.

Now that my daughter is in middle school, she stays after school for activities. So my husband and I simply ask her to text me as soon as she arrives at her destination. She'll say something like "Here and safe. See you later at pickup." Knowing she is where she's supposed to be after school does a mama's heart good.

After you've considered these questions and walked your tween through some practice rounds, continue monitoring and coaching until you're ready for the next step.

Step 2: Phone Privileges, Family Guidelines, and Contracts

Once Matt and I were confident that our tween could operate a phone proficiently, understood our family guidelines and expectations, and demonstrated that she was responsible and trustworthy, we started her off with a hand-me-down phone. That way if the phone was ever lost, stolen, or damaged, we wouldn't take a major financial hit.

At the beginning, we only gave our daughter permission to send text messages and play games. Since calling isn't cool anymore, we also allowed her to FaceTime her friends as long as she was in an open area of the house, like the family room or kitchen. I'd remind her, "Before you FaceTime, clap to get our attention so we can make sure everyone is appropriately dressed in the background." (Yes, my son likes to run around in his underwear.)

Even though Matt and I had talked with her about our expectations, we felt it was important to draw up a contract we could all sign. The contract spelled out our family guidelines, including any consequences if the rules were violated. We carefully reviewed the contract with our daughter before signing. Yes, we did. We went through each point and made sure she fully understood what she was agreeing to. This was the only serious sit-down talk we've ever had with our daughter (since open communication is an on-the-go approach). We entrusted her with a lot when we gave her that little device. Signing that contract was a big deal. We sat around the kitchen table, and she signed her name as if she were signing a mortgage.

I recommend putting your family guidelines and expectations in a written contract like we did. But keep in mind that it's also important to have an ongoing conversation with your tween about appropriate and inappropriate tech behavior. Open communication is essential.

Our children are growing up in a new digital generation where they don't think real-world rules apply to their online world. Most kids don't realize there's a real person on the other end of every screen. This is why we need to be intentional about establishing ground rules for their online behavior.

I often say to my daughter, "The online world is the real world now. Anything you text or post can be distributed to the world with one screenshot. That's real life."

It's easier to introduce technology guidelines before your kids get their own phones, but if you didn't, don't let that discourage you. My heads-up mamas are great at parenting this issue, and they never used written guidelines or contracts. They have real, open communication with their teens about their online world and discuss issues as they arise.

If your children don't have their own phones yet, you have a golden opportunity to introduce crystal-clear guidelines detailing what they should and shouldn't do with their phones and what will happen if they break the rules. You're ahead of the game!

There are tons of sample phone contracts online. Find one you like and modify it to fit your family guidelines (see the appendix for a sample contract). Matt and I established the following guidelines for our daughter, but what you decide to include in a contract may be different:

- We emphasized that a phone is not a diary. Nothing online is private. Technology is public. Anything our daughter types, texts, posts, or snaps can be screenshot and made available to the world in a second.
- We reminded her that we pay the phone bill, so we can have access to her device at any time.
- We require that she get our approval before downloading and using any new apps, music, social media, or other media.
- We don't allow any phone use in bedrooms or bathrooms, behind closed doors, during meals, or at bedtime.
- We require that our daughter turn her phone over to us each evening before bedtime.
- When our daughter first got her phone, she wasn't allowed to search online without permission. Now she can search online in an open area of the house by herself. (This will vary by age.)
- Our daughter is not allowed to change phone restrictions, settings, or passwords without our approval. (Note: I strongly recommend setting restrictions on your tween's phone and any other device from the beginning. You can do this on most phones by going to "Settings" and then "General." Select "Restrictions" and "Enable Restrictions." Then create a four-digit pass code. I don't recommend sharing this code with your child. The music setting can be changed from "explicit" to "clean," and movies and TV shows can be rated—hers is set to PG. Websites and Siri can be restricted to limit adult content. Apps can be restricted as well—hers is set to 12-plus.)
- Our daughter is required to report any cyberbullying she witnesses or hears about online. She also knows there will be consequences if she is cruel or unkind to others. I tell her she shouldn't type, text, post, or comment on anything she wouldn't say in front of me, her dad, her principal, or her teachers.

- If our daughter loses or damages her phone, she's responsible for replacing it with her own money.
- She's not allowed to communicate with online strangers. This includes texting, calling, FaceTiming, live streaming, DMing (direct messaging), or any other type of communication. She is also not allowed to respond to a message, call, or other communication if she doesn't recognize the number or person. If a cyberstranger tries to contact her, she should report it to Matt or me.
- We set clear guidelines for taking pictures. As I mentioned earlier, in our family, parental approval must be given before photos can be taken of anyone in a bathing suit, pajamas, or less.
- We require our daughter to report inappropriate or harmful online content to us, including bad language, pictures, and videos.
- We make clear there will be consequences if she breaks any of the rules. We determine what the consequences will be on a case-by-case basis, but we try to make sure the severity of the consequence matches the offense. For example, we might take away her phone after she gets home from school.
- We often emphasize that people are more important than screens, and she needs to put away the phone when she's hanging out with friends. When our daughter goes over to a friend's house, I'll say, "Remember, you're there to hang out with your friends. Put the phone away." We want her to invest in real relationships, not screen time. We also know it's important for us to practice what we preach.

Be careful not to water down your contract. For example, don't say, "Hand over your phone every night at eight o'clock," if it will actually be nine or ten o'clock on some nights. We all know our crazy, unpredictable evening schedules. So I used this wording in my tween's contract instead: "I will hand the phone to my parents at a designated time each evening before I go to bed."

If your tween breaks the phone and has agreed in the contract to pay for it, follow through. My daughter has had to pay for two screen replacements. It's a clear rule in the contract, and it teaches responsibility. If you say it, stick to it. This goes for all parenting guidelines. If you aren't going to follow through and enforce a rule, don't create the guideline in the first place.

You may need to modify the contract from time to time, adding or removing privileges, establishing new rules and guidelines, or clarifying anything your tween may not have understood. Before updating the contract, however, talk with your tween about the changes you think are necessary.

Remember, it's not just about rules; it's about relationship.

Step 3: Social Media

Social media has so many facets and talking points, it needs a chapter of its own (coming up next). But I've included it in this chapter because it's important to wait at least a few months before letting tweens open a social-media account. I recommend letting them get comfortable with texts, games, and other apps on their phones and then adding a controlled, private social-media platform. Once they've mastered the basics and know the family guidelines, social media can be added to the mix.

As cyberparents, we need to recognize that a shift in social media has taken place. Twitter, Snapchat, Instagram, and Facebook are still popular social-media platforms, but many other apps offer kids a way to connect online. These apps are also considered social media. For example, musical.ly is a popular app among elementary-age kids that lets them create their own music videos and share them online. So when your child wants a new app, find out whether it allows kids to connect with others online. This can help you make an informed decision.

Once our daughter had her own phone, we waited several months before allowing her to open a social-media account. It was a gradual process of building trust and open communication, and we didn't want to rush things. But as she proved that she was responsible and trustworthy, we looked for the right opportunity to give her more privileges and freedom. When she told us about a peer-pressure situation at school, Matt and I decided to reward her with a social-media account.

Now that she's older, she'll come to us and say, "Hey, I want this app. Is it okay?" I research it quickly and then give her my reply. If I approve the app, I let her know I'm allowing it because she has demonstrated that

I can trust her, and I remind her of the specific instance when she reported something to me. If I don't want her to download it, I'll explain the reason or tell her I need to do more thorough research.

Like the kite-string illustration I mentioned earlier, Matt and I would extend more freedom (let out more string) as she earned our trust, and we'd limit freedom (reel in the string) if she violated any of our family guidelines. Most important, we always talked through any issues that came up.

Beyond Filters and Restrictions

I used to think that monitoring my daughter's phone usage was enough. That was a mistake. Now I'm really passionate about monitoring *and* teaching (which includes lots of open communication).

Parents often ask me to recommend monitoring products, but I shy away from it. We need to think beyond filters and restrictions. Here's why: I haven't yet found a reliable product that monitors or filters everything. And phone restrictions won't catch anything inappropriate *within* an app.

For example, even though restrictions are set on my daughter's phone, porn has popped up on social media (which she reported to me). So this is an ongoing discussion. I remind my daughter, "I have restrictions set on your phone like I do on my own phone to help filter some content, but it won't catch everything. You are responsible for what you allow to enter your mind and heart."

It's important to keep in mind that all social-media apps have search capabilities, and most kids perform in-app searches (or hashtag searches) in lieu of web searches. They also communicate within apps or through direct messages (DMs) in lieu of texts. So if you're just monitoring text messages, you're probably missing most of their conversations *within* the apps.

The majority of products on the market today only filter web searches and allow wifi connections to be disabled. None of the products I've researched so far allow parents to monitor communication or searches *within* apps. In my opinion, these products offer a false sense of security.

Can you still use these products for web filtering? Absolutely. But make sure they're only a backup plan. Our first line of defense should be teaching our kids to use their devices responsibly and safely—the same approach we'll take when we teach them how to drive a car. I'm already preparing my daughter by talking about driving rules and street signs, just as we talked about online issues *before* she got her own phone. It's a step-by-step process.

Ongoing conversations with our kids go hand in hand with teaching and monitoring. That's where the hard work (the arrow) comes in.

I think of phone restrictions the way I think of dieting. I have a mom bod and would love to tone up and lose some weight. Anyone else? I want an easy fix, a miracle pill. But it doesn't exist. Supplements, vitamins, and special shakes can help, but I know that getting in shape is going to require hard work—diet and exercise.

Phone restrictions and products that monitor online activity are like supplements, vitamins, and shakes. They're helpful tools, but they're no substitute for the hard work of continual open communication with our tweens about their ever-changing online world.

Remember when we talked about the importance of teaching our kids to listen to the Holy Spirit telling them when to stay, when to speak up, and when to leave a face-to-face situation? They need to do the same in their online world. If they have Jesus in their hearts, He can show them when to download, delete, post, or report what they see online.

My son came to me recently and said, "Mom, I saw boobies on a YouTube Minecraft search."

I could see that it wasn't porn (it was a very low-cut shirt), but it was still a teachable moment.

I replied, "I'm so glad you told me. God tells us to protect our hearts and minds, so it's your job to look away when you see things like that. You did the right thing."

After our little talk, he went on with his Minecraft search.

I love teachable moments like this because my son is learning how to respond when he sees something inappropriate, without being exposed to actual porn. And you know what? He did everything right. When he saw a lot of cleavage, a red flag went off in his brain that told him to look away and report the image to me.

This was also a great opportunity to affirm his integrity. I hugged him and told him how proud I was that he was protecting his mind from bad images. Then I thanked him for telling me and reminded him, "You'll never get in trouble for being honest with me." (There may be consequences for his choices, but I always praise his honesty.)

I could have told him to delete the Minecraft app immediately, and he never would have played it again. But I would have been punishing him for being honest instead of affirming what he did right.

Once again, it's about balance. These aren't black-and-white issues. Every app is different, so that's why it's important to know the apps our kids are using and become familiar with them. If the situation warrants an intervention, I might say, "You're seeing a lot of inappropriate stuff on this app. Maybe we should reevaluate this one, since God wants us to protect our hearts and minds. What do you think?"

Instead of just monitoring and enforcing restrictions, I take advantage of teachable moments with my kids. We have ongoing conversations about our family tech guidelines, integrity, and what it means to walk in the Spirit on their own. This takes me out of the equation so they're answering directly to God. They need to do the right thing when something inappropriate flashes on the screen and I'm in the laundry room (where I feel like I live!). I want them to learn to make the right choices when no one else is looking and without relying on filters, restrictions, and monitoring devices.

Monitoring and restrictions have their advantages, but teaching a child to listen to the Spirit and follow his or her moral compass is the best monitoring device a parent could ever hope for.

10

Social Media

Popularity, Comparisons, Desensitization, Cyberstrangers

Social media is a beast of its own. As we learned in chapter 9, it's a way to connect and share online with other people. Social media isn't inherently bad. It's amazing and genius. But we need to prepare our tweens for dangers that can sneak up on them when they're using it. *Before* allowing them to access social media, it's important to lay some groundwork. Over the next several chapters, we'll cover other dangers associated with social media, but first we'll briefly address the following issues:

- Popularity
- Comparisons
- Desensitization
- Cyberstrangers

The Popularity Trap

Kids want "likes" on social media. They want to be known. To be popular, even famous. (Heck, moms struggle with this too.)

A CNN survey of more than two hundred thirteen-year-olds found that they frequently checked their social media "due to a need to monitor their own popularity status, and defend themselves against those who challenge it."[1] In *#BeingThirteen: Inside the Secret World of Teens*, a special report citing the survey results, Anderson Cooper noted the following:

- Sixty-one percent of teens said they wanted to see whether their online posts are getting likes and comments.
- Thirty-six percent of teens said they wanted to see if their friends are doing things without them.[2]

Do you know what FOMO means? Fear of missing out. That's what 36 percent of the teens in the survey feared. (Note: Tweens speak in abbreviations. So if you don't know an abbreviation, Google it.)

However, being liked on social media doesn't necessarily equal popularity. Some people are so desperate to be popular, they even buy likes. (Yes, they really do.) But social media shouldn't be about having the most likes or followers. That shouldn't be the goal. Popularity is shallow and fleeting.

The perception of social media needs to change. It's crucial that we teach our kids to be their one-of-a-kind selves. Instead of seeking to be popular, they should stay true to who they are no matter what others think. Their "task is to be true, not popular" (Luke 6:26, MSG). That's the mind-set we need to instill in our kids.

Even parents can get caught in the popularity trap. We need to remember that our purpose in life isn't to please other people or seek their approval. There's only one person we answer to: God. Our identity is in Him alone. He's ultimately the one we should seek to please. Galatians 1:10 says, "I'm not trying to win the approval of people, but of God. If pleasing people were my goal, I would not be Christ's servant."

So, what is the purpose of social media if it isn't to have the most likes or followers? For one thing, it's a fun way to share our lives with an outer circle of friends we know in real life. But. Not. Every. Detail. The most personal and intimate details of our kids' lives should be reserved only for family (their safe place). They may also share their ups and downs and some personal details with an inner circle of friends. But they should be much more cautious about what they share with their outer circle of friends, including their social-media friends. They should never share personal information online. We need to walk them through online etiquette so they know what's appropriate to post and what isn't. Maybe a picture every other day or news about what they're doing, but not a picture or post every five minutes. And if they're angry or upset, they should disconnect from social media until they cool off.

As parents, we need to make sure we have the right mind-set on popularity so we can teach our kids the real purpose of social media. If they understand that it's not about popularity, they'll be less likely to cave to peer pressure and post inappropriate pictures for attention or accept follower requests from strangers just to get another like.

I know tweens who delete pictures on their social-media accounts if they don't get a certain number of likes within an hour or so of posting. Living for the approval of others is dangerous, and it can seriously damage their self-esteem.

I also see tweens online asking for an RDH (rate date hate). Many responses go something like this: "8, No, Nah." That means an 8 out of 10 rating on looks; "No, I wouldn't date you"; and "Nah, I don't hate you." Sometimes the response is "BTFS, Yes, No." BTFS means "Break the f***ing scale" (you're off-the-charts hot); "Yes, I'd date you"; and "No, I don't hate you."

What if the response was "1, No, Yes." What would that do to a child's self-esteem?

Some other examples of online tween talk are TBH (to be honest) requests and responses like "cute or hot AF" (AF = as F***). I've also seen hateful, demeaning, and negative comments.

This kind of dialogue is one important reason we should be involved in our children's lives and continually talk with them about their online world. When I randomly see someone asking for a RDH or TBH online as I scroll through my feed, I'll say to my kids, "This could open the door for criticism and bullying. Besides, do we seek the approval of others? No."

The obsession with popularity is rampant in social media today. But my goal as a mom isn't to raise popular kids. (I worked hard to be popular when I was in school. I know what it took, and I live with a lot of regrets.) I want to raise kids who have integrity and shine like bright lights with kindness, respect, and love for all people.

Comparisons: Cancer in the Bones

Theodore Roosevelt said, "Comparison is the thief of joy." Truth. We all struggle with comparisons and feeling jealous of what others post. I know I do. I pull up my social-media account and see glamorous photos of Angela vacationing in the Bahamas for the *fourth time* this month. Oh, wait. She and her husband just bought a third house there because they like it so much. Everyone in the family is always smiling. They're all so beautiful. Never a hair out of place, and the outfits always coordinate.

Comparing our real, everyday lives with other people's social-media lives is another dangerous trap we can easily fall into. More often than not, social media doesn't reflect reality. People take pictures with filters and then edit them for a million hours until they look perfect. They certainly aren't going to post news about their bankruptcy or the affair their spouse is having, right?

If you're constantly making comparisons on social media or being overcome with jealousy, sign off. Unplug. Disconnect. Take a break and reground yourself in truth. Encourage your tween to do the same. Comparisons and jealousy can sneak up on us. We have to constantly guard against these destructive tendencies and talk with our children about them.

Here's what the Bible says:

> A peaceful heart leads to a healthy body … [but] jealousy is like cancer in the bones. (Proverbs 14:30)

> Don't compare yourself with others. Each of you must take responsibility for doing the creative best you can with your own life. (Galatians 6:5, MSG)

The *Dove Evolution* video that went viral several years ago is an excellent reminder of how dangerous comparisons can be. I love it! It's a sixty-second clip of a woman going from no makeup to complete supermodel, ready for a magazine cover. The video effectively illustrates the power of makeup and editing. It ends with this statement: "No wonder our perception of beauty is distorted."[3] I think every tween girl should see the clip so they'll realize that comparisons are often based on half truths or lies.

When I'm in the grocery checkout line with my daughter, and she's looking at the flawless pictures of models on magazine covers, I'll ask, "Do you think that's 100 percent real? Do you think that photo has been edited at all?" I want her to stop and think before she falls into the trap of comparing herself with airbrushed magazine models. Anyone can edit a photo.

When our kids are on social media, we need to have an ongoing conversation with them about their self-esteem. We don't want them to perceive themselves negatively because they're comparing themselves with an airbrushed photo. Peer pressure on social media is intense, so it's especially important to talk with our daughters about body image and self-esteem.

Our daughters often take cues from us and model our behavior. If we call ourselves "fat" or "ugly," they'll follow suit. Here's my personal rule (which I break occasionally because I'm still learning): if I wouldn't say it to someone else, I'm not going to say it to myself. We all have qualities we don't like about ourselves. I hate my nose, for example. But I've learned to be okay with it and accept it the way it is because it's how God created me. By sharing our own struggles with our daughters, we can help them understand that everyone struggles with their body image. But we don't have to give in to the Enemy's lies. Instead of belittling ourselves, we can learn to accept ourselves the way we are.

We need to frequently remind our children (and ourselves) that God hand-designed each of us. No one else in the entire world has our unique DNA. Each of us is a one-of-a-kind masterpiece with special gifts and abilities. Psalm 139 says we're "fearfully and wonderfully made" (verse 14, NIV). God created us to shine in our own way, not to be exactly like everyone else.

The Dangers of Desensitization

Our children are exposed to so much violent and sexually explicit content online (especially from news reports and videos), they can easily become desensitized. We can too. No matter how many safeguards we put in place to protect them, it can slip through. Our kids may see a suicide or murder live-streamed. Or people huddled in a mall trying to avoid a shooter. Or females being treated in a sexually demeaning way. Or a family grieving over losing a child.

This kind of content can desensitize our children to the fact that real people with real feelings are involved. Some of the images our kids see online aren't real, but many are. Because it can be difficult to tell what's real and what isn't, we need to teach our tweens to think critically and use discernment whenever they see or hear something online.

We often talk about this in our home. I remind my children that when they see something on a screen, they need to figure out whether it's legit. That's the first step. Distinguishing real and fake news is a huge problem today because of paid advertisements, satirical websites, and sponsored content. Our kids are bombarded with all kinds of confusing messages. According to a recent Stanford University study "more than 80% of students believed that [a] native advertisement, identified by the words 'sponsored content,' was a real news story."[4] We need to teach our children to recognize the difference.

Once they determine a story is actually valid, the next step is talking them through it. They still may not be seeing the entire picture or hearing the full story. To help them grasp the fuller context, we can ask questions like "What happened right before? What happened right after?"

When our kids see something fearful, such as people huddled in a mall trying to avoid a shooter, it's important to remind them that God doesn't want us to live in fear. Jesus said, "I am leaving you with a gift—peace of mind and heart. And the peace I give is a gift the world cannot give. So don't be troubled or afraid" (John 14:27).

To guard against becoming desensitized, our children must learn to put themselves in other people's shoes. If a story is legitimate, real people with real feelings are involved. I constantly remind my kids of that.

We also need to remind our children to protect their hearts and minds from disturbing images. Many of the images they're exposed to online are beyond their emotional capacity to deal with, and this can do lasting damage. Again, this calls for continual open communication as we walk with balance in the Spirit.

Cyberstrangers

Online exposure often brings our tweens into direct contact with people who can cause them personal harm. With so many apps, social-media platforms, and live-streaming videos available today, it's easy for tweens to connect on a deep level with total strangers. Nothing online is ever really private. It's essential that we talk honestly with our kids about online predators and teach them how to protect themselves. Our family guideline is that our children should never communicate with online strangers. If someone they don't know tries to connect with them online, they should report it to me immediately.

I always ask my children, "Would you open our front door to a stranger without me or Dad knowing? The same thing applies to strangers online. Don't ever talk, text, or communicate with people you don't know." This advice could literally save their lives.

Anyone with illicit or evil motives has access to our kids through social media. I'm talking drug dealers, terrorists, pedophiles, murders, sex traffickers, and others who want to take advantage of or harm our kids. In 2016, two college strangers murdered a thirteen-year-old they met online.[5] I wish this were an isolated incident, but it's becoming all too common in our world.

I don't say this to scare you. I love what one of my heads-up mamas says: "Arm, don't alarm." Cyberstrangers are a very real threat. But instead of living in fear, we should proceed with caution, continually talking with our kids and sharing age-appropriate stories to educate them.

I frequently discuss the dangers with my daughter so she'll be alert and aware. Here's a scenario that often happens online: An imposter downloads a picture of a celebrity, creates a social-media account, and posts that photo in his profile. Then he sends your daughter a request to follow her. Your tween gets so excited that a famous person wants to follow her. She can't even!

Once that imposter gains access to your child (as a follower), he starts grooming her, DMing her about life, and painting you as the bad guy trying to control everything, while he's the only one who understands and is there for her. She still thinks he's a celebrity, and soon they develop an online relationship. After their relationship develops, he sends pictures of his genitals and asks your tween for nudes. From there, anything can happen, including a face-to-face sexual encounter.

An online stranger can also access and download a photo of a child your tween knows in real life. He can then gain access to your tween by sending a friend request from that child. Except it isn't actually who your tween thinks it is. We need to alert our tweens about that possibility and instruct them to always follow up with a private text to the friend who sent the request, especially if they've been friend-requested from multiple accounts for the same friend.

I can't emphasize enough how important it is to talk about this danger with your kids. This stuff is really happening, so we have to be proactive.

Guidelines for Taming the Social-Media Beast

One of the best tools for taming the social-media beast is to establish family guidelines. I'll be sharing the general guidelines we use in our family, and you can decide what works best for yours. Remember, guidelines are just tools. The best protection is continual open communication. Since social-media platforms change so rapidly, I won't review specific ones here. If you want up-to-date information on the most popular social-media apps, I recommend following nextTalk on Facebook, Twitter, and/or Instagram.

First, let's talk about age. Most social-media platforms require users to be at least thirteen. Some even require a birth date to open an account. The obvious drawback to this safeguard is that a tween under thirteen can lie. Check the age guidelines for each platform before you decide which ones you'll allow your tween to use. As I noted earlier, if your child hasn't proved that he or she is trustworthy, hold off on allowing access.

In the previous chapter, I mentioned that we gave our middle schooler permission to set up her first social-media account because she told us about a peer-pressure situation at school. It was the perfect reason to reward her and give her a little more freedom. It was time to let out the kite string a bit. But increased freedom came with new guidelines.

My husband and I found the following guidelines helpful as we navigated through this gray area of parenting:

1. *Learn it first.* Before you allow your child to have a social-media account, set up your own account and become familiar with the platform. I spent four months learning how to use one social-media platform before I let my daughter have her own account. My heads-up mamas walked me through it, taught me how to use it, and answered my questions. (I'm tellin' you, find a heads-up mama.)

2. *Make the account private.* A private account prevents strangers from viewing your tween's time line. Typically, a stranger will only be able to see a profile picture and biography. This varies, but most social-media platforms offer the option of setting up a private account so your child's information can be shared only with followers or friends who have requested to follow your child.

Again, nothing is ever really private online, so just because your child has a private account doesn't mean something won't be viewed. Don't be lulled into a false sense of security. You should still teach your tween how to post appropriately. For example, my daughter never gives out her phone number or address or uses her last name or the full name of her school (she uses an abbreviation instead). Personal information and contact information never get posted online in our family, even with a private account.

Every fall when kids get their class schedules, they post them on Instagram. That includes full names, birth dates, addresses, school ID numbers, and school names. This is dangerous! Don't overlook what your tween may be posting online, even on a private account.

3. *Follow your tween on social media.* You already have an account set up, so follow your child. You won't have access to his or her DMs or search history as a follower, however. Those are in-app features, so parental restrictions set up on your child's phone won't work. Porn won't be blocked automatically on social media, which is why it's important to instill in your child an internal red-flag alert to report any inappropriate content to you.

I follow my daughter and many of the other students at her school. But my personal rule is not to like or comment on her friends' posts. I don't make a scene. One time I saw a sixth grader using profanity in the comments, but I didn't correct or scold him. However, later that night during dinner, I asked my daughter, "Hey, did you see [so-and-so's] comment?"

"Yep," she replied. "Totally inappropriate." End of discussion.

My daughter knows I'm in her online world, but I try to refrain from being a crazy helicopter mom, correcting everything I see. The exception is seeing someone being bullied or threatened. I have a duty to report that, but my daughter and I do it together.

I also don't post a picture of her on the social-media platform we both use unless I have her approval (since many of her friends follow me, too). I give her space. She posts on her own, and I trust her (or she wouldn't have an account). But I'm always monitoring.

Follow your tween, but don't be a stalker. We're called nextTalk (not nextStalk) for a reason, people! Find a balance. Walk in the Spirit.

4. *Know your tween's password and check his or her phone.* I check my daughter's social-media time line, search history, and DMs on a regular basis. But it's random, so she doesn't know when I'll do it. If she didn't want me to see something, she'd have to delete the DMs and search history almost every day to clear everything out.

Since search history and DMs can be deleted, make sure you trust your child. As he or she gets older, you won't need to check it as often. It's okay to let the kite string out as long as our kids prove they're responsible and trustworthy.

5. *Turn off location services.* With most apps, I turn "Location Services" to "Never" because I don't want anyone to be able to click on a picture and see my daughter's exact location. It's just not safe. However, I do keep this feature on with other apps, like "Find my Phone," because it enables me to track where her phone is if she loses it.

To change location services on most phones, close the app first. Then go to "Settings" and select "Privacy" and "Location Services." You can select "Never" or "While Using the App," but to keep your tween's location concealed, I recommend "Never." Keep in mind that you can customize each app using the location-services feature.

6. *Only allow followers your tween knows in real life.* This is a biggie for me. If someone requests to follow my daughter and she accepts, I expect her to be able to tell me who it is and how she knows the person if I ask. For example, if I'm checking her time line and see a name I don't recognize, I'll say, "Hey, who is this?"

She might reply, "Oh, that's my friend from sixth period."

Most tweens think they'll be more popular if they have more followers. I often remind my daughter, "Be selective about who you let in your world." Our tweens don't need thousands of strangers knowing their business.

7. *Don't allow your tween to follow older children you don't know.* This is a guideline one of my heads-up mamas suggested. Generally, my daughter follows friends at school who are in her grade or one grade above. Other than that, the person has to be a family friend or a high school mentor I know personally (normally my friends' teens). I don't want my daughter following high school students before she's in high school, because she sees them dating and kissing, and that makes her want to do those things at an earlier age.

8. *Decide on a case-by-case basis which adults your child may follow.* Like the guideline for people who want to follow my daughter, she's allowed to follow only those she knows in real life. With one exception: I encourage her to follow pastors, motivational speakers, and other people I know, trust, and follow. The goal is to fill her time line and newsfeed with positive content. I get so excited when my daughter texts me Bible verses she's seen on her time line. It's one of my favorite things about social media.

I'm uncomfortable with adults I don't know having full access to my daughter through social media, so I decide whether to let her follow teachers or other adults on a case-by-case basis. She and I also discuss news reports on inappropriate relationships with teachers because I want her to be on guard and aware of the dangers. We talk so she'll be prepared.

If I'm checking her time line and find inappropriate pictures other students have posted, I'll ask her about it. Many times she'll say, "I already unfollowed them after those were posted. I don't want that junk on my newsfeed." This is a parenting win. It tells me she's listening to God and following her moral compass. If your tween does that, treat that kid to Starbucks!

9. *Teach your tween that social media is real life.* As I mentioned earlier, I always tell my daughter, "If you wouldn't say something to a person's face, don't type it as a comment." I want her to remember there's a soul on the other end of every screen. It's also important that our children be aware of cyberbullying on social media and report it (we'll cover this in chapter 12).

10. *Make sure your child understands the importance of guarding his or her mind, heart, and eyes.* This should be an ongoing conversation, especially when your child begins using social media. We can set all the guidelines and parental controls we want, but if our kids want to use technology to find bad things, they can do it. They're always one step ahead of us when it comes to the online world. That's why my main goal as a parent is to teach my kids moral values and integrity, which includes guarding their hearts and minds. I'm always telling them, "You and only you are responsible for what enters your brain. Protect it. Bad images are hard to get out of your mind once they find their way in."

Your own family guidelines may look quite different from ours. Your family, your choice. The bottom line is this: no matter what social-media guidelines you establish for your family, make sure they're clear and consistently applied. Follow-through is essential.

In the end, everything comes back to open communication. Keep talking with your kids about the issues that can arise with social media. Whether you're in the car, at home, on the go, or going to bed, talk!

Now let's tackle an issue that presents one of the biggest dangers for our tweens on social media: pornography.

Pornography

Dangers, Safeguards

Social media, apps, and the online world in general expose our kids to an endless stream of potentially harmful images and information. One of the greatest threats to the safety and well-being of our children today is pornography. It's such a monstrous tsunami, I decided that it deserves its own chapter.

Pornography Is Targeting Our Children

Let's face it. No matter where we go online these days, porn is everywhere. When I first started this cyberparenting journey, I received calls from six different moms in seven days about porn they discovered on their kids' devices. The youngest child was eight years old. The oldest was eleven. Just tweens.

I field calls like these often. So when I say you're not alone, I really mean it. My heart breaks for these kids and their parents. It takes me back to my own lightbulb moment.

I define *pornography* for my kids as "any picture, video, or other material where people aren't wearing clothes, and you can see private parts."

When I was growing up, it was rare for young kids to be exposed to pornography. It was way more difficult to access because videotapes in stores could only be rented to adults with photo identification. Kids could also get their hands on pornographic magazines, of course, but they had to stash them under a mattress or in the back of a closet, which left a visible trail. Today, porn is a tap or swipe away, viewable on any device. And the search history can be deleted with no trace left behind. It's time to open our eyes and recognize the shift that's taken place.

In October 2015, *Playboy* announced that it would no longer feature nude photos in its magazine. CEO Scott Flanders said, "You're now one click away from every sex act imaginable for free. And so it's just passé at this juncture." According to the same article, "Playboy's circulation ... dropped from 5.6 million in 1975 to about 800,000 [today]."[1]

Kassia Wosick, assistant professor of sociology at New Mexico State University, notes that "porn is a $97 billion [global] industry."[2] Like any industry, it needs customers. Those customers are our kids, and that makes them targets of direct marketing. The porn industry knows that the sooner they become addicted to free porn, the more they'll crave. Once they're hooked, they'll start paying for porn, including the hard-core stuff, and all it takes is another convenient tap or swipe.

When it comes to porn, some people think, *Well, boys will be boys. Is that so bad?*

I'm a little passionate about how much I despise that statement. We must hold our boys to the same standard as our girls. Always. We can't give boys a pass and excuse their behavior just because "boys will be boys." No! Boys and girls are equally responsible for their behavior. (We'll talk about this again in a later chapter.) When boys are excused for seeing women as objects, it's the beginning of a downward spiral. Remember the knitted sweater? Pull out one little thread, and the whole sweater begins to unravel. Eventually you're left with a gaping hole.

We must also face the fact that pornography isn't just a boys' issue anymore. The porn industry is targeting our daughters as well as our sons. Porn use among girls is on the rise. Research shows that "more than half of women 25 and under ever seek out porn (56% versus 27% among women 25-plus) and one-third seek it out at least monthly (33% versus just 12% among older men)."[3]

Our primary job as parents is to prepare our sons and daughters for the battle. We can't get so caught up in the fight against porn that we forget to talk with our kids about the dangers. We need to have ongoing conversations with them about this issue and teach them how to protect themselves when porn lights up their screens. Open communication is our best weapon to fight the destructive influence of pornography in our children's lives.

The Dangers of Porn

Porn is not a male (or female) rite of passage. We need to break out of that mind-set and understand the dangers so we can truly grasp the urgent need to limit our children's exposure. I'm not being a crazy-mom alarmist here. There's plenty of research that echoes my concerns.

First of all, statistics show that porn objectifies women. A study of popular pornographic videos found that "of the 304 scenes analyzed, 88.2% contained physical aggression, principally spanking, gagging, and slapping, while 48.7% of scenes contained verbal aggression, primarily name-calling. Perpetrators of aggression were usually male, whereas *targets of aggression were overwhelmingly female*" (emphasis added).[4]

Recently the *Washington Post* published an article with some updated research on the effects of porn. The author, sociology professor Gail Dines, offered this observation: "After 40 years of peer-reviewed research, scholars can say with confidence that porn is an industrial product that shapes how we think about gender, sexuality, relationships, intimacy, sexual violence and gender equality—*for the worse*" (emphasis added).[5]

In that same article, Dines compared the porn industry to the tobacco industry, which denied the link between smoking and lung cancer for years. But just as with smoking, research continues to document the negative effects of pornography.

In April 2016, Utah governor Gary Herbert signed a resolution declaring pornography a public-health crisis.[6] The National Center on Sexual Exploitation supports this claim based on its own research and has concluded that the porn industry "fuels sex trafficking, child sexual abuse, and sexual violence."[7]

Not only are experts speaking out, but women who have worked in the industry are also sounding the alarm. In August 2016, actress Pamela

Anderson called porn a "public hazard" that has "corrosive effects on a man's soul and on his ability to function as [a] husband and, by extension, as [a] father."[8]

Additionally, Holly Madison, Hugh Hefner's former girlfriend and star of *The Girls Next Door*, wrote a book titled *Down the Rabbit Hole* that details her downward spiral from *Playboy* model to suicidal wreck. Her website gives an excellent overview of her journey:

> Life inside the notorious [*Playboy*] Mansion wasn't a dream at all—and quickly became her nightmare. After losing her identity, her sense of self-worth, and her hope for the future, Holly found herself sitting alone in a bathtub contemplating suicide.[9]

Madison writes, "Many people assume *Playboy* was my blessing, but most don't know it was also my curse."[10]

Just as I remind my kids that there's a soul on the other side of every screen when they're on social media, I want them to know there's a real person with a real-life story behind any porn video.

Ephesians 6:12 says, "We are not fighting against flesh-and-blood enemies, but against … evil spirits." Remember, Satan is like a lion waiting to pounce on our families and devour them. His goal is to steal, kill, and destroy.

Satan not only uses porn to destroy our children; he uses it to destroy the lives of people in the porn industry. Every porn star is someone's son or daughter. These people aren't the real enemy. Satan is. Pornography harms them, too.

Did you know that porn studios pay female actresses anywhere between $800 and $1,000 for a "'traditional' sex scene between a man and a woman"?[11] That's someone's daughter.

If porn puts women at risk for objectification and sexual abuse, what does it do to their self-esteem? Adult women (us!) struggle with wanting to look perfect. Our young girls pick up on this mind-set, and porn magnifies it. An article published in *Time* magazine sums it up: "A lot of girls watch porn to learn how to have sex. What they see there influences the way things should go, and how they think things should look."[12]

Sadly, research backs up this conclusion. According to the American Society for Aesthetic Plastic Surgery (ASAPS), between 2014 and 2015, the number of genital plastic surgeries among girls eighteen years of age and younger jumped from 222 to 400. That's an 80 percent increase![13]

How tragic that exposure to pornography has convinced our daughters that the beautiful, healthy bodies God gave them are somehow defective and need surgical improvements.

Another fact about porn is that it hurts intimate relationships. Multiple studies have demonstrated that porn-free relationships are stronger, and that watching porn decreases commitment while increasing the risk of cheating.[14]

In a blog article posted on Fight the New Drug, a woman in a monogamous marriage was stunned when her husband spit on her during sex. She later discovered that he had been consistently watching porn.[15] God designed sex for *mutual* respect and pleasure within marriage, but Satan uses pornography to distort our view of sex and degrade those involved in it.

The evidence is abundantly clear: pornography can create lifelong struggles for anyone caught in its web.

Pornography affects people differently and, like alcohol or drugs, can become an addiction for some. According to the *Washington Times*, "At least 25 major studies published since 2011, 16 of which were released within the last two years, link habitual use of erotic videos with deleterious developments in brain structure, often mirroring those of drug addicts."[16] In light of this sobering conclusion, we need to be aware that our tweens could develop an addiction to porn at some point in their lives. But we need more than awareness. We need to take proactive steps to prevent it.

Safeguarding our Kids from Porn

Now that we recognize the dangers of pornography and understand why it's bad for our children, how do we prevent them from seeing it in the first place? We can't. Here's the thing: our kids are going to see porn online. We must face this fact. Don't believe the lie that they won't. The question is at what age?

Now that I've dropped this bombshell, let's talk about how we can safeguard our kids.

Preparing for the Tsunami

First, we need to talk with our kids about this issue *before* they encounter it online or anywhere else. Open communication is the key. I recommend reading Kristen Jensen's book *Good Pictures, Bad Pictures* with your elementary-age children. It's an excellent scientifically based resource that teaches kids how to move bad pictures from the emotional side of their brains to the thinking side.

I read Jensen's book with my son at the end of first grade. We tackled it over the summer when our schedule was a little less crazy. (My daughter was older because I missed the earlier conversations we needed to have.)

What we learned fueled so many great family discussions. The whole concept of moving harmful things from the emotional side of the brain to the thinking side can be used for more than just pornography. Some examples include drugs, alcohol, screen and gaming addictions, toxic attitudes, sexual desires, eating disorders, and negative feelings.

Remember the "Just Say No" drug-prevention campaign? Our goal is to teach our kids how to say no when they see pornography. We want a red-flag alert to go off in their brains when they see inappropriate content online. This needs to start early so it's standard operating procedure by the time they enter the tween years. As I said earlier, our family guideline requires our kids to report any pictures of people in a swimsuit or less.

Here's how this works: One day my son was playing a car-racing arcade game at a child-friendly restaurant. It was after Vacation Bible School (VBS), and a large group of other moms and kids from our church was there with us.

He came to me and whispered in my ear, "There's a girl on the screen only wearing a bikini. I see her boobs."

I quietly slipped away to see what all the fuss was about. Sure enough, a girl in an itsy-bitsy string bikini was holding the sign for the finish line. I could almost see nipples! But I didn't make a scene. I didn't confront management and demand to have it removed. Instead, I thought about the conversations I needed to have with my son. I was so proud of him for telling me. This is real-world stuff. It's going to happen, and we need to prepare our kids for it.

Here's another example: While I was making dinner one afternoon, my son asked if he could Google a football score. I replied, "Sure, but sit at the kitchen island."

Minutes later he said, "There was a girl on a motorcycle, and she had a little string in her butt. That was all she was wearing." His eyes were as wide as a shocked emoji face.

I didn't shame him or disparage her. I simply said, "I'm so proud of you for telling me. What do you have to do when you see those kinds of images?"

His reply? "I have to protect my heart and mind. So I looked away."

Then I hugged him and joked, "Ugh, was it like dental floss for a butt?"

We cracked up (pun intended). (By the way, if you wear thongs, here's my view on the subject: your underwear, your choice. There's nothing wrong with wearing the kind of underwear you're most comfortable in. No judgment here. I'm just trying to find creative ways to talk with my boy about serious topics like this. A little humor goes a long way!)

Conversations with my son are getting a little more interesting these days. He's nine now, so we're starting to talk more about sex and how God reserved it for marriage. Teachable moments are great. Keep things as light as you can. If you make every conversation a serious life lesson, you're gonna burn your kids out fast. Keep talking and have some fun!

Boy Talk on Being Visual

Because my tween son and I have been talking about pornography since he was in first grade, he openly shares with me when he notices large racks of boobs. Not in a disrespectful or weird way, but in a "Hey, Mom, I saw this" sort of way. Here are some talking points Matt and I use to help our son process the things he notices:

- It's perfectly natural that you notice. That's how God created you.
- Girls/women are not objects. Although you're visual and notice outer beauty, it's more important to look at other qualities like kindness, intelligence, heart, personality, and how a girl treats

others. It's never okay to disrespect a girl by talking about her body parts, grabbing or touching any body part, taking pictures of her body parts, or staring at her body parts. (Say this even at a young age; it sets a good foundation.)

- One day you'll marry a girl. Then it will be okay to see her naked and enjoy all her beautiful parts, with her permission. There is nothing wrong with loving the female body. It's a beautiful creation that God designed. But it has to be treated with respect in the context of His blueprint for marriage. In the garden of Eden, Adam and Eve were naked, and it was perfectly acceptable. (We'll cover all the beautiful things about sex in chapter 17.) But until you marry, it's important not to let your thoughts get out of control or spiral into a fantasy when you notice female body parts.
- When female body parts pop into your line of sight, don't be disrespectful and stare. Turn your head away within three seconds.
- Always be a gentleman. Girls are to be treated with even higher respect than boys. Hold the door open for them, let them go first, and so on.

If your son starts this conversation with you, you can bring Dad into the discussion by saying, "I'm so glad you're telling me this. Dad is a boy like you, so I bet he can help us process this even more. Can we talk to him about it too?"

Again, your husband and your son are visual, so it's good for them to have a healthy dialogue on how to process the large racks of boobs they may be seeing on billboards, online, or anywhere else. As always, the earlier you can establish an ongoing dialogue, the better. This is a great way to safeguard your boy against porn. By the time he starts seeing hard-core porn online, it will be standard procedure to report it to you.

What to Do When Porn Pops Up

As parents, we can't take anything for granted. Even if we think we've taken all the right precautions, we should never assume that our children are entirely safe from pornography.

Please don't make the same mistakes I did. I thought I didn't need to talk with my daughter about pornography because she didn't have her own phone. I was *so* wrong! I can't tell you how many stories I hear about children showing pornographic images to other children. They're not bad children either. Something inappropriate pops up on an innocent child's phone, and that child, who wasn't prepared for it, says to a friend, "Oh no, look at this!" Then they share the image with several other kids.

I've instructed my daughter to follow these steps when pornographic images pop up on her phone:

1. Turn off your phone immediately.
2. Never, ever show a pornographic photo to another child or send it to anyone. (Most school districts have major consequences, like automatic suspension, if a child does this. Make sure you know the policy of your child's school.)
3. Report anything pornographic or inappropriate to a teacher, school official, or parent. (If you're on a school device, report it to a teacher. If you're on your own phone, turn it off until you're with a parent.)

Our kids will be more likely to do the right thing if we talk with them in advance about the steps to take when porn rears its ugly head. Role playing different scenarios can also be helpful.

The most calls I get by far are from parents in freak-out mode saying, "I found porn on my child's device. What should I do?"

First, here are some things *not* to do:

- Don't yell.
- Don't scream.
- Don't say in anger, "I'm taking all your devices away for a year." Remember, you have to mean what you say and say what you mean.

Taking away technology doesn't really accomplish anything these days. Kids go to school and use their friends' phones. They set up new social-media accounts. Our tweens are technologically resourceful. They're always one step ahead of us. You may decide to take away screens when your tween is at home. That's realistic. But keep in mind that your child is going to have online access the moment he or she leaves your house.

When we find porn on our kids' devices, we may have an overpowering urge to lay down the law. That urge is often fueled by anger. When this happens (believe me, it will), step away from the device and your child and BREATHE. Yes, you definitely need to address the issue, but reacting emotionally will only sabotage your efforts. You need to respond calmly and logically. This is important. If you've already flipped out and had a crazy-mom moment, it's okay. We've all messed up. Acknowledge your mistake, ask for forgiveness, and move on. Remember, we're not going to feel defeated.

Your job as a parent is to explain the why behind the decision to live a porn-free life and help your child continually make that choice. Let's talk about some practical ways to do this if you've found pornography on your child's device:

- *Share a story from your past.* If you have an experience to share about seeing pornography for the first time, go ahead and share it. If not, share another relevant mistake. A BIG one. But make sure it's age appropriate. Your kids need to know they're not the only ones who make mistakes. If you're vulnerable, you might be able to get past their walls.
- *Admit your part.* Again, cyberparenting has blindsided all of us. If I'm struggling to have open, honest conversations with my kids, I've found that if I first admit I haven't done a very good job teaching them how to deal with porn, they'll follow my lead. This doesn't relieve them of their responsibility, but it's a way to open up the discussion.
- *Do some pornography research and share what you've learned with your tween.* I recommend following Fight the New Drug on Facebook. This organization posts excellent articles on pornography. But don't beat your child over the head with statistics. This isn't a lecture. It's a conversation. If you need to mentally prepare some talking points about the harmful effects of pornography, that's fine (you can even use the ones we covered earlier). Just don't whip out a large presentation board or a printout. Instead of reciting a bunch of stats, share what you've learned in a personal and rel-

evant way. Give some examples of people who've worked in the porn industry who now speak out against it.

- *Encourage your tween to be totally honest with you about how much pornography he or she has viewed.* Remember, you want to be your child's safe place. Even if your tween is viewing porn daily, don't yell or start crying. Resist knee-jerk reactions. Instead, thank your child for being honest with you and let him or her know it's safe to talk with you about anything.
- *Meet with a counselor.* If your child is viewing pornography on a regular basis, ask a family doctor or a pastor to recommend a good counselor who specializes in issues like this. If the first counselor you see isn't a good fit, don't give up. Keep looking till you find one who can help you address the issue and improve open communication with your tween.

Here's the thing: Giving up pornography isn't easy if a habit or addiction has developed. It's a process. We have to walk hand in hand with our kids every day to help them break a bad habit (this applies to anything). We want them to tell us when they feel like looking at porn. They need an accountability partner to help them with their struggle, not someone reminding them how badly they've messed up.

Establish a pact with your tween so that he or she will turn to you when temptation hits. Come up with a strategy. Make a Sonic run. Go see a movie. Pray together. Let your child know that he or she isn't alone in this battle.

Remember the story I told you earlier about my friend whose husband struggles with porn? Now he sends a certain emoji when he's tempted to look at it. Their relationship is a beautiful, safe place of truth, honesty, and real struggle. We need to develop this kind of relationship with our kids.

The enemy in this battle isn't our children, other children and their families, technology, or even the porn industry. We're all in the same boat trying to figure out how to deal with pornography and its harmful effects. So let's start fighting the real enemy: Satan. He's still lurking in the shadows waiting for an opportunity to steal, kill, and destroy.

But here's the good news: our God is bigger.

12

Suicide

Stress and Anxiety, Self-Harm, Cyberbullying

Let's be real. Suicide is a topic we'd rather sweep under the rug than talk about with our kids. But it's happening every day in our tweens' world, and we can't afford to look the other way. Social media has made it even more of a threat, and like the online dangers we discussed in the previous chapters, we have to face it head-on. Once again, the key is open communication.

In 2007, "suicide was the third-leading cause of death for adolescents 15 to 19 years old; now it is second.... Only unintentional injuries, such as motor vehicle crashes and inadvertent poisonings, claim the lives of more teens."[1] As of 2014, suicide was listed as the second-leading cause of death for children and young adults between the ages of ten and twenty-four.[2] In response to this alarming increase, the American Academy of Pediatrics issued a warning about teen suicide and its risks in 2016.

I've never had a suicidal child, so I'm in no position to give advice. What I can do is share *proactive* conversations I've had with my kids about this issue and lay some groundwork for talking openly and honestly about it with our children. We need to bring this painful issue out of the shadows and face it for the sake of our kids.

If your child is suicidal, reach out to a medical doctor, pastor, or qualified counselor for help. God brings healing in all kinds of ways. Pray for your child, and seek God's wisdom and guidance. Whatever dark valley your child is walking through, he or she needs your unwavering love and supportive presence.

Fielding the Suicide Question

I'll never forget the first time my daughter asked me about suicide. She had heard about suicide prevention at school when she was in sixth grade. She had also been exposed to news stories about local teens who had committed suicide.

As conversations about suicide became the norm for us, I realized I had to lay down some foundational truths for my tween. Here's what I told her:

- No mistake or decision you make will ever cause me to love you less. I will never turn my back on you. You're going to make mistakes because you're not perfect. The key is learning from them. Don't ever be afraid to tell me about your mistakes, big or small. I will always love you.
- If someone is mistreating you or being unkind, Satan wants you to keep it a secret. He wants it to get inside your head so he can twist it and manipulate your thinking. He wants you to feel defeated and worthless. But that's not truth. The God of the universe knows you. He created you and knit you together in my womb. You're a masterpiece. By talking about the problem with me, we can bring it into the light, process it together, and remind ourselves of the truth (not just the words of other people that are often false). You are never, ever alone. I'm here. Dad is here. And God never leaves your side.
- Suicide is never the solution to your problems. Sometimes when we feel there's no way out of a situation, we don't see the whole picture. I've been there before, but as I look back now, I can see that I grew and learned the most during the worst times of my life. God is using me more today because I walked that path and learned from my mistakes. Deuteronomy 23:5 says that "[God will turn] the intended curse into a blessing because [He] loves you."
- God has you here for a specific purpose. He has a plan for your life, and you are the only one who can fulfill it. He woke you up

this morning, breathing and ready to live. God says in Jeremiah 29:11, "I know the plans I have for you.... They are plans for good and not for disaster, to give you a future and a hope." Even when you aren't sure about your future, God knows.

- You're not stuck at this school. You're not trapped in your current surroundings. If we need to, we can look at private school, a charter school, or homeschooling. There are always other options. You have a way out.
- You might feel like running away, but that never solves your problems. It only makes them worse. If you run away, I can't help. Whatever you're dealing with, we'll face it together. I'm here for you.

I know these truths are making a difference in my daughter's life. I've watched her pull up Jeremiah 29:11 on her phone and share it with other kids who are struggling and questioning life in general. Our tweens are listening, but we have to talk. Like any of these topics, we're learning to pour truth into them *before* they get into a situation where they are overwhelmed with feelings of hopelessness.

After that first difficult conversation on suicide, it's tempting to think we can coast now that we've faced the issue head-on. That would be a mistake. We need to keep talking about it and continually remind our tweens of these foundational truths so they'll hopefully turn to us for help if they ever have suicidal thoughts.

Talking with our kids about suicide when they're young doesn't guarantee they won't ever struggle with depression or suicidal thoughts later on. We always need to be on the lookout for red flags.

Some of the most common warning signs that a child may be contemplating suicide include ...

- Making suicidal statements.
- Being preoccupied with death in conversation, writing, or drawing.
- Giving away belongings.
- Withdrawing from friends and family.
- Having aggressive or hostile behavior.[3]

Always, always take suicide threats seriously. You're the expert on your child, so if he or she withdraws, find out why. If you notice that something is off, don't let it go. Talk to a doctor or see a counselor. Keep searching until you get the help your child needs.

Why They Do It

Statistics tell us that more children are committing suicide today. The question is why. There are so many complicated factors involved that it's impossible to pinpoint a single reason. Risk factors can include depression or other mental-health disorders, abuse (physical, verbal, or sexual), drug or alcohol addiction, questions about gender identity and sexuality, bullying (including cyberbullying), and even "pathological Internet use."[4]

One of my wise heads-up mamas says, "I feel like [teen suicide is] more than just one thing." She's absolutely right. Often, more than one of these risk factors work together to create a perfect storm in a child's life.

The more risk factors involved, the more likely it is that a child will think about suicide at some point. Here are some of the possible reasons for attempting suicide:

- Depression or any other mental-health disorder
- Feelings of hopelessness or worthlessness
- Sexual abuse
- Relationship problems, including isolation, rejection, or being bullied
- Substance abuse or addiction
- Parental divorce, family violence, or other problems at home
- Self-esteem or identity issues, including struggles related to adoption, sexuality, and transgender
- A chronic sense of being physically or emotionally flawed
- Unrelenting emotional pain a tween can't resolve
- Shame over major mistakes, including feelings of failure
- Loss and grief

This isn't an exhaustive list. Like an adult, a child may commit suicide for any number of reasons. Each child's life story is unique, and so are the reasons for suicide. This is why it's so important to cultivate honest, open communication when our kids are young. If they're struggling with something, we want to face it with them so the downward spiral doesn't continue.

We may not understand why our kids feel the way they do, but we can always love them unconditionally. They need to know we care and really hear their struggles. Quick fixes, snap judgments, and labels are never helpful ways to approach problems. Walk with balance in the Spirit and let Him guide you.

Since we can't possibly discuss all the issues that may lead to suicide, we'll focus on three in this chapter: stress and anxiety, self-harm, and cyberbullying. (Later in the book, we'll tackle addiction, sexuality, and transgender.)

Stress and Anxiety

Stress and anxiety are at an all-time high among adolescents today.[5] Between the social pressures of the online world and constant screen connections, AP classes (advanced placement), standardized tests, peer pressure, and a host of other issues kids are dealing with, anxiety is very real for them.

My daughter and I talk a lot about coping with stress and anxiety. In the fall of last year, she played the lead role in a school drama. The entire plot centered around her character, a lone Jewish girl who survived the Holocaust. The Nazis killed the character's parents, teacher, and friends. It was an emotionally intense role for her to play, and it led to heavy conversations about that devastating time in history.

It was a huge honor for her, but with four pre-AP classes, her stress level was maxed. There were nights filled with tears and moments she wanted to quit. At those times, the last thing I wanted to do was add to her stress. So I'd say things like, "Don't worry about your room. Clean it this weekend" and "What can I do for you? How can I help?"

I also reminded her that the stress wouldn't last forever. Then I'd try to shift the focus off her stress by saying, "Can you imagine what it will be like when the play is over, and you realize you actually did it?" (I know distraction doesn't work in every scenario, but it's great for a lot of pressure-cooker situations our children face every day.)

One ongoing conversation my daughter and I have is about taking things one step at a time. When she was overwhelmed with memorizing her lines for the play, I'd encouraged her to tackle one scene at a time and then break each scene down into one line or paragraph. Small steps forward. If she made a little progress every day, eventually she'd accomplish her goal.

Stress and anxiety that come with certain events, classes, and activities are a natural part of life, and our tweens need to learn how to cope with it in a healthy, productive manner. If your child seems stressed all the time or struggles with severe anxiety, try to determine the root cause. It could be a mental-health disorder that requires medical treatment. Stay in tune with your child and keep talking!

Self-Harming

As parents, we need to recognize that when chronic emotional issues are left untreated, it can lead to self-harm.

Self-harming (cutting, burning, pulling out hair, etc.) is on the rise among tweens.[6] In fact, it's increasing at such a rapid pace, it's hard to find accurate statistics. Self-harming is a red flag that a significant underlying problem needs to be addressed. We need to face this issue head-on and identify the root cause so it doesn't spiral out of control.

Most kids who self-harm are typically not suicidal.[7] Self-harm is "a way of coping with life," while suicide is a way of escaping from life when there seems to be no other way out.[8] Tweens typically self-harm because the outside pain takes away the inside pain. If this coping strategy stops working, a tween may conclude that suicide is the only alternative for dealing with his or her problems. So we should never assume that self-harm won't lead to suicide.

If you discover that your child is self-harming, try to stay calm (#parentfilter). Breathe. Pray. No judgments or crazy-mom reactions. Keep in mind that this is one of the ways tweens are dealing with pain today. To them, self-harming may seem normal, but that doesn't mean it is. Always take self-harming seriously and seek professional help.

We can help our children break this destructive behavior pattern by teaching them how to deal with their pain and problems in healthy, constructive ways. Open communication is essential. Have ongoing conversations with your child about the thoughts and feelings behind their self-harming behavior. Ask open-ended questions like "Why do you think you feel so overwhelmed?"

We need to start the conversation about self-harming during the early tween years before middle school begins. This prepares our tweens to combat the urge to try self-harm as a coping mechanism when stress is high and other kids are experimenting with it.

No matter what our kids are struggling with, we want to be a safe place for them to talk openly and honestly with us. We also need to let them know that God understands their pain, and they can talk to Him about it too.

Cyberbullying

One of the leading causes of suicide among young people today is bullying, especially cyberbullying. Research has confirmed this link, citing multiple studies that have "found a clear relationship between both bullying victimization and perpetration and suicidal ideation and behavior in children and adolescents."[9]

According to a survey of nearly two thousand middle-school children, "victims of cyberbullying were almost 2 times as likely to attempt suicide than those who were not."[10]

Bullying and suicide aren't new problems. But a shift has taken place in our culture that we must recognize yet again. Now our kids can be bullied while they're sitting next to us on the family sectional. Cyberbullying is a sinister threat that happens on a screen instead of out in the open where others can witness it. If our tweens aren't confiding in us, we may never know they're suffering in silence at the hands of online cowards.

It's terrifying to think that one kid's cruelty and rejection could drive another child over the edge. But we can't stick our heads in the sand and hope this problem will simply resolve itself. Cyberbullying isn't going to vanish into thin air. We have to face it.

Some people set up social-media accounts just to bully others, make fun of them, or post compromising or embarrassing photos of someone.

Because tweens mostly talk with their friends through DMing (direct messaging) in apps, it's difficult for parents to spot cyberbullying.

Wait. It gets worse. Cyberbullies can impersonate someone a tween knows in real life, downloading a photo of that person and sending a friend request. The bully uses a fake identity to wreak havoc. Let's say a girl downloads a picture of a sweet eighth grader named Beth and opens a new account with her picture. This girl then starts cyberbullying other kids at Beth's school. And those kids start bullying Beth in person because they think she's the cyberbully. But poor Beth has no clue what's happening online.

See how confusing this can get for tweens if we're not involved in their online world and continually talking with them about these issues?

Online impersonation is a huge problem. In the social-media chapter, I talked about cyberstrangers downloading pictures of celebrities and then asking to follow your tween. What if your tween accepts and begins DMing with a person she thinks is a celebrity? Eventually nudes are asked for, and your tween sends a picture of herself in a bra. Guess what happens then? That stranger is going to start bullying and blackmailing your tween. He'll say, "If you don't send me more photos, I'm posting this online."

Don't be naive. These things happen often online. Google "blackmail for nudes" and note all the questions from panicked kids trying to figure out how to respond to being blackmailed online. See how this can spiral? Our tweens can get themselves in trouble so fast online and then flip out because they don't know what to do. It can even drive them to attempt suicide.

While I'm on the subject, what do you think the punishment is for impersonating someone online? It varies from state to state, but in New York and California, "online impersonation is a misdemeanor punishable by thousands of dollars in fines and up to a year in jail. In Texas, the crime is a third-degree felony that could land perpetrators up to ten years in prison."[11]

Our tweens need to know that they can be legally punished if they impersonate someone online. Kids often do this as a prank or joke, but it's no laughing matter. The consequences are very real.

So are the consequences of cyberbullying.

In April 2016, I was asked to be part of a special town-hall meeting on cyberparenting, hosted by News 4 San Antonio and Fox 29 in San Antonio, Texas. Matt Molak, whose son David committed suicide because of cyberbullying, was a special guest on the panel, along with Nico LaHood, Bexar County district attorney; University of Texas Health Science child psychiatrist Dr. Thomas Matthews; and Texas senator José Menéndez.[12]

Nothing makes cyberbullying real like meeting the parents of a teen who committed suicide because of the relentless bullying he faced. His parents were aware of what was happening, and they even switched schools to resolve the problem. They were good parents. And they were so broken. I'll never forget the sadness in their eyes.[13]

In David's case, he supposedly became a target at school because of his attractive girlfriend. His family found numerous online messages calling him derogatory names and threatening him. They reported this to David's school, but even though they had proof of the cyberbullying, Texas had no law to prosecute this kind of offense.

David's brother, Cliff, wrote this comment on social media following David's death: "In today's age, bullies don't push you into lockers[;] they don't tell their victims to meet them behind the school's dumpster after class[;] they cower behind user names and fake profiles from miles away constantly berating and abusing good, innocent people."[14]

Don't think this can't happen to your family. It can happen to any of us. When I met these sweet parents, everything about cyberbullying changed for me.

The Molaks are using David's legacy to help others. In November of 2016, David's Law was introduced in the Texas legislature. If passed, the bill would make cyberbullying a misdemeanor and would require school districts to have a policy that gives them authority to investigate and report cyberbullying incidents regardless of where they occur.[15]

Yes, we need to make sure our kids aren't being cyberbullied. Yes, we need to talk with them about it. But you know what opened my eyes more than anything else on that panel? Anyone can be a bully. Bullies can be the kids next door. They may even be our own children. Don't fall into the trap of thinking, *It's not my child.*

We not only need to teach our children to report bullying; we need to teach them not to be bullies themselves. Tweens frequently take "funny" jabs at each other, and then someone takes it to the next level or won't let it go. My middle schooler just told me that kids often say "Kill yourself," or "KYS," as a joke. We must teach our tweens that words matter. Things can spiral out of control fast, so we need to be on guard.

Maybe our children aren't the bullies. But what if they see bullying online and ignore it? What if they're part of the group message that is attacking another child?

Teach your child to speak out for the one being bullied. Jesus said, "Whenever you did one of these things to someone overlooked or ignored, that was me—you did it to me" (Matthew 25:40, MSG).

If our tweens know God and are walking in the Spirit, they'll answer to their own moral compasses and treat others the way they want to be treated themselves. It's all about the Golden Rule: "Do to others as you would like them to do to you" (Luke 6:31).

Cyberbullying is a heart issue. As parents, we must teach and model respect when we disagree with one another. No name calling. No personal attacks. Tweens model what they see.

Solving this problem is going to take *all of us* working together. Learning together. And continually talking with our kids.

Now that we've brought the issue of suicide into the light, let's keep the conversation going. Our kids need to know they can tell us anything because we're their safe place.

Addictions

Alcohol and Drugs, Screen and Gaming Addictions

It's important to talk honestly with our kids about addictive behavior in general. In our family, we talk about people we know who have lost their lives to addiction. Years wasted and families torn apart because someone abused alcohol and drugs. My husband and I share these real, personal life stories with our kids because we want them to understand that one bad decision to "just try it one time" at a party can alter their entire lives.

Talk openly and transparently with your children about this issue. Share your own struggles. I've found that talking about bad habits is a great way to address addiction in that first conversation.

I tell my kids about my struggles with changing bad habits so they can see I'm just like them. When they were little, I would share my struggle with drinking Diet Coke in the morning instead of coffee. I also have a bad habit of checking my phone right when I wake up. Often there's a text or e-mail I need to respond to. But when I'm busy doing that, my son (who always wakes up first) will grab the iPad to check football scores. Instead of greeting each other when we wake up, it turns into two people on screens. We end up losing quality family moments because of the bad example I set.

Cussing is another example I've used with my kids, especially during elementary school. They'll say, "Why aren't we allowed to use the words *freaking* or *fricking*?"

I reply, "Because it creates a bad habit, and when you get older, you'll be tempted to use the real f-word in their place. Why start the habit and then have to break it?"

I don't just answer their questions with "I told you so." I try to explain my reasoning because I want them to understand why we have our family guidelines.

Alcohol and Drug Addiction

Now that my kids are older, I share even more details of my past struggles with them. I have an addictive personality and used to drink lots of alcohol in high school and college. When I drank, I made tons of bad decisions, so now I choose not to drink anymore. Some people can drink in moderation and have no problem with it. I'm not one of those people, so I refuse it altogether. However, I don't shame people who drink.

For example, when we go to a party, my kids will sometimes ask on the way home, "Did you see so-and-so's mom drinking a beer?"

I reply, "Well, some people can drink and know when to stop. So that's okay. Every person gets to decide for themselves. When you're twenty-one, you'll get to make that decision for yourself." Balance.

As my kids are exposed to bigger issues like alcohol, drugs, and pornography, we continually go back to our habit conversations. I remind them that if they can avoid a bad habit in the first place, their lives will be easier. Bad habits can lead to addictions, so they need to be "alert and … sober," always on guard (1 Peter 5:8, NIV).

Remember the *Good Pictures, Bad Pictures* book I recommended for talking with our kids about pornography? The chapter "What's an Addiction?" explains the process of moving things from the feeling part of the brain to the thinking part.[1] It's an excellent resource, so make use of it when you're talking with your tween about changing a bad habit or overcoming an addiction.

Many times kids will say things like "Trying it once won't hurt me" or "All my friends are doing it." But when they let their guard down and become complacent, a spiral begins, and then we have a problem. Like the first thread pulled on a knitted sweater.

This spiral can easily happen with drugs like marijuana. I don't want to get into the messy political debate. Medical experts can guide us on legalizing medical marijuana. I'm more concerned about the perception kids have of recreational marijuana and the effect this national discussion is having on them. I hear from parents all the time that their kids don't think marijuana is harmful. So I did a little research to see if this claim is actually true.

According to the National Institute on Drug Abuse (NIDA), a recent survey "highlighted continuing concerns over the … softening of attitudes around some types of drug use, particularly a continued decrease in perceived harm of marijuana use."[2]

Softening = complacency = slow fade.

You may be thinking, *What's the big deal?*

Well, for one thing, it's a scientific fact that recreational marijuana use can lead to addiction and adverse effects on brain development. NIDA notes that "regular use [of marijuana] by teens may have a negative and long-lasting effect on their cognitive development."[3] In addition, the Partnership for Drug-Free Kids observes that "marijuana, just like any other drug, can lead to addiction. It affects the brain's reward system in the same way as all other drugs of addiction."[4]

These risks alone should get our attention, but there are other adverse effects to be concerned about as well. According to the American College of Pediatricians, "Marijuana … is a risk for both cardio-respiratory disease and testicular cancer, and is associated with both psychiatric illness and negative social outcomes."[5]

The normalization of marijuana in our society is creating a perfect storm of complacency, abuse, and addiction. But as parents, we can't afford to be complacent. We need to be alert to the dangers and prepare our kids by including marijuana in our conversations about addiction.

We also need to talk with them about the growing problem of prescription and over-the-counter (OTC) drug abuse. The National Institute on Drug Abuse for Teens states that "after marijuana and alcohol, prescription drugs are the most commonly abused substances by Americans age 14 and older."[6] Since these drugs are legal, kids assume they're not as harmful as illegal substances. Often they're combined with alcohol or other drugs as a cocktail. This is extremely dangerous because it can lead to addiction and overdose. Abusing prescription and OTC drugs is a slippery slope that can lead to a lifelong struggle.

Drug and alcohol addictions are notoriously difficult to break, but don't lose hope if your child is struggling with one. Many resources are available to help you and your family address these issues. There are also treatment centers and counselors who have special training in this area. Don't go it alone. Seek professional help. Most important, love your child unconditionally and keep the open communication going. Seek God together and trust Him to guide you as you walk with your child toward healing.

Talking with our tweens about the dangers of drug and alcohol addictions is essential, but we also need to have an ongoing conversation about a new cyberparenting challenge: screen addiction. That's what I want to camp on for the rest of this chapter.

Screen Addiction

As we learned in the previous chapter, "pathological Internet use" (which I generally refer to as screen addiction) is one of the risk factors for suicide among young people. But did you know that gaming can fall into that category too, if it's excessive?

According to a government survey of teens, "self-reported daily use of video games and Internet exceeding 5 hours was strongly associated with higher levels of depression and suicidality."[7] That's a sobering statistic, isn't it? Especially when you consider that the survey was taken in 2009. A more recent study on screen time, conducted in 2015, found that "on any given day, American teenagers (13- to 18-year-olds) average about nine hours (8:56) of entertainment media use, excluding time spent at school or for homework. Tweens (8- to 12-year-olds) use an average of six hours' (5:55) worth."[8]

Does that alarm anyone else? An older study says that five hours a day of online use could put our kids at a greater risk for suicide and depression. Yet newer research (in our quickly changing, screen-obsessed world) shows that tweens currently spend an average of six hours a day on a screen. That's a BIG red flag!

Technology has multiplied the fears and concerns parents have always had about addiction. Now when we talk to our kids about this issue, we have to think about screen addiction, too. I often weave this into our conversations and say something like, "Did you know that you can become addicted to screens like you can drugs? There are even screen rehab facilities for people who can't break their own addictions. So we need to maintain a balance with our screen use and make sure we can function without our phones and devices. Remember, real people and relationships are so much more important than screens."

What are the warning signs of screen addiction? Dr. Kellyann Petrucci recommends asking the following questions:[9]

- Is your child restless, irritable, or moody when [he or she isn't on a device]?
- Does your child skip activities or cut out early so he or she can get back to the screen?
- Is your child's schoolwork suffering because of too much time on digital devices?
- Do you catch your child "cheating" on the screen limits you've set [ignoring or exceeding them]?

I can think of a few more:

- Does your child become withdrawn, angry, or even violent when you restrict screen time or try to implement new guidelines?
- Have trust and open communication suffered because of the amount of screen time your child is engaging in?
- Has your tween developed an attitude since he or she started spending more time on screens?

You know your children better than anyone. Do you notice any red flags? Does your tween seem obsessed with screen time? Are you observing behaviors or attitudes that never used to be a problem? Or have problems gotten worse with increased screen time? If so, you may need to review your family guidelines and place more restrictions on screen time.

In our home, we sometimes implement screen-free hours as a safeguard. On Sunday, our family day, we'll often say, "It's screen-free Sunday." For us that means no phones, iPads, tablets, or other devices. We do allow TV watching (and even some gaming) as long as we're all doing it together as a family. We don't have standing screen-free days because our schedules change so frequently, but it's something we implement when we notice we're getting too dependent on those little devices.

It's always a good idea to review family screen guidelines from time to time and talk about them together. Be honest and open with your child about your concerns and discuss the changes you think are needed. If your child has a screen addiction, don't be surprised if you get pushback on limiting screen time. Tears. Begging. Anger. Threats. Silence. You name it.

Stay calm and cool (#parentfilter). Explain the new guidelines clearly and make sure your children understand them. Then follow through with implementing them and be prepared for withdrawal symptoms. Yep. Withdrawal symptoms.

Dr. Richard Graham, who started a technology addiction program in the United Kingdom in 2010, found that "young technology addicts experienced the same withdrawal symptoms as alcoholics or heroin addicts, when [their] devices were taken away."[10]

Symptoms may include moodiness and irritability, depression, restlessness and anxiety, anger, temper tantrums, and even violence. Every child is different, so don't expect your child to have the same symptoms as another child. But if screen withdrawal is anything like drug or alcohol withdrawal, you may be in for a nasty stretch. Remain calm and keep that parent filter in place. You and your child will get through this.

Now that you're aware of the addiction, you can intervene before it spirals into darker territory, so don't give in to discouragement or despair. Love your child no matter what. Walk with him or her through the recovery process, whatever it takes. Seek help from a counselor or psychiatrist who specializes in addictions. Get referrals from your family doctor.

Remember, nothing is impossible with God. Trust that He can turn this curse into a blessing in your child's life and yours. Yes, it takes courage, patience, tough love, lots of prayer, and even professional help for a loved one to conquer an addiction. But with your support, your child can do it.

My Game Boy

Y'all, one of my biggest concerns for my boy is that he loves to game. Loves it! He says he's going to be an app developer when he grows up, so he "needs" to practice now. (Sounds like parent manipulation to me.) Oh, this has been a struggle. His gaming is a huge red alert in my brain. I pray about it a *lot*.

On the one hand, I don't want to be crazy overprotective and not let him experience the gaming world. But on the other hand, I want to make sure he's able to self-regulate. It's a balance. The Holy Spirit keeps me centered and on point.

I recently read an article in the *Washington Post* about a fifteen-year-old boy who became so addicted to gaming that his parents had to send him to a summer wilderness therapy program to "reconnect with himself and the real world around him."[11] His obsession with gaming began five years earlier but intensified over time. At the height of his addiction, he'd react with violent outbursts whenever his parents asked him to turn off his gaming console and engage in other activities. For years his parents "felt their son slipping away … consumed by the virtual worlds shared by millions of strangers."[12] The decision to send him to a treatment program was radical, but they were desperate. They couldn't let this destructive addiction go on day after day and year after year.

Many parents of tweens are becoming alarmed over their kids' compulsive gaming, and screen use in general. According to experts, there has been "a steep rise in the number of parents worried that their kids are in fact addicted."[13] To address this exploding problem, treatment programs and counselors are beginning to specialize in this new type of addiction.

Psychologist Kimberly Young says, "I don't think we know exactly how many [children] are suffering from this, but we know it's a big problem."[14]

The *Post* article went on to say, "Boys tend to be more susceptible to compulsive gaming than girls, but any kid who is trying to avoid overwhelming stress—bullies at school, a difficult home environment, social anxiety [and loneliness]—might be especially drawn to video games. Experts also see a correlation between obsessive video game use and traits associated with ... anxiety and depression, although the exact nature of the connection is not fully understood."[15]

In addition, a 1998 study indicated that "video games raise the level of dopamine in the brain by about 100 percent," which essentially mirrors the increase from sex.[16] No wonder gaming is addictive!

News reports like this made me think more deeply about how I approach my kids' screen time at home. The young man in the *Post* article couldn't regulate his gaming. He became increasingly detached from the real world, including his family and friends and the activities he once loved.[17]

If I'm teaching my children to listen to God about when to stay, when to speak, and when to leave social situations, then I should also be teaching them to listen to Him about self-regulating their gaming and screen time. I can't become complacent! This is too important.

Last summer, I tried an entirely new approach to screen time: I didn't set any limits. *Gasp!* Now before you think I've lost my mind, I didn't give my kids free rein. We were continually talking about their screen use. My goal was to teach them to self-regulate. I think of it like preparing them to say no to pornography, drugs, and alcohol. I can't always be there, so I want to give them the tools to know how to respond.

With regard to gaming, I don't want my kids to be unable to walk away from screens because I'm not there to regulate their screen time. So I ignored all those rules on social media for parenting screen time. I threw out the system where my kids can earn thirty minutes of screen time for every thirty minutes of reading time.

I replaced the rules and guidelines with conversation.

I'm not saying there's anything wrong with earning systems. And for younger kids, it's a great place to start. Each child is different, and every family gets a choice. There's no right or wrong here.

Remember when I talked earlier in the book about focusing less on rules and regulations and more on helping our tweens develop an internal sense of right and wrong (a moral compass)? Well, I applied that approach to my kids' screen time.

When my son got grouchy after excessive screen time, I'd say, "You probably need to turn that off. Let's play a board game instead." Or "Will this game matter in five years?"

I kinda handled it the way I handle pornography. Instead of implementing rules, I talked my kids through it, teaching them to navigate this issue on their own. I want them to learn personal responsibility and how to regulate their own screen time.

Here's what this looked like in our home:

- I implemented the idea when my kids were eight and twelve years of age.
- I made sure all parental controls for our video-game consoles were set to block online interaction with strangers. I didn't allow connecting online or playing games online with others.
- My kids played video games in our game room, right off our kitchen. They were close by, so I could hear everything. They also had to leave the door open when they were gaming. (Do you picture me lurking around the corner like a stalker? No! Not me.)
- I didn't allow any mature or adult-rated games. My tweens mainly played Mario, Star Wars, football, soccer, and Minecraft. We used the official video-game rating system to determine which videos were acceptable:

  C = young children
  E = everyone
  E 10+ = ages ten and up
  T = teen (ages thirteen and up)
  M = mature (ages seventeen and up)
  A = adults only (ages eighteen and up)
  RP = rating pending[18]

When my kids got grouchy playing games, I knew they were playing too much. But instead of imposing rules, I'd say, "What do you think is making you so irritable?"

Without fail, they'd reply, "Too much screen time."

I love this because they recognized it on their own without my telling them how bad too much screen time can be or regulating it for them. I didn't need to nag. They were learning how to regulate themselves.

Most days they gamed a little and then turned to something more creative. During the school year, there isn't much time for gaming because of homework and extracurricular activities. But over the summer, they learned to turn the video games off on their own—and even got bored with them.

Whenever I asked to play a board game or card game with them, they almost always said yes even if they were in the middle of a video game. I discovered that if I initiated quality time and put my own screen down, they were ready to spend time with me. My kids crave face-to-face time as much as I do!

It's also important that we model the behavior we want our kids to engage in. I struggle with screen addiction too. It's so easy for me to open my social-media platforms for a second to check just one thing and then get caught up in a post and the comments. Twenty minutes later, I could've missed an important conversation with one of my kids.

I know my children can relate to my struggle, so I'll straight up say to them, "I put my phone in the other room because if it's near me, I'll be checking it. And I want to unplug and just be with y'all tonight. You're more important than that screen. Let's snuggle or visit or chat." I'm on screens way too much, but this is one way I try to be a good role model.

When I'm on a deadline or there's a crisis, I sometimes give my kids a heads-up. If I'm multitasking, and they want to watch a movie with me, I'll say, "I'll watch the movie, but be patient with me. I've got this thing going on, so I'll have to check my phone over the next couple hours."

Teaching our tweens to self-regulate when it comes to screen time or any other activity is a process that begins with trust and open communication (like using the starter conversations on bad habits we talked about earlier). As they learn to walk in the Spirit and follow their own moral compasses, we can let out the kite string a bit and allow more freedom. We still need to be alert for the warning signs of addiction, but we'll sleep better at night knowing they're aware of the dangers and understand the importance of guarding their hearts and minds.

14

Mass Shootings and Terrorism

School Lockdown Procedures, Fear, Death, Stereotypes

Although statistically speaking it's unlikely that our children will be directly involved in a mass shooting or terrorist attack, they often have direct access to the horrific details. An endless stream of images and video footage appears on news reports and social media whenever these kinds of events occur. In 2015, for example, there were 333 mass shootings in America (at schools and other locations).[1] And as of December 2016, the number of mass shootings increased to 363. (A *mass shooting* is defined as "four or more [people] shot and/or killed in a single event [incident], at the same general time and location, not including the shooter.")[2]

Social media normalizes these events and even live-streams footage of people running from a shooter or being gunned down. This online content can have a traumatic impact on our children, especially our elementary-age kids. When they see disturbing images, they naturally have questions. They need help processing this information so it doesn't desensitize them to these events.

Even adults find it difficult to discuss topics like mass shootings and terrorism, so how can we talk about it honestly and openly with our children without traumatizing them? Let's brainstorm some ideas together.

Conversation Starters Close to Home

I've found that the easiest way to start a conversation on these issues is to simply ask my kids about the emergency procedures at their school. Most public schools have practice drills to rehearse what students and staff should do in an active-shooter situation. In schools, these are typically referred to as *lockdown drills*.

Talking about school lockdown procedures and practice drills moves the topic from a broader focus to a closer-to-home focus kids can relate to. Once the conversation is rolling, it can evolve into deeper discussions on terrorism and mass shootings.

Here are five steps you can take to open up the conversation with your tween:

1. Become familiar with your school's policies and procedures before talking with your child about lockdown situations. Having this information will help you navigate the discussion at home, since you'll be using the same terms and definitions the school uses.
2. Talk to your child about where to go and what to do in a shooting scenario. Make sure your instructions echo the school's procedures.
3. Reassure your child that he or she is never alone. God is always there even if you aren't. He's "an ever-present help in trouble" (Psalm 46:1, NIV).
4. You know your child better than anyone. If your child suffers from anxiety or panic attacks, talk with your pediatrician about how to approach this topic without increasing his or her anxiety. It's important not to be a dramatic, emotional mess when you have this conversation. Remember to remain calm and use your parent filter.
5. Make sure the terminology and level of graphic detail you use are age appropriate. For elementary-age children, I prefer using the term *bad person* instead of *shooter* or *gunman*. If your child is older and can handle more detail, using the actual terms may be fine. For example, my middle schooler and I have honest, detailed conversations about ISIS, the Columbine shootings, and other incidents related to mass shootings and terrorism.

The questions on shootings and terrorism that our kids are discussing in peer groups and classes are often very real and direct. They know what's happening in the world and have honest questions that deserve honest answers. Again, we should be their go-to source of information on these topics. Their safe place.

One time my daughter told me, "We were talking about Columbine at school, and some other kids asked me, 'If a gun was pointed at your head and you were asked if you were a Christian, how would you respond?'"

If our kids are talking about these issues with friends and peers at school, we need to talk about them at home, too. Remember, no fear. Face it!

Let's cover the first three steps in a little more detail.

1. *Know your school's policies and procedures.* The top priority for school administrators is to keep our kids safe. To minimize casualties in any emergency situation, they look at every possible angle and come up with the best contingency plan. They want to do everything they can to protect our children if the worst happens.

Why am I pointing this out? Because as parents we need to realize that even though we may not agree with every school policy or procedure, administrators and teachers are concerned about our children's safety too. We're on the same team. Understanding the reasons behind the procedures is important. For example, my son told me that the procedure at his school is to quickly assemble everyone in a classroom and lock the door. (This is why they call it a lockdown.) Students are then told to huddle in a corner and stay quiet. When the door is locked, it can't be opened again until someone in authority (a school official or police officer) has deemed the area safe.

My immediate question was, "What happens if you're in the bathroom and can't get to the classroom before it's locked?"

My son casually replied, "Then I hide in the bathroom by myself. The teacher can't unlock the door because the bad person could try to use me to get the door open so he can hurt other students."

I cringed at the thought. My knee-jerk reaction was *I can't believe our school policy would leave a child behind.* But I didn't share this with my son.

Later I talked in detail about the procedure with my husband and some teacher friends. They wisely reminded me that the school's job is to *minimize* the number of fatalities and casualties overall. They assured me that teachers are going to do everything in their power to get every single student into that classroom before it's locked. They care about our children. They're shaping the next generation. They don't want anyone to be harmed.

But unfortunately, they have to think about the worst-case scenario. *What if the gunman is walking down the hallway toward the classroom, and the teacher has no time to reach every student?* In that split second, the teacher has to save as many lives as possible. Which means the classroom door must be locked quickly, even if a student is left outside.

When my friends explained the reasons for this procedure, it made complete sense and helped me take my mama-bear emotions out of the equation.

As you learn about your school's procedures, you may be tempted to get upset like I did. But calm your knee-jerk reaction and keep reminding yourself that school officials care about your children too and don't want anyone hurt. We're working together to protect all the kids.

The fact that we even have to discuss these horrific issues with our children makes me sick to my stomach. But if we're going to assign blame for the evil in the world, let's blame the true schemer behind it: Satan. Remember, "our struggle is not against flesh and blood, but against . . . spiritual forces of evil" (Ephesians 6:12, NIV). Evil is real in this world. We're in a battle between good and bad. But our fight isn't with one another (flesh and blood); it's with Satan himself.

2. *Talk to your child about where to go and what to do in a shooting scenario.* When I realized that my son might be locked out of his classroom in an active-shooter situation, I had to talk with him about what to do. I know this worst-case scenario is highly unlikely, but I had to go there. I had to know deep down in my heart that I had prepared my child for the worst.

So I asked him, "What would you do if you were locked out of the classroom?"

We talked about trying to find a janitor's closet or standing on a restroom toilet, locking the stall door, and staying very, very quiet. I told him never to approach a shooter or try to take him down. (My son truly thinks he's a superhero, so it needed to be said.)

We also talked about ways he could protect himself if he was ever attacked. He knows that hitting or kicking someone is allowed only for self-defense. Once when we were having a serious conversation about a bad person trying to kidnap or hurt him, he jokingly said, "So in this situation, can I kick him in the penis?" (Okay, I'll admit it. My son really just likes saying the p-word and even has a song about it, but sharing it would violate our confidentiality rule.)

I laughed and replied, "Well, you're assuming it's a boy. If it is, here's the thing. You don't seek him out. You hide from him. But if he finds you in that locked restroom stall, kicks down the door, and is getting ready to hurt you, fight back like crazy. So yes, kick him in the penis."

Immediately he jumped up and shouted "Yes" with a little karate kick of excitement.

It's important to keep things light when we're talking with our kids about these kinds of topics. Add some humor. We don't want to create anxiety or fear. We must keep the conversation as casual and calm as possible.

After my son enjoyed his little joke, we moved into more difficult territory.

Tearing up a little, I said, "So, you're locked out of your classroom, and you're hiding in a restroom stall, standing on a toilet. What would you think about? What happy memories could you focus on?"

He answered, "Our Disney trip when you got sick on the Star Wars ride. And the first time we went skiing, when you and Dad went tumbling down the mountain."

We laughed even though it was a very serious conversation. Okay, I was crying, too, but I wasn't sobbing or being dramatic. I was just sad that I had to discuss this with my elementary-age child. We can be real with our children and stay calm at the same time when we discuss tough topics like this.

I explained to my son that I was crying because it hurt my heart to even think about him in this situation and not being able to be there to fix it. Then I took the conversation a little deeper.

3. *Reassure your child that he or she is never alone.* I wanted to prepare my son physically and mentally for an active-shooter situation, but most

important, I wanted to prepare him spiritually. I reminded him, "You'd have someone with you greater than me. The God who made you and walks with you every step of your life will never, ever leave your side."

Then we read this verse together:

> Be strong. Take courage. Don't be intimidated. Don't give [your enemies] a second thought because GOD, your God, is striding ahead of you. He's right there with you. He won't let you down; he won't leave you. (Deuteronomy 31:6, MSG)

Our goal as parents should be to teach our kids where to turn whenever they're worried or afraid. We want them to turn to us, of course, but God is their ultimate safe place, the only one who is with them 24/7. We need to talk about what it means to trust Him in their everyday world, no matter what is happening. His power to help them when they're in danger goes way beyond any earthly powers.

If we're going to tell our kids to remain calm in an active-shooter situation, our actions should match our words. We should practice what we preach.

During a lockdown at your child's school, instead of going into crazy-mom mode, allow emergency personnel and school officials to do their jobs. They've been trained to handle situations like this, and they'll bring your child to you as soon as it's safe.

Rushing onto school property or arguing with police officers who won't let you enter only makes the situation more stressful. Breathe. Pray. Trust God. When fear of the unknown throws you into a panic, your faith in God can help keep you grounded and carry you through.

Going Deeper

I used the school lockdown drill as a conversation starter with my son and tried to keep things light. But as our discussion turned more serious, we talked about God's promise in this verse:

> Don't be afraid, for I am with you.
> Don't be discouraged, for I am your God.
> I will strengthen you and help you.
> I will hold you up with my victorious right hand.
> (Isaiah 41:10)

My child said, "I get that God is with me all the time, but why does He even allow bad things to happen in the first place?"

Wouldn't we all love a simple answer to that complicated question?

I replied, "That's a great question. One reason is that God gives us choices. It's called free will. We get to choose good or bad. Will we follow God and love others, or will we be filled with hate and do harm to others? Our decisions determine the course of our lives and affect other people. Obviously, a bad guy who entered your school would be choosing hate and evil. And because of his choices, others would suffer."

You child may ask a more complicated question like "But why doesn't God stop the bad guy or kill him?" To this I would respond, "God's plan was to give us free will so we can each live how we choose. We may not always understand why God doesn't stop bad things from happening, but He promises to make things right in the end. Our job is to trust Him. One day Jesus will physically come back to this earth, and each person will be held accountable to God for their choices. Each person will face His judgment."

This could lead to a conversation about death, though I wouldn't dive into this topic unless your child brings it up. Even then, what you say should be age appropriate. Since there isn't a script to follow for discussions like this, we need to rely on God for wisdom and let His Spirit guide our words.

When I discuss death with my kids, we talk about how everyone is going to die someday. Take Lazarus, for example. Jesus raised him from the dead, but guess what? He eventually died again.

No human being on this earth is going to live forever. But here's the amazing thing about our faith in Christ: we don't need to fear death because Jesus Himself conquered it, and heaven will be our eternal home when we die. Death for those who believe in Jesus is just the gateway to a perfect place with no more pain and no more tears. That's why the Bible says, "To live is Christ and to die is gain" (Philippians 1:21, NIV).

Talking about the evil choices people make is also a great opportunity to teach our kids not to stereotype people or put them in boxes. By that I mean not every Muslim is bad just because radical Islamic terrorists are killing people. We should never stick a label on any group. For instance, if a self-proclaimed Christian says something hateful and demeaning, I'll tell my kids, "We don't believe that. We don't want to be lumped together with that person, right? So don't do the same thing to others."

God has given every human being the right to choose good or evil, and each individual is responsible for his or her actions. Only God knows each person's heart.

At the same time, our kids need to be aware of the dangers of terrorism. They shouldn't label people, but they should treat *all* strangers with caution, regardless of religion or race, and take steps to protect themselves. Why? Because of this important fact: most radical terrorist groups recruit online.[3] One or more of these groups may try to contact our children on social media. It happens. Explain that this is one of the reasons we don't allow followers we don't know in real life and why we avoid communicating with cyberstrangers.

Terrorism is a seriously terrifying subject, and you may be thinking, *I don't want to destroy my child's innocence by talking in depth about it.* Believe me, I get it. But don't let your fears prevent you from having conversations about it. Our kids are already talking about this topic with their friends and in their classes at school. So instead of avoiding it, face it head-on and show your children that you're a safe place to bring their fears and questions.

Like every other issue we've discussed in this book, there's no script for talking about terrorism and mass shootings with our tweens. The conversations I have with my kids on these topics take place as we go about our daily activities. We talk about them while we're hanging out on our back porch, swimming in our pool, or sitting in our kitchen. I'm always on the lookout for teachable moments and opportunities to connect on a deeper level.

Remember what we learned earlier? It's essential to build open communication and instill values in our tweens *before* the teen years hit. This is one of the best ways to protect their innocence. But Satan manipulates us into thinking the exact opposite and convinces us that we should avoid tough discussions. Then we become complacent, and it leaves the door wide open to cyberstrangers and all the other dangers we've been talking about. We need to keep our guard up!

Since I started the conversation with my kids about mass shootings and terrorism, we've brainstormed how to deal with any situation when they're full of fear. They know that God is always with them no matter what they face. And that calms my fears because I know they're spiritually prepared if the unimaginable happens.

15

Attitude and Body Changes

Brain Development, Puberty, Periods, Wet Dreams

Attitude. You know, the tone of voice, the eye roll, or "that look." I want to start yelling like a crazy person when either of my kids responds as if I'm an idiot. Their attitudes really push me over the edge. Can you relate?

But attitude goes both ways. I'll never forget the first time God spoke to my heart about my own sass. It had been a rough morning. I was irritable because I hadn't slept well, and I used a short tone with my kids before dropping them off at school. I was feeling convicted. Then these words popped into my head: *If you want your kids to have less attitude, you have to model it first.* Ouch!

When our feelings control our attitudes, our relationships with our kids suffer. Attitude creates a wedge between us, and then a downward spiral ensues. Complacency sets in, and instead of talking with our kids, we go into avoidance mode. Eventually, relationships are in turmoil, and we end up glaring at one another across the great divide.

One of my heads-up mamas says that attitude in our tweens is like "feelings in HD." I love that! Feelings are magnified, and everything is SO DRAMATIC. As adults, we have to be the voices of reason. So when our tweens give us attitude, we need to respond with truth and logic. We also need to recognize and try to understand the rapid changes they're experiencing. We must learn to walk with balance in the Spirit. Jesus will keep us centered.

Before we tackle how to handle the attitude, I want to dive into the reasons behind it. Where are our sweet kids, and why are they acting like aliens?

The Bubble

Has your middle schooler ever appeared ditzy, as if his or her head is in the clouds?

When my once-responsible daughter started acting this way, it was new to me. Then I read *Middle School: The Inside Story* and learned all about "The Bubble."

This book is a great resource. It has saved me so many times when I've wanted to scream and pull out my hair. Times when my daughter was in the middle of a story and stopped all of a sudden. Or when I asked a question, and she looked at the clouds and didn't even hear me. Then I'd remember: the Bubble.

Authors Sue Acuña and Cynthia Tobias explain:

> It's typical for middle schoolers to hear only the part of the story that applies to them. We like to call it The Bubble.... There are so many changes coming at them at once, they have to spend almost all their time trying to figure out what's happening and what to do about it. They still need us—in some ways more than ever. We can't live in their Bubble—it's strictly single-occupancy. But we definitely should be regular visitors, occasionally poking our heads inside.[1]

So how do we cope with the Bubble? Never yell. Remain calm. This takes *so* much patience. I can't even.

Acuña and Tobias give parents some valuable advice: "When you give important information ... have [your tween] repeat it to you." Then they offer this gem:

> No need to battle The Bubble; it's going to disappear in its own time and way. But your friendly visits periodically will remind your

> [tween] that you—and the rest of the world—are still there. It shouldn't be used as an excuse for being rude or inconsiderate, but you may be able to trace a lot of frustrating behavior to The Bubble.[2]

This information has been life changing for me as a parent. If I recognize the Bubble, I'm able to remain calm. If I overreact, yell, or become frustrated, open communication shuts down very quickly. Recognizing how to deal with the Bubble is a *huge* key to open communication with our tweens.

The Brain under Construction

Understanding what's happening to tweens' bodies during this stage of development also helped me show more grace and forgiveness. Here's one important piece of information I discovered: the prefrontal cortex—the front of the brain—"plays a role in the regulation of complex cognitive, emotional, and behavioral functioning."[3] It's the part of the brain that's responsible for functions like judgment, abstract thought, and impulse control.[4]

Research has shown that "adult and teen brains work differently. Adults think with the prefrontal cortex, the brain's rational part, but teens process information with the amygdala, the emotional part. And it's the prefrontal cortex that responds to situations with good judgment and an awareness of long-term consequences."[5]

And guess what? The prefrontal cortex doesn't fully develop until our kids are in their midtwenties.[6] The brain develops from back to front, so the prefrontal cortex is the last part of the brain to fully develop.[7]

But there's another important fact we can't afford to miss. Research shows that "a spurt of growth in the frontal cortex [occurs] just before puberty (age 11 in girls, 12 in boys)."[8]

Wait … what?

So when our kids are eleven or twelve, the part of their brains that's responsible for judgment and impulse control experiences a surge of growth? A light went off in my head. Those are the foundational years when it's so important to instill truth and moral values in our kids. It's also when they're most likely to engage in online activity by themselves. That's the exact period of time in my daughter's life when I was so complacent.

Well, that explains a lot. The perfect parenting storm.

The Joys of Puberty

On top of all those changes is puberty, which "usually occurs in girls between the ages of 10 and 14 and between the ages of 12 and 16 in boys."[9] These are the general ages. According to some medical organizations, it can occur earlier—age seven or eight for girls, and age nine for boys.[10] Again, each child's development is unique.

Girl Talk about Puberty

What happens to girls when they go through puberty? As estrogen (the female hormone) increases, they develop breast buds first and then pubic hair, which is typically followed by their first period.[11]

This is totally normal. Talk with your daughter about her changing body. Tell her when you started noticing your own body changing. If you have a funny story about shaving your legs or armpits, share it, and use terms like *routine maintenance* and *natural.* Talk about when you started your period. Prepare your daughter for this event and make sure she keeps a pad in a non-see-through bag at the bottom of her backpack—just in case. Have her wear a pad for practice so she knows what it's like. Role-play with her about asking to see the nurse if she starts her period at school.

I tell my daughter to say to her teacher, "I'm having tummy troubles and need to see the nurse." If the teacher asks additional questions, she can say, "I think it's a *girl* tummy issue."

Simple as that. Remind your daughter that every girl will go through this. Standard operating procedure.

Start the body-change conversation with your daughter when she enters fourth grade, at the latest. That was when I got my daughter the American Girl book *The Care and Keeping of You: The Body Book for Girls.* I let her read it on her own first and then told her we could discuss anything she had questions about. I kept reassuring her that our conversations were confidential, and I would never share them with anyone. I didn't, unless we needed to ask our pediatrician or doctor together about a specific issue. I also assured her that even though some of her questions might seem embarrassing to her, they were perfectly natural.

When discussing your daughter's period, explain that this is the beautiful way God created women so they can have children after marriage. Use this opportunity to talk about the importance of following God's blueprint for marriage. (We'll cover this in chapter 17.)

Let her know that mood swings go along with having a period, but she needs to resist letting her feelings control her actions and attitudes. Share your own struggles with mood swings and apologize when you mess up. Make sure you're modeling the behavior you expect her to have.

When I'm having a particularly tough time with my emotions, and I know it's related to my period, I share this with my daughter. I might say, "I feel like yelling and being crazy mom right now. But I'm trying to think logically because I know it's just hormones making me feel wacky. This is the time of month that requires extra patience on my part."

If you've already laid the groundwork for open communication with your daughter, you won't feel so uncomfortable talking about puberty, periods, and mood swings. And your girl will appreciate having someone in her corner who understands what she's going through.

Boy Talk about Puberty

What does puberty mean for boys? Their bodies get bigger (including their penises), their voices change, and hair starts sprouting everywhere. To be more specific, pubic hair appears around age twelve, armpit hair around fourteen and beard growth around sixteen.[12] Each boy is different, so these changes can happen earlier or later than the average age. Hormones make boys' testicles bigger as well, and their testosterone levels increase.[13] Erections are common and completely normal for boys during puberty. (We'll cover masturbation in chapter 17. Remember, no topic is off limits.)

Does that make you feel old and nauseous? It does me. My baby boy … NOOOO!

Okay. We have to take our emotions out of the equation and talk about erections and wet dreams. (The first couple of times I spoke publicly about these topics, my neck would turn red, and I felt like I was going to break out in hives. But the more we talk about this stuff, the easier it gets. I promise. We can do this, sister!)

Reassure your son that all guys have erections. Don't shame him or make fun of him. Actually, Dad might be the best one to have this conversation with your son. Suggest that your husband share a funny or embarrassing story from personal experience. This will help your son feel like he's not the only one in the world experiencing these changes. This could end up being one of their inside jokes. (You know dudes. They like to joke about everything.)

Wet dreams begin when the body starts manufacturing more testosterone. (It's similar to beginning a period when a girl's body starts producing more estrogen.) Like erections, wet dreams are perfectly normal for boys during puberty. It's one of those gray areas in parenting.

I love what one of my heads-up mamas says: "The black-and-white issues are clear. Prepare your child for the gray."

We often avoid talking with our kids about the gray areas because we don't know what to say or how to handle them. No more avoiding. We need to be proactive in addressing each issue our tweens are dealing with. Seeking advice is a good step.

Dannah Gresh points out the following in her book *Six Ways to Keep the "Good" in Your Boy*:

> The body ejaculates [semen] naturally. It's involuntary, and a boy should know to expect it or he may be frustrated and insecure when it happens.... A boy who is not masturbating and thus is getting no release through self-gratification is likely to experience more wet dreams.[14]

That's good to know. I always thought wet dreams were bad. Her information helped me think of them as a positive alternative to masturbation. If your child isn't having wet dreams and you're worried that he's masturbating too much, don't freak out. Remember, this is a gray area. Not every boy has wet dreams, but that doesn't mean something's wrong.[15] If you have concerns about your son's erections or wet dreams, talk to your pediatrician.

So how do you handle wet sheets when your boy wakes up? Don't shame him. Your guy needs to know that wet dreams are a normal, healthy part of his development. Don't make a big deal about it.

I love the input and advice from other moms in our group. For example, if your boy says to you in the morning, "I need to throw my sheets in the washer," don't cause a scene or ask a bunch of nagging questions. Clear out the washer and let him take care of it.

One mom said, "I secretly get my husband when I see wet sheets. He'll go into my son's bedroom by himself and say, 'I got your back, man.'" Dad changes the sheets and throws them in the washer. No big scene.

I mean, precious, right? Who knew this conversation would end on a sappy note? You never know where open communication is going to take you.

Dealing with the Attitude

So now we understand why our once innocent and sweet tweens are different. We've got the Bubble, the prefrontal cortex, hormones, and body changes covered. But does that excuse our tweens for giving us attitude and walking all over us? Heck to the no.

It boils down to a concept you're very familiar with by now: walking with balance in the Spirit. That's what we need to do when we're dealing with tween attitude. We need Jesus to keep us centered. In line. On point. At times we'll need to address the attitude directly, and at other times we'll need to let it go and love our kids with grace. To figure out whether to discipline our tweens or extend grace, it helps to rely on the Spirit of God living in our hearts.

Most of the time, I want to be sympathetic because of the Bubble, the prefrontal cortex, and the hormones, but I also know that when I let one little thing go, it can start a downward spiral. Things can quickly spin out of control. I've seen this happen over and over.

I've learned some important lessons about dealing with tween attitude.

Mostly about what not to do. When my daughter was a tween, I tried yelling, crying, and taking away her phone. None of it worked. Trial and error, but I still couldn't get it right. For example, one night we were about to walk into Hobby Lobby to get materials for a school project. My tween's attitude was all over the place. I started crying and said, "It really hurts me when you talk to me like that."

She was upset, but it was all about me and my feelings. I didn't handle the situation correctly. I knew that deep down. But as I prayed about it, God showed me something big.

My tween had some eye roll and tone going on one day (this was probably weeks or months after the Hobby Lobby incident). Oh, it was making my blood boil! But I collected myself and removed my feelings from the equation. Then I calmly and quietly said to her, "Crazy mom wants to come out right now. But I'm going to move my knee-jerk emotions from the emotional side of my brain to the logical side. Thinking logically now, I'm actually quoting James 1:19 to myself: I should be 'quick to listen, slow to speak, and slow to get angry.'"

She smiled and then apologized. I could tell from her face that she was glad I knew that verse. Again, God's Word has the answers. Why do I miss it? Because I'm not listening.

When I do things my own way, I keep messing up. But when I actually live out God's Word (listen to Him and do what He says), it changes everything. Not only did God supply the appropriate response to my tween's attitude, but I finally modeled for my girl how to behave when those crazy knee-jerk emotions take over. And she was dealing with a ton of them at the time. (She still is as a teen!)

The advice from the book *Good Pictures, Bad Pictures* about moving things from the emotional side of the brain to the thinking side of the brain helped too.[16] Can you tell I love that book?

One final talking point on this subject. Sometimes when I see the attitude coming out in my kids, I'll say, "You have every right to be tired and cranky, but it's still not okay to be mean or disrespectful. If you wouldn't talk to your teacher with that tone, don't use it on me."

#LearningTogether. It's a process.

I also try to show them grace and forgiveness even when they don't deserve it. Even when their attitudes make my blood boil. Why? Because I know I don't deserve grace and forgiveness for all my mistakes, and yet God extends those things to me. Matthew 6:14 says, "If you forgive those who sin against you, your heavenly Father will forgive you."

We need to be honest and open with our tweens about how their words and attitudes affect us. But we also need to forgive and show grace.

When your tween cops an attitude that threatens to bring out crazy mom, ask God to help you walk with balance in the Spirit. Whatever you do, don't engage in the fight and become a twelve-year-old again. (We can all go there, right?) Don't scream. Don't let your feelings control your attitude. None of that will improve your relationship.

Instead, remain calm. Respond with grace. Walk away. Bite your lip. And when you do respond, "speak the truth in love" (Ephesians 4:15). Always be the bigger person. Remember, you are the role model.

16

Dress Codes and Dating

Sexualization, Character versus Appearance, Love

Oh, dress codes. Like everything else in our society, we're pressured to pick a side. Are we shaming girls and letting boys get off scot-free?

There are lots of arguments about dress codes in parenting circles these days. Specifically, that dress codes target girls, while boys aren't held responsible. I'm so tired of the fighting. Why does everything have to be so divisive?

Instead of getting sidetracked with the debates, how about actually addressing the issue and looking at the facts?

To see how we got here, let's take a trip down memory lane.

A Little Dress-Code Research

Pull out your smartphone or tablet. If you're snuggled up in a comfy place and don't want to get up, don't move. I wouldn't get up either. Just take my word for it now, and you can do the Google searches later when you're waiting in the carpool line.

For those of you who have your devices handy, start off by Googling "Isiah Thomas 1981 Indiana Hoosiers." (I'm a proud IU alumnus. Can you tell?)

Click on "images" at the top of the results page and check out the length of the men's basketball shorts back in the eighties.

Got it? Okay, now Google "Indiana University Hoosiers current men's basketball team."

Do you see the difference in the length of the men's shorts? They've gotten a *lot* longer over time, haven't they? Tons more coverage.

Now let's take a look at cheerleader outfits. Google "Sandy's cheerleader outfit in *Grease*." (By the way, *Grease* was released in 1978. "Oh, Sandy! Oh-Oh-Oh-Oh Sandy." Who else wants to sing that song?)

Look at the actual images from the movie and notice how long Sandy's skirt and sweater were.

I have to add a disclaimer before we go any further: I'm not picking on cheerleaders. I was a cheerleader in middle school! I know they work their butts off. Most professional cheerleaders not only have amazing bodies and athletic talent, but they've trained their entire lives to achieve their spot on the squad.

Okay, let's get back to cheerleading outfits. Google "Current NFL cheerleaders." (Make sure you've clicked on "images" at the top of the search window.)

Would you agree that cheerleading outfits today are much skimpier than they were in 1978? Don't get me wrong. I'm not saying it's right or wrong; I'm making a factual observation. And the fact is this: Guys' uniforms today cover up more skin. Shorts are way longer now than they used to be. Girls' uniforms, on the other hand, cover up less skin. Skirts have gotten shorter, and tops have gotten smaller. Of course, I realize the everyday dress code for males and females isn't quite the same as athletic uniforms. But do you see my point?

So I wonder ... why are girls exposing more skin, while guys are covering up more? If we're going to be a skin-loving world, let's at least be equal. Where are the booty shorts and crop tops for boys?

What are we doing, world? Why are we exploiting our girls and making them sex objects while, at the same time, we're covering up our boys?

Of course, I'd rather we all just cover up. That way we'd be forced to look at the heart instead of outward appearances. But can y'all see where I'm coming from on this? Our culture promotes and glorifies clothes that exploit girls. Sexist much?

Why did I mention NFL cheerleaders? Well, last year my family went to our first NFL game because my son is a football fanatic. It was *so much* fun! But approximately three rows in front of us was a young teen with two adults I assumed were his parents. As the cheerleaders performed, this young teen took out his phone, zoomed in on one of the cheerleader's breasts, and snapped a picture. The adults around him seemingly had no clue. It made me sick to my stomach. I couldn't help but think, *What if that was my baby girl who was treated like a sexualized object after training her whole life to be an NFL cheerleader?*

If my daughter wanted to be a cheerleader, I'd fully support her, but I'd warn her that some people will look only at her outward appearance instead of recognizing all her hard work, athletic ability, and talent.

We live in a sexist world. It's a sad fact of life—one of the many problems in our culture today. When I saw the teenage boy take that picture, I immediately thought, *Did that get Snapchatted or shared on social media?*

Dress codes and sexualization are important cyberparenting issues we need to talk about honestly with our children before the hormones start raging.

God's Perspective on Dress Codes

Let's turn the culture off and tune in to God's Word for answers.

Here's what the Bible says to girls:

> Women [should] be modest in their appearance. They should wear decent and appropriate clothing and not draw attention to themselves by the way they fix their hair or by wearing gold or pearls or expensive clothes. For women who claim to be devoted to God should make themselves attractive by the good things they do. (1 Timothy 2:9–10)

> Don't be concerned about the outward beauty of fancy hairstyles, expensive jewelry, or beautiful clothes. You should clothe yourselves instead with the beauty that comes from within, the unfading beauty of a gentle and quiet spirit, which is so precious to God. (1 Peter 3:3–4)

As moms, we need to model these things for our daughters. It's okay to love makeup, jewelry, and shoes. But do we love them more than God? Do we focus more on our appearance than developing godly character? Material things aren't bad unless they become an idol in our lives. Do we worship them more than God? Is our outward appearance more important to us than reflecting His heart in the world?

God is pretty clear on this one: Girls, wear decent and appropriate clothing. Don't use your outward appearance to draw attention to yourself.

Now, what does the Bible say to boys? Let's take a look:

> Do not lust in your heart after [a woman's] beauty or let her captivate you with her eyes. (Proverbs 6:25, NIV)

> Anyone who even looks at a woman with lust has already committed adultery with her in his heart. (Matthew 5:28)

This principle is the same for all guys, married or single. No man should look at women as sex objects or lust after them. Remember, guys are visual, so what they see is going to cause the biggest problems for them.

Just as the Bible teaches *mutual* submission, it also teaches *equal* responsibility regarding dress codes. How did God know that women would be dressing provocatively, and guys would have trouble looking away? How did He know to include all these relevant verses in the Bible to help us navigate this issue? Because He's God. He created each of us and knows our internal struggles. He knows the sinful, fallen world we live in and where it's going. He knows.

So instead of looking to social media for answers, we need to go to the Source of truth. Only He has the answers to our questions.

One other key passage applies to both girls and boys:

> Temptation comes from our own desires, which entice us and drag us away. These desires give birth to sinful actions. And when sin is allowed to grow, it gives birth to death. (James 1:14–15)

Well, isn't that the truth? James was describing that downward spiral we experience when life spins out of control because of our bad choices. Like the knitted-sweater example, one little thread gets pulled, and the entire sweater starts unraveling.

Temptation comes from our own desires.

Why do girls dress provocatively? The reasons may vary. When I was a teenager, I wanted attention from guys. I desired to be noticed, though I didn't realize it at the time. I understand it now, but I wish I'd known it then and made different choices.

As moms, we need to model humility and modesty in front of our sons and daughters every day. I'm not going to tell you how long your shorts need to be or whether it's okay to wear a string bikini. (Your bikini, your choice.) Seek God, and He'll tell you. Remember, this isn't about rules; it's about relationship. Your relationship with God.

Keep in mind that our daughters will copy the way we dress. We are their example. We need to teach them how to dress in a way that will attract guys who have character and will value them for who they are, not for how much skin they show.

Boys are tempted in different ways by their desires. Why do they sometimes look at women as objects or have trouble looking away from inappropriate images? Again, they're visual. But that's still no excuse for giving in to temptation and treating girls like sex objects.

We need to teach our sons to look at a girl's heart more than her outward appearance. We want our boys to respond to a girl's character, not what she's wearing or how she looks. But how do we instill this foundational truth in our sons? One important way to drive this home is through open communication. We need to continually remind them that even though it's natural to notice outward beauty, it's not okay to disrespect a girl. As we teach our sons to seek God, they'll develop their own moral compasses and learn to listen to God's Spirit.

As we discussed in chapter 11, when my son notices large racks of boobs, I tell him to look away, to not stare, and to focus on inner beauty more than outward appearance. (You can review the other talking points in the pornography chapter.)

I want to raise a son who notices a girl's heart, not just her figure. I want him to treat girls with respect, not as objects. My son and I have had lots of conversations about what that looks like.

When he tells me about seeing girls who are showing lots of skin (in public and online), we don't talk badly about them. I tell him, "People dress like that for different reasons. I used to dress like that. Mommy was young and immature. I wanted attention from boys. But the thing is, I got attention from the wrong kinds of boys because of the way I dressed. Those boys cared about my outward appearance more than my heart. But what I was truly seeking was someone to look at my heart and fall in love with me as a person."

My husband and I use everyday situations to instill chivalrous values in our son. I know some people think that teaching chivalry is old-fashioned and outdated. But what's wrong with instilling more respect and politeness in the world today? I think we desperately need to bring it back.

When we open the pizza box every Friday night at dinner, Matt will often say, "No, son. Ladies first, always."

I'll never forget when my preschool-age son held the door open for an elderly couple at a restaurant. As soon as I saw him do it, I said, "Wow, sweetie, you're such a gentleman." He beamed.

Even now, he frequently holds the door open for strangers when we're out and about. I praise him all the time for his chivalry and kindness.

You can never go wrong with positive reinforcement. It encourages repeat behavior.

I teach both of my kids empathy, but I especially want my son to develop sensitivity to others. Our culture teaches boys to be strong and tough, so we tend to overlook qualities like empathy and sensitivity. Why can't we teach them to be strong and sensitive? It doesn't have to be either/or. It can be both.

Several years ago the dog of my son's friend died. We talked about how awful it must've felt. Then my son came up with the idea to make his friend a card. I was so proud of him and told him what a great idea that was.

When we talk about girls, my tween son mostly thinks they're gross.

But I know the time is coming when his opinion will change. My daughter often tells him, "Wait until middle school. Most boys have big crushes by then."

That's a nice segue into the topic of dating.

To Date or Not to Date

Right now I'm planting seeds about the kinds of girls my son should look for when his interest in dating eventually ignites.

I tell him, "When you think about girls, you need to look for the ones who are smart, kind to everybody, and don't try to impress others. They're a rare find, so you'll have to search for them. They're normally not the obvious choice."

You know what I want for my kids when it comes to dating? First of all, I *don't* want them to be asked out on a date because they're popular, dress provocatively, or try to impress everyone around them. I want them to be asked out because they're humble, kind, and compassionate to everyone. I want them to be asked out not because they force their way into the spotlight but because their quiet integrity and character shine in the world, and someone special recognizes and appreciates those qualities.

Philippians 2:3–4 says, "Don't be selfish; don't try to impress others. Be humble, thinking of others as better than yourselves. Don't look out only for your own interests, but take an interest in others, too." I love this verse! Those are the qualities I want my kids to look for when they start dating.

Like so many other topics we've discussed, it's important to lay the groundwork for open communication about dating when our kids are younger. Obviously, my kids aren't dating yet, but we're already discussing this issue. Beginning the conversation early gives us time to prepare our tweens and instill in them the values we want them to exhibit when they start dating, *before* the raging hormones and feelings enter the picture. Let me share with you how my husband and I handle this issue.

We told my daughter in late elementary school that there would be no dating in middle school. She might have crushes, which is perfectly normal.

And she might have a "boyfriend" she'd want to sit with at a football game or hang out with at a dance. But we made it perfectly clear there would be no actual dates in middle school.

I tell both my kids, "Crushes are a normal and natural part of growing up, but you shouldn't be crazy in love. Keep a balance." There's that word again: *balance*.

I actually like the idea of crushes in middle school because it opens up a lot of good dialogue with my children about qualities to look for in the opposite sex. Tweens often crush on the most popular girl or the hunkiest guy in school, so we need to emphasize qualities like respect, character, and integrity. Our children can learn to recognize these qualities in the words kids use, how they treat others, and the way they carry themselves.

Tweens may talk about "dating" whether or not they actually go on dates. We may laugh about it, but middle-school relationships are *not* a joke. I mean, the other day I saw a photo on Instagram of a seventh-grade couple in bathing suits hugging. The caption said, "Ten months. She's all I've ever dreamed of."

And a million middle-school kids were commenting "Goals." (Kids use this word all day long in texts and online to comment on something they aspire to or want to accomplish.)

This is normal middle-school culture. I'm not sharing this to shame the boy and girl. I'm telling you because we need to prepare our own kids. They're encountering real peer pressure to have serious dating relationships in middle school. It's a thing.

Matt and I decided that we're going to allow dating in high school. We haven't given our kids an exact age because we don't want to lock ourselves into a commitment. We need to be just as clear and accurate about dating guidelines as we are with the phone contract. We don't want to get specific about ages and then have to change them later. For example, we're not going to tell our daughter she can start dating at eighteen when we may decide she's ready at sixteen. Likewise, we don't want to say sixteen and then decide she isn't ready at that age.

We've told our kids, "Dating will be allowed in high school, but we'll determine the age when we get there. And we don't want you going crazy in love in high school. We want you to keep a balance. This will be practice for the real thing."

This is another gray area. Some parents don't allow dating until late high school or college. There is no right or wrong here. The guidelines may look different for each family and child. I love the advice one of my heads-up mamas gave me for preparing our dating guidelines: "I want my kids to learn and practice dating while they're under my roof. I don't want to send them to college far away and not be able to walk them through this process."

My heads-up mama also warns me that this dating conversation gets really tough in high school. Rape. Abuse. Dating violence. See why having a heads-up mama is so valuable?

In one of my groups, a mom asked me, "What happens if my daughter falls for a teen boy who hasn't saved himself for marriage?"

Great question. This is what I told her: "First, I would show grace and love. Second, does the boy who had premarital sex regret it? Or does he think premarital sex is normal and okay? If this kid's values line up with your family values, and premarital sex was a mistake, then it might be okay for your daughter to date him. But I think you'd still need to have lots of discussions with your child about the importance of waiting to be married." Again, we need the Holy Spirit to keep us balanced.

"I Can't Help Falling in Love with You"

Before we wrap up this dating conversation, I want to talk about love for a moment. Plastered all over social media today are statements like "Love is love," "You can't help who you love," and "All you need is love." These simple, feel-good expressions sound wonderful on the surface, and they can tap into strong emotions, but what do they really mean? And do they apply in every situation and context?

If we take emotions out of the picture and look at these statements logically, it sounds as if people are saying they have no choice in the matter.

Who they love is beyond their control. But this mind-set can have dangerous implications for tweens, especially if they start viewing these sentiments as foundational truths that apply to every situation.

Let's say a mom discovers private direct messages in her middle-school daughter's social-media app between her and an online stranger who is approximately fifty years old. After exchanging hundreds of messages with her and building a relationship, he's now pressuring her for nude photos. When the mom confronts her daughter and tells her the relationship is wrong, the middle schooler bursts out in anger, "But I love him. Love is love. I can't help who I love."

Her concept of love is so distorted that she truly believes she's in love with this older man she met online. She's convinced she has no choice. She simply can't help it. With all the tween emotions and hormones involved, it's difficult to separate feelings from truth. Can you see how Satan uses feelings to manipulate and twist a child's concept of love?

This is why it's so important to start talking about love and dating with our children as early as possible. Paving the path for open, honest communication now is much easier than being blindsided later when these issues hit us in the face and all kinds of feelings are involved. We need to teach foundational truths about love when our kids are young so that sweet social-media sentiments will be less likely to swallow them up when their emotions are running high.

I can tell you right now, I thought I "loved" a lot of people when I was young. I was attracted to them. I felt like I loved them, but they weren't healthy or good for me. Please tell me I wasn't the only lovesick teen making all kinds of bad choices!

Basing love on feelings *alone* is a slippery slope. A blog article on PsychCentral summed it up well: "Feelings … can be fleeting.… Love is all about choices."[1]

I want my kids to look for character instead of following their feelings. Yes, physical attraction is important, but this is about balance. That's why we spend a lot of time talking about the qualities they should look for in future dates and mates. Some people make a list of all the qualities they want in a spouse. I encourage my kids to make a mental list of four or five key things. But there's one nonnegotiable I encourage them to keep at the top of their list: the person they have a crush on, date, or marry needs to know Jesus (not religion) and want to listen to Him. That person's life should reflect godly character. It doesn't mean the person will be perfect, but the light of Christ should be shining brightly in his or her life.

17

Sex Talks and Masturbation

God's Blueprint, School Curriculum, Gray Areas

Three years after my fourth grader asked that very detailed question about sex, she was finally ready for the answer.

You know what her response was? "I'm so glad I made the decision to wait to hear that information. Because I can't undo that image in my brain now."

Her question opened the door to some important conversations about sex. I wanted my daughter to understand God's original blueprint for sex before we talked about anything else.

The Architect's Word on Sex

So what does God say about sex? Let's dig into His Word and wrap our minds around His original design for marriage:

> The LORD God made a woman from the rib he had
> taken out of the man, and he brought her to the man.
> The man said,
>
> "This is now bone of my bones
> and flesh of my flesh;
> she shall be called 'woman,'
> for she was taken out of man."

> That is why a man leaves his father and mother and is united to his wife, and they become one flesh. (Genesis 2:22–24, NIV)

> [The Scriptures] record that from the beginning "God made them male and female.... This explains why a man leaves his father and mother and is joined to his wife, and the two are united into one." Since they are no longer two but one, let no one split apart what God has joined together. (Matthew 19:4–6)

> Because there is so much sexual immorality, each man should have his own wife, and each woman should have her own husband. The husband should fulfill his wife's sexual needs, and the wife should fulfill her husband's needs. (1 Corinthians 7:2–3)

> Marriage should be honored by all, and the marriage bed kept pure, for God will judge the adulterer and all the sexually immoral. (Hebrews 13:4, NIV)

It's clear throughout Scripture that God's blueprint for sex is between a man and woman inside a committed marriage. A safe place. If everyone in the world followed God's commands and kept their commitments, we'd have no fear of STDs (sexually transmitted diseases). Think about that.

But we live in a world where people screw up. Literally. (Sorry, I couldn't resist.)

Okay, let's set the stage for talking about sex with our tweens. Keep in mind this isn't going to be a one-time discussion. We need to start the conversation when our kids are in elementary school and keep talking about it until they're married. I'm totally serious. Never miss a teachable moment with your child.

Learn from my mistakes. By the time I started the conversation with my daughter in fourth grade, she'd already been exposed to sexual content. Middle school is so dang tough anyway that you don't want your tween to get swallowed up in confusion about sex.

If any questions come up about dating or marriage when your child is young, you could simply say, "God says marriage is between a man and woman." You could also read one of the scriptures I just mentioned.

This will lay the groundwork for your first talk about sex.

Routine Sex Talks

Let me be very clear. Sex talks with our kids aren't formal presentations with charts and graphs. They're personal conversations. None of the sex talks I had with my daughter were sit-on-the-couch discussions. We talked on the go, in the middle of routine activities. Always.

I can't stress it enough: stay calm and relaxed. Remember the parent filter? You might be nervous on the inside, but try to be cool and collected on the outside. If you're calm, your tween may feel less awkward. If you're a mess, he or she will avoid talking about sex at all costs.

Don't forget that talking about sex isn't something you'll check off your mental to-do list and never discuss again. It's a continual process of teaching your child about God's blueprint for sex and what a healthy marriage looks like.

Some parents take their kids on a special retreat or weekend to talk about sex for the first time. If you feel you need something like that to start the conversation, go for it. Your family, your choice. As far as I'm concerned, anything that gets parents talking with their kids is a step in the right direction.

But my approach to sex talks is very different. I'll be honest. I'm not a fan of taking our kids to some secluded spot to talk about sex. To me it sends the message that they need to create a special place or time to talk with me about it. And if I have to carve out a whole weekend for the talk and read a book to prepare, it's going to be pushed back on my calendar. I just don't have that kind of time.

I've discovered that if I can incorporate this conversation into our normal, everyday lives, like all the other issues we talk about, it becomes seamlessly routine. Trust me, I talk about sex way more now than I want to.

Listen. Open communication isn't about following a scripted dialogue. These are real-time conversations with our kids as they're struggling to figure things out. We should walk with balance in the Spirit and allow God to guide our hearts and words.

Kitchen Talks

One of the first sex talks I had with my daughter took place in our kitchen. We were hanging out making dinner together one evening, and I asked her an open-ended question. I didn't use a lead-in phrase like "I need to talk with you about something important" or "We need to talk." When we say those words, an alarm goes off in our tweens' heads that screams, "NO! Get out of here fast!"

Instead, I casually asked, "When you hear the word *sex*, what does it mean to you?"

She replied, "Is it like male or female and something you do when you're married?"

I could tell she felt uncomfortable talking about it, so I said, "Yes, you're right. It can mean male or female. It can also mean something you get to do when you're married. It's not a bad thing if you do it within God's plan. In fact, it's pretty awesome. But it's something God created for marriage between a man and a woman. It's how a baby is created. Like in Genesis 4:1 when Adam and Eve had sex and made a baby. It's natural, and God says it's okay within marriage."

I was referring to this verse in Genesis: "Adam made love to his wife Eve, and she became pregnant and gave birth to Cain. She said, 'With the help of the Lord, I have brought forth a man'" (NIV).

Then I simply ended the conversation by saying, "When you have questions about sex, will you ask me? I'll be 100 percent honest because I want you to get the correct information. You'll probably want more details soon, and I'm here to answer your questions."

That was it. No big deal. I served dinner and moved on to a different topic.

On-the-Road Sex Talks

After that brief sex talk with my daughter, I kept praying she would feel safe with me. Months went by before she finally asked more questions while we were driving in the car. Remember Deuteronomy 6:7? "Talk about [these commands] when you are … *on the road.*" Oh, I'm telling you. God knows.

She'd been thinking about how babies are formed, and her questions were getting more detailed.

I calmly explained, "God made men and women different. Guys have a penis. Girls have a vagina. God created them beautifully, and they fit together like a puzzle."

I still laugh about that. I have no idea where the puzzle analogy came from.

We talked very simply about how it takes one sperm from a man and one egg from a woman to make a baby. That's how God designed it.

That was it. No more questions. Once again I ended the conversation by saying, "You'll probably want more details soon, and I'm here to answer your questions. I'm your safe place."

Then I moved on to another topic. I didn't beat it to death. I planted the information and moved on.

Let's take a brief intermission from these on-the-road sex talks and review some helpful talking points for discussing sex with your tween:

- *Open-ended questions are usually best.* For example, ask "What do you think sex means?" Try to avoid questions that require yes or no responses. If your question is met with silence or a shoulder shrug, you could say, "If you ever hear new words you don't understand, will you please ask me? I want to be your source of information so you can be sure it's right. You need to protect your heart and mind, so please don't ever Google a word on sex, because bad words or images could pop up that you might not be able to get out of your mind. I also want you to know that all of our talks are confidential. I want you to be able to ask embarrassing questions and feel safe. I'm here for you."
- *If your child doesn't want to talk about sex, don't force the discussion.* Change the subject. Don't be frustrated or irritated. Ask your tween about something else. Try broaching the topic another time. Ask God to open the door in His time and help your tween feel safe talking with you.

- ➠ *If your child engages in the conversation, keep your responses simple.* You may also need to define terms or provide some clarity depending on what your child thinks about sex. Make sure you understand what he or she is asking. Then keep your answer simple. For example, one of my mentor moms loves to tell the story of a child who asked, "Where do babies come from?" The mom went into a fifteen-minute anatomy explanation, and when she finished, the kid looked at her and said, "Bobby came from Illinois. Where was I born?" Ha!
- ➠ *Pay attention to your child's conversation cues.* If your tween loses interest in the topic or stops asking questions, don't push to keep the conversation going. Move on to talk about homework or football or another topic.
- ➠ *If your tween wants to sign a purity pledge, don't let it become a substitute for sex talks.* I don't have a problem with purity rings, symbols, or pledges. I'm for anything that helps instill moral values in our children. But a purity pledge isn't a substitute for ongoing conversations about sex. Please don't fall into that complacency trap. I signed a purity pledge, but no one ever talked to me about sex. If signing a purity pledge is important to you and your kids, then do it. But talk with them continually about sex too.

There are no scripted sex talks. Every child is different, so don't expect the conversations with your tween to look the same as mine. Topics will even vary from talk to talk. So instead of trying to anticipate questions and rehearse answers, ask God to guide the discussion. Relax. You've got this, Mama!

Now let's get back to the sex-talk story.

Several months went by, and by this time, my tween was in fifth grade. One evening we were on the road again when she asked a very detailed question about how the sperm gets to the egg. It was obvious she needed details on how this works.

I knew it was time to tell her exactly how the penis and vagina fit together. I was gripping the steering wheel and sweating like a beast. I had to use my parent filter.

As she processed that the penis actually goes into the vagina, a light-bulb went off in her brain, and she said, "Pull the car over. I'm going to throw up."

I chuckled and replied, "I know it seems gross. But one day God is going to bring a guy into your life, and you'll fall in love and get married. Then you'll get to have sex in a safe relationship. It will be beautiful."

She said, "Can I just stay single? I don't want to do all that."

I said, "Of course you can. It's your life and your decision. But I'm always here to talk."

It's normal for kids to think sex is gross or weird. It's also normal for girls to think it will hurt. Try to paint a beautiful picture for them, because that's how God designed it.

My daughter and I laugh about that conversation now, but I can tell you, she was pretty grossed out at the time. That night she couldn't even look at me and my husband without a very weird look on her face. Bless her.

When a friend of mine with three kids told her oldest daughter about sex, her daughter screamed, "Oh my gosh! You had to do that *three* times?"

My friend was thinking, *Yeah, three times a week!*

Getting Down to Details

Once you've covered the basics on how sex works between a man and woman within marriage, you're ready for more detailed questions.

By sixth grade, my daughter had sex education at her public school. I attended a curriculum meeting for parents and was so disappointed that more parents didn't attend. (Don't miss out on those meetings at your tween's school!) In our district, parent night takes place later in the year, so I was exhausted by that point. I was just trying to make it to the finish line (the last day of school).

Hear me on this: as parents, we've got to keep running this race even if we're tired, because when they cover sex education at school, it's prime time to talk, listen, and answer our tweens' questions. They're absorbing all this new information, and some of it may be presented differently from the way we've presented it at home. We need to make connections between the definitions of sex our kids are getting at school and our moral beliefs about sex.

My kids attend a public school in Texas, and the curriculum our district uses is called *Worth the Wait*.

At the meeting, I was able to review each day's curriculum and was impressed with our district and the teacher who presented the information. But I was also surprised that the definitions of *anal sex* and *oral sex* were given in sixth grade. Instead of letting my feelings take over, though, I listened as the teacher explained why they needed to define these terms.

She said, "Kids don't think they count as sex and don't realize they can get STDs from them, so we must define these terms earlier."

That made perfect sense. I already knew that everything is happening earlier because of online exposure.

So after arriving home that night, I told my sixth grader, "You're going to cover some new definitions about sex at school next week. So we're going to discuss these definitions over the weekend."

Since it was bedtime, I didn't launch into the details. I simply gave my daughter a heads-up. I didn't want her lying in bed unable to sleep because of the images and questions whirling around in her head. (Note: it's okay to give a heads-up once you've established ongoing conversations with your tween, but don't do it with that first sex talk.)

That weekend Matt and I had a great conversation with our daughter on the back porch. It was kind of like a sit-down conversation (only because we needed a private place to talk away from my son). Matt and I explained the definitions of oral and anal sex to her. In detail. We described how it happens between a man and a woman and between two men and two women. We also talked about STDs and the importance of following God's plan for marriage to avoid getting them. Then we talked about how God's Word related to the scientific information her teacher would be sharing in class. (As parents, we need to make this connection clear.)

After our talk, we answered her questions. One of them was "Can my teacher say that sex is reserved for marriage?"

I replied, "Well, I don't know. Your teacher will probably refer to abstinence because it's scientifically proved that it's the only way to 100 percent protect yourself from STDs. Your teacher may not talk about spiritual reasons you should wait to have sex until you're married. But isn't it cool that God's Word lines up with science again? I mean, if no one had sex outside of marriage, the way God created it, there would be no STDs. Your teacher will explain that as abstinence."

If your child asks a question you're unsure how to answer, you can always say, "Let me think about how best to explain that to you. Can I get back with you tomorrow?" Then make sure you follow up. It shows your child that his or her questions are important to you.

As our kids get older, they'll ask more detailed questions about sex, and they may talk about slang words they've heard. For example, if your child asks, "What's a blow job?" you could say, "Remember when we talked about how oral sex is with a person's mouth and another person's genitals? Well, a blow job is with a person's mouth and another person's penis."

They'll think it's gross. Which is a perfect opportunity to say, "And because it's a form of sex, you can get STDs from it."

Kids are curious about sex, so we need to be open and honest with them. Trust me, you don't want your tween Googling "blow job" and seeing pictures. I know questions about topics like this can be terrifying, but it's really a *good* thing. Your child is asking YOU!

Should both you and your husband be involved in sex talks? I think that depends on your family situation. Matt works a lot, so I'm with the kids after school and handle most of these conversations while I'm fixing dinner or when we're driving in the car. Then I tell Matt about them after the kids are in bed, or whenever it works best for both of us. Timing!

My husband is supershy about discussing sex. He's learning right along with me that open communication is essential. So when we needed to explain anal and oral sex to her, it surprised me when he said, "I want to be involved in that conversation."

Y'all, he was amazing! He told her, "Any guy who tries to have sex with you before you're married (including anal or oral sex) is not marriage material. You need a guy who respects you and your values and cherishes your decision to wait."

I fell in love all over again! I was *so* impressed. I don't know how he found the right words. Oh, wait. Yes, I do. Walking in the Spirit. My hubby submits to the living God. Our secret weapon.

As my son is getting older, Matt is taking the lead in our conversations with him. Love it! I also love that we can talk about sex as a family now. It's awesome to see my daughter instilling truth in my son. Matt says she sounds like a little Mandy.

Just the other night when my kids were watching TV, a commercial with an aggressive sex scene came on, and she told my son, "Turn your head. You have to protect your heart and mind. That is not okay to see."

Even if you don't think your kids are listening to you, they are. You're shaping little souls.

As I said earlier, Matt and I never keep secrets from each other. But we have a little pact that if my daughter tells me something she's not comfortable talking to her dad about, she lets me know. I then tell him about the conversation and ask him not to bring it up with her. He respects that boundary.

Same thing with my son. Now that he and my husband are having more conversations about sex, there are things my son doesn't want me to ask about. Matt and I respect our kids' boundaries, but we also keep each other informed.

The M-Word

Talking about masturbation with our kids is tough. It takes practice. But I've found that the more I discuss it with other parents, the more comfortable I am addressing it with my own children. So don't let embarrassment keep you from talking with your inner circle about how to address this issue with your tween.

Masturbation is "the stimulation or manipulation of one's own genitals" for pleasure.[1] We tend to think of it as a boy issue. Nope. It's a topic we need to cover with our girls as well. As porn use increases among girls, so does masturbation. Remember our discussion about gray areas? Well, masturbation is definitely a gray area.

It seems to me that we have four possible ways to respond when we talk about masturbation with our tweens:

1. "It's natural. Do it."
2. "It's wrong. Don't do it."
3. "It's not something that should be a habit, but it may happen."
4. We can stay silent on the issue and let our kids figure it out for themselves.

Option 4 seems like the easiest approach, doesn't it? We think that if we ignore the issue, it will somehow resolve itself. Wrong! We've decided to face it. So let's discuss the other three responses.

1. *"It's natural. Do it."* This is an all-in response that accepts masturbation as "a natural and harmless expression of sexuality for both men and women."[2] God designed our bodies with the capacity to feel pleasure when our genitals are stimulated. So we should never shame our kids or give them the impression that the bodies God gave them are somehow dirty or sinful. Never! Instead, we should assure our tweens that the changes they're experiencing sexually are completely natural. But just because something's natural doesn't mean they should engage in it. For example, I naturally get angry, but that doesn't mean I should give my emotions free rein. I need to get my anger under control. Our job as parents is to teach our kids about sexual control and seeking God so they can decide for themselves what's right or wrong.

2. *"It's wrong. Don't do it."* Many people sincerely believe that masturbation is wrong, but this response can be shaming and judgmental. It's important to keep in mind that there are Bible-believing folks on both sides of this issue, and Scripture doesn't specifically refer to masturbation as a sin. In fact, this word doesn't even appear in the Bible. God clearly warns us to "flee from sexual immorality" (1 Corinthians 6:18, NIV), but He's silent on whether masturbation falls into that category. For me, it's important to focus on teaching my kids to seek God's wisdom and guidance regarding gray areas like this.

3. *"It's not something that should be a habit, but it may happen."* In my view, a balanced response to this issue is the best approach. We need to be

real and honest with our kids about masturbation. A safe place where they can talk about it openly, without shame or fear over how we'll respond. We don't want to shame our tweens and make them feel they can't confide in us. That will only start a downward spiral of lies. We also don't want them to feel isolated. They shouldn't have to wrestle with this issue alone. On the other hand, do we want to actively encourage them to masturbate? The key once again is *balance*.

I love how Dannah Gresh discusses masturbation in her book *Six Ways to Keep the "Good" in Your Boy*:[3]

1. God didn't create sex as a "solo sport." Masturbation misuses our natural sexual desire for a relationship God designed to be between a man and a woman.
2. "Masturbation focuses on a selfish desire" rather than giving our bodies to our spouses in marriage as 1 Corinthians 7 tells us.
3. "Masturbation can lead to addictive habits that include excessive masturbating, porn use, or a fantasy life that's not healthy."

Our kids need to know that sex as God designed it is about mutual pleasure, not pleasing ourselves. This is *so* important. Let's review what 1 Corinthians 7:2–3 (NIV) says: "Each man should have sexual relations with his own wife, and each woman with her own husband. The husband should fulfill his marital duty to his wife, and likewise the wife to her husband."

God created sex exclusively for the *mutual* pleasure of one man and one woman in marriage. Even though masturbation may not be sinful, it can be selfish. Instead of promoting masturbation—or shaming our kids over it—we should encourage them to seek God so they can fully enjoy sex the way He intended it.

Our tweens also need to know that anything done in excess is usually bad or harmful. Remember our earlier conversation about addictions and forming bad habits? Masturbation can become an addiction for some kids and even open the door to pornography and sex. So it's essential to continually remind them that they're responsible for their bodies and for protecting their hearts and minds.

When I asked my mentor for advice on masturbation, she said, "Well, I want to eat a pint of ice cream every day, but I don't because it's unhealthy and not a good choice." I love that analogy. Except I want to eat chocolate instead!

Before we tackle two more complicated topics, I just have to say something. I'm so proud of you, girl. You're facing tough issues, and you're still reading. We can do this!

18

Sexuality

Love and Truth

Y'all, I want to be real with you. This topic was *tough* for me to write about. So tough that it almost caused me not to write this book. Sexuality has become so politicized in our culture that everyone feels they have to pick a side. Emotions are running high. It's such a hot-button issue right now that my mind has been spinning with fear-based scenarios of how people might react. I know my words could be taken out of context, and people might label or bully me or my family if they disagree with my views.

You want to know what I really think? It's none of my business how consenting adults live their lives. I have no right to judge anyone. God gave each of us free will to live the way we want, and we're ultimately accountable to Him.

My job is simple: to love God and love others.

So why did I write this chapter? Because early online exposure has caused a seismic shift in parenting. Like my daughter, kids today are asking complicated questions about sexuality at very early ages, and as parents, we need to know how to respond.

For me, it was extremely important to address this issue *before* my daughter started middle school. I wanted to make sure she had a solid foundation of truth, so I first explained God's blueprint for sex toward the end of her elementary-school years. Then I gradually moved into other aspects of sexuality when she was in early middle school.

You may feel overwhelmed and afraid to talk about this topic with your kids. I felt the same way. But fear is *not* an option. So let's face this thing together for the sake of our children.

Clarifying the Terminology

First, let's cover some general definitions we need to know when we talk with our kids about sex:

- *Sexual orientation:* "a person's sexual preference or identity as bisexual, heterosexual, or homosexual."[1] The term *sexuality* is more common today. I use both of these terms interchangeably in reference to sexual attraction or sexual acts.
- *Heterosexual:* "a tendency to direct sexual desire toward the opposite sex."[2]
- *Homosexual:* "a tendency to direct sexual desire toward another [member] of the same sex."[3]
- *Bisexual:* "a tendency to direct sexual desire toward both sexes."[4]
- *Asexual:* a person without sexual feelings or attraction to either sex.[5]
- *Pansexual:* a person who is "capable of being attracted to multiple sexes and gender identities."[6]

I included *asexual* and *pansexual* in these definitions because kids are also encountering these terms in their online world. For example, Miley Cyrus announced to the world in 2015 that she's pansexual.[7] Guess what happens when our kids hear this word? They want to know what it means, so they either Google it or ask us. That's why we need to be their go-to source. Their safe place.

Now that we've established some key definitions, let's tackle how to approach the supercharged topic of sexuality with our kids.

Laying the Groundwork for Open Communication

What we teach our children about sexuality could influence their attitudes and perceptions for a lifetime, so we need to carefully consider our approach. The way I see it, the four possible options we discussed in the previous chapter for dealing with masturbation apply to this issue as well:

1. We can be all in and accept everything.
2. We can be shaming and judgmental.
3. We can adopt a balanced approach based on love and truth.
4. We can stay silent and let our kids figure it out for themselves.

Let's talk about silence first. We may choose to avoid the topic because we don't know what we actually believe. Or we may be afraid of being labeled a bigot if we express our views. The last thing we want is to raise judgmental, bigoted children, so ignoring the issue often seems the wisest—and easiest—solution. But if we want to be their go-to source of information instead of social media or their peers, ignoring the issue and avoiding their questions is *not* an option. Silence only ends up confusing our children.

So let's move on to the polar-opposite responses: being all in or being judgmental. I think we can easily eliminate the judgmental option from our list. If we become judgmental toward those who have a different view of sexuality than we do, we're choosing a path of hate. But hate is *never* the answer. No matter what we believe about this issue, let's choose love instead of hate. We want to be Jesus parents, not Pharisee parents, right?

The other response is to go all in and accept everything. But if there are no limits, everything ends up in gray territory—five million shades of gray—with no black-and-white boundaries. No right or wrong. No moral compass. Just a dangerous slippery slope of confusion. If everything goes, what will we teach our kids about sex, when it's okay to start having it, and with whom? Can you see how complicated things get when there are no guidelines or limits?

Ultimately, each of us has to decide how to discuss this issue with our kids. Your family, your choice. But I recommend a balanced approach. That's how Jesus lived. He was "full of grace *and* truth" (John 1:14, NIV). He continually taught that we should always love and never judge. Judging is God's job, not ours. At the same time, He spoke the truth. This is the approach we need to model for our kids: love and truth.

Let's break down these two simple steps.

Step 1: Teach Love

Jesus taught that we should treat others the way we want to be treated (see Matthew 7:12 and Luke 6:31). This is the Golden Rule. But He also commands us to love everyone:

> You have heard the law that says, "Love your neighbor" and hate your enemy. But I say, love your enemies! Pray for those who persecute you! In that way, you will be acting as true children of your Father in heaven. (Matthew 5:43–45)

> You must love the LORD your God with all your heart, all your soul, all your strength, and all your mind [and] love your neighbor as yourself. (Luke 10:27)

Love is so important to God that He wants us to get it right. It has to be more than just words. We have to really mean it and model it in our lives. We need to teach our children that even when they don't understand or agree with someone, they should always default to love. Always.

Jesus knew we'd struggle with judging others, so He gave this warning: "Do not judge others, and you will not be judged. For you will be treated as you treat others" (Matthew 7:1–2).

Judging means to condemn or pass judgment on others. When we judge other people, we're actually putting ourselves in God's place.

The apostle James said,

> Don't speak evil against each other.... If you criticize and judge each other, then you are criticizing and judging God's law.... God alone, who gave the law, is the Judge. He alone has the power to save or to destroy. So what right do you have to judge your neighbor? (James 4:11–12)

Again, judging is God's job. Love is ours. That doesn't mean we shouldn't teach our children to walk in the Spirit so they can discern right from wrong and good from evil. That's what a moral compass is for.

Jesus said, "Just as you can identify a tree by its fruit, so you can identify people by their actions" (Matthew 7:20). The Pharisees destroyed others with their hate and judgment. Jesus broke down barriers and changed everything with His love. Teaching our tweens to show discernment *and* love is one of the most important things we can do.

God knew. God knows.

So when we talk about sexuality with our kids, how can we be Jesus moms instead of Pharisee moms and teach them what love looks like? Let me give you an example.

One time my daughter told me about another eleven-year-old who claimed to be bisexual. (When I asked my daughter for permission to share this story, she said, "No worries. Lots of kids say they're bi.") My knee-jerk reaction was to tell my child to stay clear of this kid. But I bit my lip and listened. Instead of letting my feelings dictate my response, I prayed and asked God for wisdom. Then I discussed the situation with my husband.

The next morning I said to my tween, "You know that child you were telling me about? I need you to show her extra love and make sure she doesn't get picked on or made fun of. Will you do that for me?"

After that conversation, my daughter started standing up for this child whenever others were making fun of her. Months later, my tween told me she saw this girl crying, so she texted her uplifting words and funny emojis. I was so proud of my daughter for showing love, courage, and integrity. That's how Jesus loves and shines through us.

My initial reaction was to bubble-wrap my child and respond like a Pharisee mom. But once I took my feelings out of the equation and turned to God for wisdom, I was able to respond with a balanced Jesus-mom perspective.

If I had been a Pharisee mom and told my daughter to avoid this child, she would have missed out on a beautiful opportunity to show love. Just think of all the opportunities our kids will have to show love if we act like Jesus moms.

Our natural human response is to judge others because it takes the focus off our own faults. Love isn't always instinctive; it must be taught. That's why it's so important to love like Jesus and model it well for our children.

One day I was reading a familiar account in the book of John that left me speechless. I mean, it was like a mic-drop moment for me.

A man and woman were caught in the middle of an adulterous act. The religious leaders dragged this woman in front of a group of townspeople Jesus was teaching. Imagine the humiliation and shame she must have felt as her sexual sin was exposed to the world.

What if you were caught in an embarrassing sexual sin and dragged before your church or coworkers? The thought alone is horrifying.

The religious leaders said to Jesus, "This woman was caught in the act of adultery. The law of Moses says to stone her. What do you say?" (John 8:4–5).

No-brainer there. The woman had broken the Law, after all. No gray area or wiggle room. She deserved the consequences for committing a sexual sin. (I sound like a Pharisee, don't I?)

But Jesus was silent. Pin-drop silent!

While everyone was standing there, He bent down and wrote in the dust with His finger. Can you imagine the tension?

Then He surprised everyone with this amazing response: "Let any one of you who is without sin be the first to throw a stone at her" (verse 7, NIV).

You guys, that makes me want to cry. Jesus and His radical love are revolutionary! How in the world has Satan convinced us that God is the bad guy? Because we've become complacent and forgotten how good and loving He is.

The story could have ended there, but it didn't. There's more! Did the people start throwing stones? No. They began walking away one by one. Jesus had challenged them to look at their own sin, and they were convicted. Even the self-righteous religious leaders knew they had no right to throw stones.

Only Jesus and the adulterous woman remained. Then He said, "Where are your accusers? Didn't even one of them condemn you?" (verse 10).

She replied, "No, Lord" (verse 11).

At that moment, Jesus could've thrown the first stone. He was the only person who had lived a sinless life (Hebrews 4:15). According to the Law,

He would have been justified in stoning her because that was the punishment for adultery. But He didn't.

Instead, He replied, "Neither do I [condemn you]. Go and sin no more" (John 8:11).

The religious leaders wanted the woman to be humiliated, condemned, and stoned for her sins. Instead, Jesus showed compassion, mercy, and love. The barrier-breaking, redemptive love of Jesus transformed this woman's life. She deserved judgment and condemnation, but He covered her sin with love and forgiveness. He wiped away her guilt and shame. He is a God of second chances.

This is a teachable moment for us as parents. In just a few verses, we learn a major life lesson: don't throw stones.

I constantly remind my children that our job is to love and not throw stones. We don't have the right to judge others. Jesus was the one who addressed the woman's adultery and told her to leave her sinful lifestyle. No one else had the right to point an accusing finger and condemn her.

If we're going to worry about anyone's sin, it should be our own. That's why I wrote a whole chapter on looking in the mirror.

When our kids see something in the world or online that they don't agree with, how should they respond? With discernment and love. If they're walking in the Spirit, Jesus will keep them balanced and centered.

Once our kids get the love lesson, it's time to talk about truth. Love and truth go hand in hand. The truth *never* changes or negates God's command to love.

Step 2: Teach Truth

Truth is a tough subject because most people have different ways of defining it. So if your definition differs from mine, I respect that. Your family, your choice. Our family defines *truth* based on what the Bible teaches. It's our moral compass for deciding what's right and wrong.

My tween has asked me some really tough questions on sexuality. One time she said, "I know I'm supposed to love everyone and never bully, but is being gay wrong?"

I calmly replied, "It doesn't matter what I think. Let's look at what God says. That's truth. That's how we determine right and wrong."

Then I gave her the following verses to look up:

> Do not practice homosexuality, having sex with another man as with a woman. It is a detestable sin. (Leviticus 18:22)

> If a man practices homosexuality, having sex with another man as with a woman, both men have committed a detestable act. (20:13)

The Old Testament is a complicated book, and some people believe it isn't relevant anymore. But it has great value because it teaches us about God's moral laws and lays the groundwork for the New Testament. It's true that *ceremonial* laws, like offering an animal sacrifice to pay for sins, aren't practiced today because Jesus covered our sins once and for all when He died on the cross. But *moral* laws in the Old Testament are still relevant, like "Honor your father and mother" (Deuteronomy 5:16).

After my daughter read the Old Testament passages on homosexuality, we looked at what the New Testament had to say:

> [People] traded the truth about God for a lie.... Even the women turned against the natural way to have sex and instead indulged in sex with each other. And the men, instead of having normal sexual relations with women, burned with lust for each other. Men did shameful things with other men, and as a result of this sin, they suffered within themselves the penalty they deserved. (Romans 1:25–27)

> Don't fool yourselves. Those who indulge in sexual sin ... or commit adultery, or are male prostitutes, or practice homosexuality ... none of these will inherit the Kingdom of God. Some of you were once like that. But you were cleansed; you were made holy; you were made right with God by calling on the name of the Lord Jesus Christ and by the Spirit of our God. (1 Corinthians 6:9–11)

> We know that the law is good when used correctly. For the law was not intended for people who do what is right. It is for people who are lawless and rebellious, who are ungodly and sinful.... The law is for people who are sexually immoral, or who practice homosexuality, ... or who do anything else that contradicts the wholesome teaching that comes from the glorious Good News entrusted to me by our blessed God. (1 Timothy 1:8–11)

The Old and New Testaments say the same thing: engaging in homosexual sex is a sin. But hear me on this: it's no different from any other sexual sin.

I know that some people have different ways of interpreting these passages, or they believe that the word *homosexuality* has been translated incorrectly, but I think the Bible as a whole is crystal clear that sex is intended exclusively for marriage between a man and a woman (see the verses in chapter 17). So that means *any* sexual act outside of God's original blueprint is sin, including heterosexual premarital sex and adultery. God doesn't compartmentalize sin and say that one kind of sexual sin is worse than another. Thankfully, because of Jesus, God extends grace and forgiveness to *all* of us, no matter what sinful choices we've made.

I base my beliefs about sexuality on God's Word, but that doesn't mean I hate people who don't share my beliefs or advocate disrespecting and bullying them. I have gay friends in my life whom I deeply love and respect (my kids love them too).

We can believe in biblical truth and still love others. Our fight isn't against groups, agendas, platforms, or people. It's against Satan and his hate-filled schemes.

Dave Willis, author of *The Seven Laws of Love*, notes that "loving someone doesn't mean you agree with everything that person does. It means your concern and commitment to that person is not conditional upon his or her behavior."[8] We need to continually teach our children to walk in love even when they meet people they disagree with.

So how do we teach our tweens to stay grounded in truth and yet love without being judgmental? Let's go back to the story of the woman who committed adultery: don't throw stones. This can apply to any situation.

For example, years ago one of my children asked why an unmarried woman was pregnant. First I wanted to make sure my child was grounded in truth, so we read some Bible verses about God's design for sex between a man and a woman inside marriage (see chapter 17). Then I said, "We don't know this woman's story. But remember Mary, the mother of Jesus? She wasn't married either, but God had a specific plan for her life."

Finally I added, "If this woman did something different from God's blueprint for marriage, it was her choice. She gets to live her life the way she wants. Our job is to show love and not throw stones."

We can learn a lot from Mary's story. Do you think she was judged for having a baby out of wedlock? Absolutely! And yet it was God's plan.

I know there was only one virgin birth, but do you see my point? We shouldn't condemn, judge, or throw stones because we don't know the full story. We aren't God, and we don't know His plan for a person's life. His ways aren't our ways (see Isaiah 55:8).

Another time my tween asked, "Mom, I heard there's a pregnant eighth grader at our school. What should I do if I see her?"

I almost went into Pharisee-mom freak-out mode, but I collected myself. My Jesus-mom response was "Show her extra kindness. We don't know the whole story. Maybe someone forced her to have sex. If she did choose to have sex, it was her choice, and she has to live with the consequences. Show her love and respect. Don't EVER let anyone make fun of that girl. She's got a tough road ahead. Stand up for her always."

Never let anyone convince you that you're a hateful, close-minded bigot because you're teaching your kids scriptural truth right along with love the way Jesus modeled it. Don't buy into that lie or let Satan manipulate you into silence. Don't let fear keep you from having real, honest conversations with your tween about sexuality. Your child desperately needs to hear from you on this. Trust me.

As parents, we can never go wrong if we teach our children truth *and* love.

Tackling the Tough Questions

In schools all across America, kids are talking about sexuality because it's trending online. So don't miss out on teachable moments with your tween.

How can we tackle the tough questions our children ask? In our family, I always try to answer questions with as much detail as my child needs. Only you can determine how much detail is appropriate for your child's age and maturity level.

Here are some Q and As to help guide your discussions after reading the Scripture passages I presented earlier:

Q: *"What do you think about the legalization of same-sex marriage?"*

A: (Note: This question can be answered in any number of ways, but I prefer focusing on the spiritual and relational sides of the issue instead of the political side.) "Ecclesiastes 7:18 (MSG) says, 'It's best to stay in touch with both sides of an issue. A person who fears God deals responsibly with all of reality, not just a piece of it.' Balance is important. On one side of this issue, same-sex couples want the same right to marry as opposite-sex couples. On the other side, same-sex marriage doesn't line up with God's Word and how He defines marriage. First Corinthians 6:12 (MSG) says, 'Just because something is technically legal doesn't mean that it's spiritually appropriate.' So where does that leave us? Here's the bottom line: God created everyone equal and gave us free will. We're personally accountable to Him for how we live our lives. So even if I morally disagree with something that goes against what the Bible teaches, my job never changes. *I'm still called to love everyone.* No one should ever be discriminated against, treated with disrespect, or bullied. We should follow the Golden Rule Jesus Himself gave us: treat others the way we want to be treated."

Q: *"The Bible says that sex should only be between a man and a woman, but is there any scientific evidence to support it?"*

A: "Yes, science does support what God's Word teaches. It always takes an egg and a sperm to produce a child. God designed it this way. Even with adoption, surrogacy, artificial insemination, and laboratory methods, a baby is always formed by combining one egg and one sperm. It's that simple."

Q: *"Are people born gay?"*

A: "I'm not God, so I don't know. It's between each person and his or her creator. God gives us free will to live our lives the way we want. My job never changes: I'm supposed to love."

If my kids press for more information on this specific question, I respond, "That's tricky. Again, this is really between each person and God. But I do know that having sex is a choice. For example, if a married woman chose to have an affair with a man who wasn't her husband, that would be a sexual sin. (I'd only use this example with my older child.) It's no different from any other sexual sin. No matter what feelings are involved, that doesn't make it okay. So acting on any sexual attraction outside of what God defines as marriage is wrong. That goes for heterosexual, homosexual, bisexual, pansexual, or any other sexual we may come up with in the future. Same sin. No different."

Q: *"Why does God limit sex to marriage between a man and a woman?"*

A: "Well, we don't know why. He's God. We're not. The Bible says His ways aren't our ways (see Isaiah 55:8). We do know this: God isn't trying to be mean; He wants to protect us. He gives us guidelines to keep us safe. You know, like I won't let you have Snapchat yet. I'm not withholding that to be mean because I hate you. I'm giving that restriction because I love you and want to keep you safe."

Q: *"What does LGBTQ stand for, and do we agree with that group?"*

A: "It stands for 'lesbian, gay, bisexual, transgender, and questioning.' Questioning means that a person isn't sure. As Ecclesiastes 7:18 (MSG) says, 'It's best to stay in touch with both sides of an issue.' We need to stay balanced and find areas where we can agree. And we absolutely agree with the LGBTQ community that no one should be bullied or treated with disrespect. Our views about sex differ from the LGBTQ community because we believe that sex is reserved for a man and woman inside a biblical marriage. It's okay to see things differently, but we should always try to find common ground and show mutual respect. Remember, our job is not to throw stones. We're called to love."

If you don't know how to respond to your tween's question, never make up an answer. It's perfectly okay to say, "I don't have it all figured out. I'm not God. But I follow His Word and use it as my moral compass to help guide my decisions." You could also say, "Let me do some research on how best to answer your questions, and I'll get back to you." (Always remember to follow up.)

One of my main goals as a parent is to raise loving, respectful children who are kind to everyone. My heart breaks when I hear of young teenagers committing suicide because they were gay or transgender, and hate-filled people were bullying them.

Hate is always the wrong choice. Always. Our job is to love, not hate.

One time my tween overheard someone in her fifth-grade class say, "God hates f*gs."

I was beyond furious. Comments like that aren't tolerated in our home, and I'll call them out every single time. It goes against everything Jesus taught.

I told my child immediately, "It's not okay to say that. That's not Jesus and what He stands for. The real Jesus came to this world and died on a cross for everyone. He is about loving others and not throwing stones."

I can tell you from personal experience that it's completely possible to love others and stand for truth at the same time. I do this with my own family all the time. I deeply love my spouse and children and would lay down my life for them. And they sin like no one's business (I do too, by the way). I hold them accountable when they make mistakes, but that doesn't change my love for them.

So yes, it's possible to love people and speak the truth (see Ephesians 4:15). I practice it every day with my family.

Whew! That was a challenging discussion, wasn't it? But don't kick your heels back just yet. We have one more complex topic to talk about.

19

Transgender

Disorders of Sexual Development (DSDs),
Gender Confusion

This was another difficult chapter to write. Everywhere we turn, it seems, transgender issues are in the news and on social media. The transgender bathroom legislation is a hot-button topic across the country right now, and as I was working on this chapter, *National Geographic* launched a cover story about a nine-year-old transgender child. Transgender has become a highly politicized and emotionally charged issue in our culture. Yet again, we're being pressured to pick a side.

We can't afford to sweep this issue under the rug and hope it will go away. Our tweens need help navigating these murky waters. And so do we! Thankfully we have the Holy Spirit to guide us.

I've addressed this topic in a separate chapter because transgender shouldn't be confused with sexual orientation. Basically, sexuality deals with sexual attraction and sexual acts, while transgender is about *gender* identity and perception. This is an important distinction to grasp before we discuss transgender with our kids.

So, are some people actually born the wrong gender? What does science say about this? How do we approach the transgender issue with our children? We'll explore these questions and lots more in this chapter. We'll also dive into some specific research and differing views on the subject and explore what the Bible has to say. There's a *lot* to talk about, so buckle up!

When it comes to discussing the transgender issue with our tweens, I recommend using the same two-step approach from the previous chapter:

1. Teach love.
2. Teach truth.

As we've already learned, even when we don't understand or agree with someone else's view on an issue, our job is to love. A phrase I use often with my kids is "Default to love." I also try to work these reminders into our conversations:

- Never tease or bully someone who is different.
- Treat others the way you want to be treated (the Golden Rule).
- Never throw stones. Judging is God's job, not yours.
- Recognize that each person has a unique story and DNA according to God's design. Don't label or stereotype people or try to force them into boxes and categories.
- Speak the truth, but LOVE, LOVE, LOVE. Ask God to fill you with His love for people who are different from you.

Conversation Starters

A good conversation starter for talking about transgender with tweens is defining what it means. According to the dictionary, a transgender person is someone "who identifies with or expresses a gender identity that differs from the one which corresponds to the person's sex at birth."[1]

The American Psychological Association (APA) defines *gender identity* as "a person's deeply felt, inherent sense" of being male, female, or "an alternative gender."[2]

So a person's sex is male or female, but gender identity is how people view their gender. For example, a person may be born male (sex) but view himself as female (gender). We need to understand the difference.

How is one's sex determined as male or female? Let's take a trip back to middle-school science class. We all have twenty-three sets of chromosomes (forty-six total). All but the twenty-third set relate to the characteristics that make each of us unique (hair and eye color, etc.). The twenty-third set determines sex—XX for females, and XY for males.[3]

Once again, science confirms God's Word. Genesis 1:27 says that "God created human beings in his own image.... Male and female he created them." When we're born, we're either male or female. That's a biblical and scientific fact.

For that first transgender conversation with your tween, I recommend sticking with these basic facts. Just as you talked about God's blueprint for sex before discussing other sexual orientations (e.g., homosexual, bisexual, etc.), discuss God's simple design for male and female before moving on to other questions. Set a foundation of truth.

In addition to Genesis 1:27, here are two other Bible verses you could read together:

> [God] created them male and female, and he blessed them and called them "human." (Genesis 5:2)

> From the beginning "God made them male and female." And [Jesus] said, "This explains why a man leaves his father and mother and is joined to his wife, and the two are united into one." (Matthew 19:4–5)

One thing is clear from these verses: God created humans male and female.

If your child doesn't ask for more information, leave it there for now. I'll offer some research in the next section to guide your conversations if your child wants to know more.

Remember, if you don't know the answer to a question, don't make up something and risk giving your child the wrong information. It's important to get this right. If you don't know what to say, it's okay to respond, "I'm not sure about that. I'm not God. There are some things we won't know on this earth."

Digging for Clues

Before we can go deeper into this conversation with our kids, we need to roll up our sleeves and do some homework. The more I research this topic, the more complex I realize it is. My search for answers has led me down some pretty divergent paths. I've explored what genetics, medicine, and psychology have to say about transgender, and I've even traveled back to New Testament times to find clues.

I've discovered *so much* on this whirlwind journey, but I still have a lot more to learn. I also have many unanswered questions. One important truth I've been reminded of in my search for answers is that the more complicated the issue is, the more we need to love. We can never go wrong instilling love in our kids.

Transgender isn't just a research topic. It involves real people, many of whom are going through a very painful struggle. We may not understand because we haven't walked in their shoes. But we can always respond with love and respect.

Talking openly and honestly with your kids about such a complex topic won't be easy. But don't let that scare you into silence. Instead of hoping they won't come to you with transgender questions, conquer your fear by getting better informed and seeking God's wisdom. Trust me on this. You don't want to wade into these murky waters without Him. Let the Spirit guide your research and conversations. He's got this, and He'll help you figure it out.

So grab your shovel, and let's start digging for clues.

Scientific Discoveries

One of the first discoveries I made was that some people have biological disorders that make it difficult to determine their sex as male or female. For example, they could have genitals or reproductive organs of one sex and chromosomes of another sex. Various terms, such as *hermaphrodite*, have traditionally been used to describe some of these disorders, but two of the most common terms used today are *intersex* and *disorders of sexual development* (DSDs), which encompass all of the currently known disorders.

According to the American Academy of Pediatrics, "an estimated 1 in 2,000 children born each year ... [have] a disorder of sex development (DSD)—a group of about 60 conditions in which biological sex, or being male or female, is not clear."[4] These conditions may be identified at birth or puberty, or they may not be discovered until later in life. For example, if an adolescent girl doesn't start her period during puberty, doctors may discover a DSD.[5]

Do some DSDs constitute a third sex? This is a subject of debate among experts, but most agree that even with the existence of DSDs, scientific evidence indicates that we are born either male or female. It all goes back to the XX (female) or XY (male) chromosome.

The American College of Pediatricians states that "the exceedingly rare disorders of sex development (DSDs) ... are all medically identifiable deviations from the sexual binary norm, and are rightly recognized as disorders of human design. Individuals with DSDs do not constitute a third sex."[6]

So if people are born either male or female, why do some people question their gender? What causes transgender? The Crossport Gender Support Group notes that "theories of both psychological and biological causality have been forwarded and it is quite likely there are different causes for different individuals."[7]

It does appear that in some cases, DSDs can lead to transgender. There are documented cases of babies born with DSDs who became confused about their gender later in life and identified as transgender.[8] Let's say, for example, that a child is born with ambiguous genitals. Doctors and parents determine that the child should be raised as a girl. But later on, this person struggles with gender-identity issues and finds out that she was actually born with an XY chromosome. So she decides to undergo sex-reassignment surgery that will give her male genitals to match the XY chromosome she had at birth.

It's important to keep in mind that not everyone born with a DSD questions their gender. And people can struggle with their gender even if they don't have a DSD.[9]

See how complicated this can get?

Y'all, I'm no medical expert. I'm just a mom trying to answer my kids' questions. But as far as I can tell, here's the bottom line: We don't know exactly why people are born with DSDs, but we do know that DSDs are real. Just as real as any other developmental disorder at birth. We also know that every person is unique, and even though DSDs don't automatically lead to gender confusion or transgender, in some cases they do.

We have more information available on DSDs today than at any other time in history, and genetic research continues to increase our understanding of these complex conditions. But there are still many unanswered questions.

If your child was born with a DSD or any other disorder, I'm 100 percent certain that God knows and loves your child, and He has a plan for your child's life. Nothing caught Him by surprise. He wove your little one together in the womb, and no one else in the entire universe has your child's exact DNA. Your child is an original. A masterpiece.

Transgender Clues in the Bible

The Bible clearly says that we're created male or female, but does it say anything about transgender? The word *transgender* doesn't appear in Scripture, but if we dig a little deeper, we discover a reference to eunuchs in the New Testament. A eunuch is "a man or boy deprived of the testes or external genitals."[10]

According to the Bible, being a eunuch isn't a sin. It's a state or condition, not a sexual act. I know this is complicated, but stay with me. In Matthew 19:12, Jesus made a very interesting comment: "Some are born as eunuchs, some have been made eunuchs by others, and some choose not to marry for the sake of the Kingdom of Heaven. Let anyone accept this who can."

In this passage, "three classes of eunuch are mentioned, namely, born eunuchs [without testicles from birth], man-made eunuchs [testicles removed after birth], and spiritual eunuchs [celibate]."[11] So when Jesus stated that some men are born eunuchs (without testicles), it sure sounds as if He was talking about a DSD, even though that term wasn't used in His day.

We always have to be careful about lifting a single Bible verse out of context and using it to prove a point. But I think this passage could offer a valuable clue about people who are born with DSDs.

Mixed Messages and Gender Confusion

In light of what we've discovered about DSDs and transgender so far, you may be wondering where I stand on this issue. You probably won't be surprised to hear that I think a balanced approach is essential. There are too many factors involved to take a black-and-white approach. We simply don't have all the answers.

There are two sides to the transgender issue that make it even more confusing and complicated to talk about with our children. On one side, kids are struggling with their gender because they were born with a DSD, another biological disorder, or a psychological disorder. They have a real disorder that is causing them to question their gender.

On the other side are kids who think transgender is cool and trendy. Many of them are questioning their gender not because they have a biological disorder but because they're being bombarded with mixed messages from our culture (often on social media). They're hearing that "everyone has a right to choose whatever gender presentation *feels* best."[12] But this is a slippery slope.

As we've learned repeatedly on this journey, we can't always trust our feelings. Satan often uses them to manipulate us and distort our perspective. We've also learned that kids' brains aren't fully developed, which makes judgment and decision making difficult. This is why it's dangerous to base decisions on what "feels best." Kids' feelings change *all the time*.

I don't know about your kids, but my tween son can't even figure out what color we should paint his room. We've been talking and getting paint samples for over a year, and he still can't decide. He keeps flip-flopping. Every day he wants a different color.

With the brain still under construction, how can our kids be expected to sort through all the mixed messages they're getting about gender identity? They need our help to cut through the confusion and walk in truth.

A growing number of children aren't just questioning their gender; they actually want to undergo sex-reassignment treatments or surgery. This is alarming because many of these children may just be confused because they're immersed in a digital world filled with conflicting messages about gender.

Did you know that "as many as 98% of gender confused boys and 88% of gender confused girls eventually accept their biological sex after naturally passing through puberty"?[13] This is an important reason to apply the brakes and think things through before allowing a child to have sex-reassignment surgery.

A number of health-care professionals have expressed concern about this growing trend. Many believe that sex reassignment is not only unnecessary but also involves serious risks that could have life-altering implications. In 2016, members of the Youth Gender Professionals stated,

> We are concerned about the current trend to quickly diagnose and affirm young people as transgender, often setting them down a path toward medical transition.... We feel that unnecessary surgeries and/or hormonal treatments which have not been proven safe in the long-term represent significant risks for young people. Policies that encourage—either directly or indirectly—such medical treatment for young people who may not be able to evaluate the risks and benefits are highly suspect, in our opinion.[14]

Here's another sobering statistic to consider: "A thirty year follow up study found rates of suicide are nearly *twenty times* greater among adults who undergo sex reassignment in Sweden which is among the most LGBTQ-affirming countries" (emphasis added).[15]

Y'all, we can't afford to stand on the sidelines while our kids are struggling with this issue. We need to be a safe place for them to talk about gender issues and work through their feelings. If we're their go-to source for information on this topic, we can help them navigate through all the mixed messages and remind them to seek God's truth.

Should kids undergo sex reassignment because they're unhappy with the way God created them, or because they feel uncomfortable in their own skin when they hit puberty? Our job as parents is to help them understand the changes they're experiencing and appreciate the bodies God gave them. Kids may think that if they change their bodies, life will be perfect. But that's a lie. The grass isn't always greener on the other side. We'll always have struggles in life. That's why we need to teach our kids to find their identity in God alone. They are beautiful masterpieces God created to shine in their own unique ways.

If a boy doesn't like trucks or playing sports, should he be reassigned as a girl? What if he's just a boy who loves wearing pink and playing with dolls? Why is that wrong? No one should label kids who don't fit a certain gender mold. Each child is hand-designed and adds value to this world. We should love, not label.

In the middle of all the confusion and debate over the transgender issue, we must never forget that real people are struggling with their gender. Kids with real biological disorders are crying themselves to sleep at night because they're frightened and confused. Others are caught in a web of mixed and confusing messages and need our help to figure things out. No matter what causes people to question their gender, we should treat everyone with compassion and respect.

Tackling the Tough Questions

My husband and I regularly discuss transgender issues with our daughter. We don't give her canned answers to complex problems. We present the facts but say, "This can get confusing. Gender identity is between each person and God. Each person's story is unique. Some people are born with disorders that cause them to struggle with gender. Other people struggle because they want to be different. But guess what? That doesn't change our job. We're supposed to love, not throw stones."

As transgender issues continue to trend on social media, we need to take advantage of teachable moments with our tweens. Don't shy away from tough questions out of fear. Face them head-on. We're in this together.

The possible questions our tweens could throw at us are endless, but the open-communication guidelines never change: Remain calm. Don't yell. Listen. Pray. Walk with balance in the Spirit.

Here are a few Q and As to give you an idea of how I might respond to some challenging questions:

Q: *"Why are boys allowed to use the girls' bathroom now?"*

A: "Well, this is a political fight. Both sides have valid points and concerns, but normally the truth is somewhere in the middle. Here's what you need to know: If a transgender child uses your bathroom, always treat him or her with respect. Kids who are struggling with transgender issues need to be loved, not judged or bullied. I do have concerns that kids who aren't transgender will try to take advantage and use an opposite-sex bathroom to take pictures or do other inappropriate things. If you ever see anyone in a school bathroom doing anything inappropriate, leave and tell a teacher."

Q: *"Why did Bruce Jenner become a lady?"*

A: "I don't know Bruce Jenner personally, but everyone gets to choose how to live their lives, even if we don't understand or agree. God gives each of us free will. Bruce Jenner could have a biological disorder we don't know about. Remember, our job is always to love. My concern is that stories like these make transgender so trendy that kids who don't actually have a disorder will want to be transgender just because it's cool. But that's dangerous because people who question their gender are at a greater risk for suicide. We need to stay balanced and not let our feelings swing too far one way or the other. And we should never disrespect, hate, or bully anyone."

Q: *"My friend doesn't want to be a girl anymore. What should I do?"*

A: "Love and respect her. Some kids are born with a disorder that causes them to struggle with their gender. Sometimes they don't even know they have the disorder until later in life. Others want to change their gender because they think it's cool. We should never judge another person. That's God's job. Ours is to love. We don't know what your friend may be struggling with. If she asks what you think, you could share with her that God created each person male or female, but you also know things happen that make people question their gender. Let her know that God loves her and understands what she's struggling with. He's always there to help us with our problems. Philippians 4:7 says that God can give us peace that "exceeds anything we can understand."

The transgender battle rages on, and everyone is being pressured to pick a side. We can debate this issue all day long, but the truth is, we don't have all the answers. Each transgender story is different. God knows and understands it all far better than we ever will.

Our job is always the same: Love God. Love others. And don't throw stones.

Sleepovers

Gun Safety, Sexual Abuse

After those two very heavy chapters, I feel like I can breathe again. Parenting isn't for the weak. Facing it is hell sometimes. So to lighten things up, I'm going to take you on a trip down memory lane.

When I was a tween, I loved stretching out on my Strawberry Shortcake cover and snuggling up next to my three best girlfriends at a sleepover. We ate pizza and sweet treats and giggled into the late-night hours. And we pranked the first girl who went to sleep by putting her bra in the freezer.

Sleepovers are one of my favorite childhood memories. But now they're a whole new cyberparenting responsibility with unique risks and issues to talk about with our tweens. They're also a great opportunity to practice open communication.

A friend's tween came home from a sleepover and told her mom, "The girls were in a separate room FaceTiming an old man they didn't know, who lived in another country. It was weird, Mom. They were telling him where they lived and where we went to school. He was asking so many questions."

Sleepovers. Parents everywhere hate you now. Simple childhood pleasures have turned into this huge issue we have to parent differently because of online exposure. The world has changed, and we have to recognize the corresponding shift in parenting.

The Pros and Cons of Sleepovers

As I see it, we have four options when our tweens get invited to other homes for sleepovers:

1. Say no sleepovers at all.
2. Allow sleepovers only at the homes of close friends whose families we know personally.
3. Allow most sleepovers and try to meet at least one of the parents first.
4. Say yes to all sleepovers, whether we know the parents or not. No boundaries.

My husband and I have chosen option 2. But we've realized that no matter which option we choose, there are pros and cons.

Here's one example: When my tween transitioned into middle school, her friend group changed. She still has her core group of friends (with whom we allowed sleepovers), but new friends are joining the group. On the one hand, it's wonderful because I know my tween and her friends aren't being cliquish. They're including others.

But on the other hand, I don't know the new families. They're probably fine, but I'm not comfortable letting my daughter spend the night with a family I've never met. Because of our family guidelines, it seems like I'm picking and choosing families I trust, and that can appear judgmental. But nothing is further from the truth. I simply don't know some families. In hindsight, it would've been easier to say across the board, "We don't allow sleepovers in our family at all."

If you allow sleepovers in some homes like we do, trust your instincts and the Holy Spirit's guidance. If you decide against allowing your tween to go to a sleepover, talk about it. You could honestly say, "I don't feel comfortable with this, and my job is to protect you and make sure you're safe."

Matt and I are currently reevaluating our family sleepover policy and praying about whether to make some changes. I've explained to my middle schooler many times that she has different friends now, and I don't know their families. I've been up front and honest about my uneasiness, so she's fully aware there might be a future change in our guidelines.

On the flip side, my daughter already has some great memories of sleepovers with her close friends. I love that. And it's a relief to know she formed those memories in homes where she was safe and secure.

Talk through the pros and cons of each option with your spouse and come up with a family policy on sleepovers. Once again, aim for balance.

Prepping Your Tween for Sleepovers

If you decide to allow sleepovers at other homes, it will require more conversations with your tween. Here are some talking points you can use in casual conversations before a sleepover:

- You're responsible for what you allow in your heart and mind. Make good decisions as you watch things online or stream movies with your friends.
- Please change clothes behind closed doors where no one has a phone. Remember, a picture can be caught in a mirror accidentally while you're dressing and posted to social media.
- Cyberstrangers are real. Please don't communicate with online strangers or give out personal information. Kids have been kidnapped or murdered after developing an online relationship with a stranger.
- Some kids won't get invited to this party. So be respectful and think about their feelings as you post details on social media. I'm not saying you can't post, because other kids probably will, but just keep in mind how others will feel.
- Proverbs 16:28 says that "gossip separates the best of friends." It hurts people and destroys friendships. So please make sure you keep yourself in check as you sit around and talk about everything happening at school. Be nice. Don't bash others.
- Be respectful and listen to the adults in charge. But those adults should never ask you to do anything inappropriate, illegal, or immoral. If that happens, you need to text me immediately so I can protect you.

➡ You get to go to sleepovers because I trust you. But I don't expect you to be perfect. None of us are. You can tell me anything, and I will always love you even if you make a mistake.

Remember, this is a conversation, not a lecture. Talk through these issues together and ask for your child's input. Make sure to listen. You might learn something new!

Sleepover Pointers

I've learned a lot from other moms over the past several years. Here are three of my favorite sleepover pointers that other parents have shared:

1. Create a secret code so that if your tween ever feels uncomfortable at a sleepover, he or she can discreetly let you know. If your child doesn't have a phone and needs to ask the host to call you, role-play scenarios to help him or her know exactly what to do. For example, your tween could tell the host parent that he or she forgot to feed the dog and needs to call and remind you. (Before my daughter got her own phone, her secret code was to say she wasn't feeling well.) The upside of technology is that if our tweens have their own phones, they don't need to ask the host to call us anymore. Our kids can secretly text us and say, "I'm feeling really awkward. Can you come get me?"
2. Most parents agree that it's acceptable to drop their tweens off when the party starts and pick them up around 10:00 or 10:30 p.m., as long as they arrange it with the host parents in advance or when they drop off their kids. It's okay to be the only parent picking up your child at ten o'clock. Don't cave to parent peer pressure!
3. When you're hosting a sleepover, have all the kids leave their phones on your kitchen counter. This will keep them from Googling something inappropriate. Make clear they can have access to their phones at any time, but you still want to protect them while they're under your roof.

This last piece of advice moves me right into my next talking point. Many of us would love to become the house where all the kids hang out. Right? I know I would. As one of my mentors told me, "Have a stocked fridge and pantry, and the tweens will come." But we must recognize that being the hang-out house comes with a new level of responsibility and risk now.

All the kids will be bringing phones with them. And all of them will have social-media accounts. The last thing I want is for a child to be exposed to pornography, make contact with a pedophile, or have an inappropriate picture posted on social media while hanging out at my house!

Remember our old sleepovers? We would prank-call people from the phone book. Well, now tweens live-stream with strangers from all over the world. We must be on guard.

As parents, we need to be proactive and set clear guidelines for technology in our homes when other children visit.

For my daughter's twelfth-birthday sleepover, it was the first time every single girl had her own phone. Guess what I did? I e-mailed the parents ahead of time, informed them of my sleepover guidelines, and politely asked that everyone comply. These were my only requests:

- That all the girls leave their phones on the kitchen counter so they could visit with one another face-to-face.
- That the girls not post on social media, so kids who weren't at the sleepover wouldn't get their feelings hurt.

All the parents informed their tweens of these guidelines before the sleepover, and the girls happily complied. So if you establish sleepover guidelines, make sure to notify the families in advance.

I failed miserably at this the year before. I didn't contact the parents beforehand, so some kids had phones at the sleepover and some didn't. I asked the girls to put their phones on the kitchen counter, but they were coming in at different times, and I could never really get them quiet. So learn from my mistakes: notify parents ahead of time of your expectations on phones.

Again, we're talking about tweens here (late elementary age and middle schoolers). Family sleepover guidelines will change as our kids get older.

The more online integrity they demonstrate, the more freedom we'll be able to give them.

Two other important sleepover issues come to mind at this point: gun safety and sexual abuse.

Gun Safety

No matter where you stand on this issue politically, the reality is that some people have guns in their homes. Do you know if they're locked away?

My own kids have spent the night at other homes, and I never asked the families about guns. It never crossed my mind until I heard Noah's story.

Noah was at a sleepover when his friend accidentally shot and killed him. He was just thirteen years old. His mother, Ashlyn Melton, is now a spokesperson for the ASK Campaign (Asking Saves Kids), created in collaboration with the American Academy of Pediatrics.

When Noah's mom spoke on *The Today Show*, she said, "In all those years of play dates and sleepovers, I never had anyone ask me about my guns, and I never asked anyone else about theirs. I didn't think to ask. I would have never let my child go there if I had known they had guns lying around unsecured."

She went on to say, "I am a gun owner. I believe in gun locks and following strict safety procedures around guns."[1]

My husband is also a responsible gun owner, and the guns in our home are safely locked away. My children don't know the combination. This isn't about Second Amendment rights or taking sides on guns. It's about asking a simple question to protect our kids.

If your child is going to spend the night at someone else's home (even the homes of grandparents or cousins), you shouldn't be afraid to ask about guns. If you're embarrassed, blame me. You can say, "I'm reading a book this crazy mom wrote, and she talked about kids playing with real firearms at sleepovers. So I thought I'd ask if y'all have any weapons. Oh, and you should buy her book." (I need all the promo help I can get!)

You can even go a step further and say, "I'm fine with guns, but I just want them locked up and away from the children."

Be proactive. Don't be afraid to ask questions and talk with other parents about this issue. You can do it in a nice, respectful, and sincere way. Not everything has to be a debate.

Sexual Abuse

Most of this book focuses on questions our children will ask as a result of early online exposure. It's unlikely they'll ask about sexual abuse (unless they hear someone use the term and want to know what it is). But I want to raise the issue so we can have a preventive conversation about it.

A school counselor once told me that most sexually abused kids who came to her office had been abused at sleepovers by older siblings in the home. Because of this, she has a family policy of no sleepovers.

Sexual abuse can happen anywhere—church, school, sleepovers, in our neighborhoods. Anywhere. If our tweens are old enough for sleepovers, it means they're spending more time away from us. And that makes them a target for sexual abuse. So this is an important issue to talk about with our kids. Remember, it's not a one-time discussion. It's an ongoing, routine conversation with your child.

According to the National Center for Victims of Crime, "the prevalence of child sexual abuse is difficult to determine because it is often not reported; experts agree that the incidence is far greater than what is reported to authorities.... Studies ... show that 1 in 5 girls and 1 in 20 boys is a victim of child sexual abuse.... Children are most vulnerable ... between the ages of 7 and 13."[2]

When my kids were little, I started telling them, "No one should touch private parts." I said it was okay for a doctor to do so, as long as my husband or I was in the room. Bath time was always a great opportunity to bring up this issue.

But like so many other discussions we have with our kids, we may be tempted to check this one off our mental to-do lists and never bring it up again. We can't afford to fall into the trap of complacency.

As the research suggests, children are most vulnerable to sexual abuse between the ages of seven and thirteen. That's the same age range when I became complacent and thought I could coast. Remember?

But Satan is lurking in the shadows, waiting to steal, kill, and destroy.

As our kids get older and begin spending more time away from us, we need to continually remind them that they need to protect themselves from sexual abuse. Keep telling your child that it's never okay for anyone to touch or violate his or her body.

I remind my kids, "No matter what a person threatens you with, even if they say they'll hurt or kill me, you still need to report it to me. I'm your safe place. Tell me everything, and we'll figure it out together."

I love the sleepover advice from Gregory Ramey, a child psychologist at the Dayton Children's Hospital in Dayton, Ohio: "Pick your child up if she calls you during the night" and "be around in the morning."[3]

If your tween doesn't want to go to a sleepover or expresses fear about being with someone, never force it. Listen to your child and don't assume that he or she is just being difficult. I even respect this with carpooling. If one of my kids says, "Please, I can't ride home with that kid anymore," I respect his or her wishes because there's usually a reason. Try to get your child to talk about why he or she wants to avoid a person or situation.

Also, if your tween goes to a sleepover, be available the next morning to talk. You don't have to bombard him or her with questions, though. Your child may be exhausted from staying up too late. But you need to be available to talk the next day.

After a sleepover, I try to casually ask questions like these:

➡ What did y'all do?
➡ Did you prank-call (or live-stream/FaceTime) anyone?
➡ Did anyone call strangers?
➡ Did you see anything inappropriate online?
➡ What movies did you watch?
➡ Did y'all text anyone from school?

These are just suggestions. Focus on having a casual conversation with your child. Don't ask all your questions at once. Your tween will feel like he or she is being interrogated. When you do ask a question, let your child fully respond before jumping to your next question. Listen and remember to stay calm no matter what he or she tells you. Be a safe place for your tween. If your child is tired and doesn't want to talk, don't force it. Talk later, after your tween feels more rested.

If your child ever confides in you about being sexually abused, take him or her to a doctor immediately. Don't question it. Your child's safety comes before any other concern you may have. Face it! The truth will set you free.

The person who abused your child made an evil choice and should be brought to justice. Abusers themselves are often victims of sexual abuse or may be struggling with a porn addiction. It's important to bring this issue into the light so that everyone can get the help they need.

Do whatever you need to do to help your child heal from sexual abuse. Talk with a qualified counselor who can help him or her process the trauma. A knee-jerk reaction for many parents when they discover that their child has been sexually abused is to become overly protective. You may also need to work through your own emotions and concerns with a counselor. Sexual abuse harms everyone in a family, and each of you will process the experience differently.

No matter what, love your child and assure him or her that you'll walk through this together with God's help. Deuteronomy 31:6 says, "Be strong and courageous! Do not be afraid and do not panic before [your enemies]. For the LORD your God will personally go ahead of you. He will neither fail you nor abandon you."

In your pain and confusion, don't stop trusting God. He cares and wants to walk you through this to a place of healing and peace. I personally know families who have overcome sexual abuse. There's hope.

Whether you allow sleepovers in your family is entirely your choice. If you have additional talking points on this topic, our nextTalk group would love for you to join the conversation. We're continually learning together on this cyberparenting journey and sharing each other's ideas on social media.

21

Rejection and Your Child's Tribe

Frenemies, Conflict Resolution, Characteristics of a Healthy Tribe

Breaking news alert: your child is going to face rejection in this world. It deeply hurts a mama's heart. Let's face it. Being a tween is rough. It's an awkward stage of life where peer acceptance is incredibly important.

Many kids are hypersensitive to rejection, but they have to risk it if they're going to make friends. Social media has only magnified the issue. In our tweens' online world, rejection is "in yo' face" all the time.

In this chapter, we'll walk through different kinds of rejection and talk about how we can help tweens deal with it. Some kinds sting more than others, especially when our kids experience rejection from a friend in their own tribe. We'll also discuss the different kinds of relationships and the importance of teaching our children how to develop a healthy inner circle of friends.

When Our Kids Don't Make the Team

First, I want to talk about the kind of rejection that happens when our kids try out for something they desperately want but don't make the cut. Trust me. It will happen. Whether it's trying out for a sports team, a play, or some other activity, our kids will face rejection. Prepare yourself for this reality and ask God for wisdom and guidance to help them learn from it.

Recently my daughter came home and said, "Basketball team cuts were made today. I saw a seventh-grade boy crying after school."

"Please tell me no one was laughing at him," I replied.

"No, everyone was actually being very nice."

"I'm so glad," I said with relief.

I could relate to how that seventh grader felt. I was a cheerleader for three years in middle school, but when I tried out my freshman year in high school, I didn't make the team. A month later my mom and I moved to a new town, and I tried out at my new school. I didn't make that squad either. Within a few months, I was rejected twice for cheerleading, had moved to a new school, and had no real friends. It was tough. But at least I didn't have to relive the rejection month after month.

What do I mean? In today's online world, almost every kid who makes a team will post a picture on social media. Nothing's wrong with that. They have every right to be proud and excited. But it hurts those who were cut.

Whenever those kids go online, they see posts of team friendships being formed, but they've been left out. Four months later, there's the team at the championship game—all over social media. It's in their faces all the time. Rejected again and again. It doesn't take long for self-esteem to crumble. Not making a team may seem minor to us, but in a screen-crazed world, it can be a huge deal for our kids.

See how the online world can magnify rejection? We must recognize the shift and help our tweens deal with rejection in a healthy way. We can't prevent it (no, we're not going to bubble-wrap our kids), and we can't fix it. But we can help them work through their emotions and learn what to do when it happens.

If your kids confide in you about feeling rejected, stop and listen first. Don't lecture or speed past their pain to the glowing life lessons they can learn from the experience. After you've invested time validating their feelings and letting them know you care, you may have an opportunity to share a painful memory of a time you were rejected.

When we share our own stories of rejection, our children know we can relate to their pain. We can understand at least a little of what they're going through. It's also important to talk about how they feel when social media keeps throwing the pain back in their faces. This helps them understand why they may be feeling defeated.

From there, turn the conversation into a teachable moment. Talk about how everyone experiences rejection, but the important thing is how we handle it. We can let it destroy us and make us bitter, or we learn to become more accepting and compassionate toward others because we know what rejection feels like.

Warning: Frenemies Ahead

Trying out for something and being rejected is one thing, but when other children reject our tweens, it's even more painful. It not only happens at school; it happens online 24/7. One of your tween's friends throws a party and posts the pictures on social media. Only she didn't invite your child. Your son's friend suddenly starts bullying him and posts disparaging remarks about him for everyone to see, all because this kid likes to make other people laugh (at your son's expense).

It's going to happen. We need to be ready to pick up the pieces when it does and help our tweens work through it.

What if someone in our tweens' inner circle rejects them? Maybe even a BFF? This kind of rejection is the absolute worst of all.

The *Urban Dictionary* defines a *frenemy* as "an enemy disguised as a friend."[1]

Here's a real-life example of a frenemy situation I witnessed on social media: Two girls were best friends. Inseparable for years. They got into a fight, and then one posted a picture about best friends and tagged almost every girl in the whole school, except her actual best friend. Ouch!

Girls are going to have drama. Boys sometimes too. Some drama is normal because none of us are perfect. But if a relationship turns into a nonstop roller-coaster ride of being friends one day and enemies the next, we need to discourage it. No relationship should be a constant fight. It's unhealthy.

One day my son jumped in the car after school and said, "Mom, there were two girls crying today at lunch. They wouldn't even eat. They were in a fight about something. But by pickup, they were best friends again, and everything was fine. I don't get girls *at all*." I almost died laughing.

How do I deal with the rejection drama with my kids? First I say, "Well, your friend is still learning. We all are. It's your job to love, forgive, and show kindness. Try to talk through it together."

I don't shame my kids' friends, because I'm only hearing one side of the story. Maybe there's a legitimate reason for their behavior. Do my children know why they've been rejected? It's important that they seek out the person who hurt them and have a heartfelt conversation about what happened.

We need to teach our kids to talk through misunderstandings with their friends and practice biblical forgiveness. (We need to model it in our own lives, too.) Even if the other child doesn't ask for forgiveness, our kids can still follow Jesus's example. Often, if they're willing to take the first step toward reconciliation, God will turn the curses into blessings. Once again, open communication is the key.

Oh, how I wish I'd known the value of open communication when I was growing up. It would've saved me a lot of pain over lost friendships. But instead of working through problems and taking an honest look at myself in the mirror, I'd react with anger and selfishness. I missed so many great life lessons (and lost so many friends) because I wasn't listening to God or walking with balance in the Spirit.

Hear me on this: friends are going to make mistakes. Like when my boyfriend broke up with me to go out with my best friend. (My kids *love* to hear this story. I can laugh about it now.) Your kids will make mistakes in relationships, and their friends will too. Some friendships are mended; others aren't. That's life. But if our kids learn how to mend fences when they're young, they'll be more likely to experience healthier relationships throughout their lives.

It's incredibly painful to watch our kids struggling with rejection, isn't it? Especially when it comes from a frenemy. When we see how much our children are hurting, the mama bear comes out in us, and we want to do more than empathize with how they feel. We want to take matters into our own hands and fix the problem. But instead of turning into a crazy mom, we need to apply the parent filter. Why? Because if we handle things right, these experiences can become teachable moments for our kids.

If I notice that one of my kids' close friendships is becoming a continual roller coaster of conflict and emotion, I'll say, "This relationship is causing a lot of turmoil. It might be a good idea to step away for a little while. This friend could still be an outer-circle friend. Maybe you can connect on social media occasionally if you want to. Your inner circle needs to be a healthy place."

If a frenemy situation is causing constant turmoil or has escalated to bullying, don't be afraid to reach out to a school counselor or administrator. Just make sure your child knows in advance that you're contacting the school. Otherwise, he or she may feel blindsided if an administrator arranges a meeting to get your child's side of the story.

Often, the best thing we can do is encourage our kids to face a frenemy situation head-on and try to work through it themselves first. It's tough to confront a frenemy, but I often tell my kids, "Doing the right thing is normally not the popular thing. I'm so proud of your integrity and character. I know it's hard to stand up, face the problem, and do what's right."

When our kids are treated like outcasts, they feel alone, but that's a lie from Satan. We need to remind them they're never alone. God is always right there with them no matter how they feel or how they're treated. We want them to always seek God and turn to Him with their problems. He's their ultimate source of help and wisdom. He understands more about their frenemy situation than they do, and He's able to heal relationships. In fact, that's what He wants to do.

Teachable Moments

When we talk with our tweens about dealing with rejection, it's important to take advantage of teachable moments in a way that will benefit them over the long haul. Following are some thoughts to keep in mind.

Don't Try to Fix It

I know this is tough, but your child doesn't need you to call the coach and demand that he or she make the team. Resist the temptation to think you *always* need to confront the kid who sent your tween a rejecting message on social media or call a parent whose child was mean to yours. Each situation is unique and may warrant a different response.

Of course, if the problem continues, that's different. Work out a plan with your child to tackle it together. And be careful not to embarrass your tween.

As painful as rejection is, our kids can learn so many important lessons from it. For example, they can learn to trust God when things don't work out the way they think they should, and they have to go down a different path. It's a life lesson we don't want to take away from our children.

Our kids may not understand God's plan in the middle of their rejection and pain. That's where trusting God comes in. They absolutely need to process feelings of hurt and betrayal. It's okay for them to acknowledge their sadness and disappointment. But they shouldn't get stuck in the sadness or let rejection get the better of them. They need to apply the same lessons we've been learning throughout this book: face it and seek God in the pain. Talk about the problem openly and honestly. Then move on and trust that God knows what He's doing.

When our children are struggling with rejection, it may be difficult to hear the words "God has another plan for you." So I've found it's sometimes best to share rejection stories from my past and let my kids learn from my experiences how God worked everything out. For example, when I'd share the story of my boyfriend breaking up with me to date my best friend, I'd say, "But it all worked out. I met Daddy, and he was the perfect choice for me. God knew what He was doing."

Sharing our experiences and modeling healthy ways to handle rejection are powerful tools in our parenting arsenal. Instead of trying to fix our kids' pain, we need to pull out those tools more often.

Teach Biblical Conflict Resolution

Tween drama is gonna happen, so one of the best things we can do as parents is teach our children how to resolve conflict. Jesus even gives us a blueprint to follow in Matthew 18.

Let's say your daughter has a tween friend in her inner circle who is making bad choices and is being distant. Your daughter is concerned about her friend's choices, but she also feels hurt and rejected. She doesn't understand why her friend is acting that way. Situations like this happen all the time, and they can quickly get out of control.

Matthew 18 outlines four important steps to follow in a conflict situation:

Step 1: Go to that person "privately and point out the offense" (verse 15). Your tween first needs to have an honest conversation with her friend and explain her concerns. I recommend not having a conversation like this through texts or DMs because it can be screenshot. The conversation needs to be live-streamed, FaceTimed, or face-to-face. Role-play with your child and work out what she might say. This isn't about pointing fingers; it's about talking openly and honestly with a true friend.

Your child might start out by saying, "I know I'm not perfect. So I expect you and others to hold me accountable when I'm making mistakes. I also care about you and the choices you're making. I wanted to talk with you about it in person instead of talking behind your back. I would never do that to you." Then she could express her specific concerns to her friend and how she feels distance in their relationship. Role-play constructive ways she can let her friend know how rejected and hurt she feels without putting her friend on the defensive.

Remind your daughter that it's important to give her friend a chance to respond. Listening is just as important as talking. She could repeat what her friend tells her to make sure she understands. Emphasize staying calm during the conversation, no matter how her friend responds (the kid version of the parent filter). If the conversation goes well, the other steps may not be necessary. If it doesn't, move on to step 2.

Step 2: Bring one or two friends with you and try again to reason with your friend. If your daughter's initial efforts to resolve the problem are unsuccessful, she'll need to follow the advice in verse 16: "Take one or two others with you and go back again, so that everything you say may be confirmed by two or three witnesses."

A word of caution: Your child's friend could feel judged or ganged up on, so your daughter needs to clearly express her love and concern. The tone has to be right. This talk should *not* be confrontational. Remind your tween that "harsh words make tempers flare" (Proverbs 15:1). Walking with balance in the Spirit is key here. Your daughter could start the conversation by saying, "I tried to talk with you privately, but it didn't work. I care about you, and I'm really worried about the choices you're making. I'm your friend, and I want you to be okay. So I asked two of our BFFs to join our conversation."

Again, role playing how to approach the situation can be helpful, and it's also a good idea to spend time together in prayer beforehand, asking God to guide the conversation and soften this friend's heart. Also remind your daughter to listen to her friend and not interrupt while she's responding. If her friend still won't listen, it may be necessary to move to the next level.

Step 3: Get a parent involved. Verse 17 says, "If the person still refuses to listen, take your case to the church." In this scenario, it means the person in charge. Your daughter shouldn't talk with her friend's parents alone. You should talk about it first and then approach this friend and her parents together with your concerns. As always, do this *in love*. Express concern, not judgment. Ask Jesus to keep you and your daughter centered. (I don't get parents involved unless I'm extremely close to them, or there's a life-threatening situation like suicide or a child meeting up with an online stranger.)

Step 4: If nothing works, move on. This is always the last resort. Verse 17 goes on to say, "If he or she won't accept the church's decision, treat that person as a pagan or a corrupt tax collector." I'm always telling my kids, "You are not responsible for other people's choices. You only get to control how you handle a situation. After you've tried your best to resolve a conflict, the ball is in their court. You don't get to control their response."

If the conflict isn't resolved even after talking with the parents, then your daughter's friend will likely move from her inner circle to an outer circle. Or they might stop being friends. Remind your daughter that regardless of what happens, it's still her job to love and show respect. She should never treat an ex-friend in an unkind or hateful way. Colossians 3:13 tells us to "make allowance for each other's faults, and forgive anyone who offends you. Remember, the Lord forgave you, so you must forgive others."

Her friend may come around in time, and if she does, your daughter should respond with *open arms*. That's true forgiveness.

Keep on Talking

In our home, we talk about all different types of rejection and friend changes. It's an ongoing conversation, and I often share age-appropriate examples from my own friend circle (with permission, of course). We don't wait until a friendship is in ruins or someone doesn't get a role in the class play to talk about rejection. We discuss it often.

For example, after school one of my kids said, "Today we had to pair up for a class project, and I didn't have a partner. It felt like no one liked me, and I had no friends. It was embarrassing."

When this kind of thing happens, we need to talk through it with our tweens. To them, rejection is a BIG DEAL. It's devastating. To us, it's normal, everyday life.

You know what I said to my tween? "Well, I remember not having a partner for class projects, and that was the worst. But on the flip side, it keeps us humble. When all your close friends are in one of your classes, and you always have a project partner, you need to remember the child being left out. You know how it feels now." The pain of rejection can teach our kids an important lesson about being compassionate toward others.

Philippians 2:3–4 says, "Be humble, thinking of others as better than yourselves. Don't look out only for your own interests, but take an interest in others, too."

When our kids experience rejection, they develop empathy for others. Instead of trying to bubble-wrap them, we need to let God use hard experiences to teach them humility and compassion.

As parents, we need to work together to raise a loving generation of kiddos who accept people who are different from them. We need to talk often about cliques so our tweens know it's not cool to leave others out. Because one day they'll be on the outside of the circle. Rejected.

You may be thinking, *Isn't it a contradiction to teach our kids to choose their inner circle carefully and then tell them not to leave others out?* Like everything else, this requires balance. We want our kids to be selective about their inner circle, but at the same time, we don't want them to be cliquish. I think it's possible to do both by treating everyone with kindness and respect. They may share more personal things with their inner circle, but that doesn't give them an excuse to be cliquish.

Developing a Healthy Tribe

We can't rejection-proof our children, but we can teach them how to develop a healthy inner circle of friends. When I talk with my kids about different kinds of relationships, I've found it helpful to compare them with rings on a dartboard.

The center ring, or bull's-eye, is our kids' relationship with God. This is the most important relationship in their lives. We need to talk about it continually (remember Deuteronomy 6:6–7) and encourage our kids to know God on a deep level. That means spending time with Him on a regular basis (praying and reading the Bible) and learning to walk in the Spirit. Ultimately, our children answer to God and His voice, not ours.

The second ring after the bull's-eye is our families. Our children need to understand that family always comes first after our relationship with God. This is their safe place, where they can ask or tell us anything, and we'll keep their confidence (unless something illegal has happened or a child's safety is at risk). Continual open communication is essential for healthy family relationships. We should also model the foundational truths we're teaching our children.

The third ring is our children's inner circle of friends. All kids need an inner circle—a tribe—where they feel safe and can be themselves. It's important to have ongoing conversations with our children about essential qualities to look for in friends (like honesty, integrity, and good character), and how to find peers who meet those qualifications. Let's face it. Our tweens' tribes tell each other almost everything, so we want to make sure the kids they spend the most time with are a good influence.

The Bible gives great advice on friendship and building an inner circle: "Walk with the wise and become wise; associate with fools and get in trouble" (Proverbs 13:20). Share this verse with your child and talk about what it looks like to "walk with the wise."

The fourth ring is our kids' outer circle of friends. This group will mainly consist of social-media friends our children know in real life or buddies they hang out with in class. This level of friendship is for sharing fun things and general, everyday stuff, but not personal information or intimate details of their lives. As our kids get to know their outer-circle friends better, they may become inner-circle friends.

The fifth and final ring is everyone else. No one is left off the board. People on the periphery of our children's lives may have very different values from the ones we've taught at home. So we need to remind our kids that no one has the right to be disrespectful or unkind. Ever. Our job is to love and be kind to everyone, not to reject, judge, or bully.

We must teach our children to accept kids they may not necessarily like or understand, and stand up for the kids others may reject. It's never okay to participate in rejection or intentionally exclude others from group activities. Our children should always show empathy and understanding toward others who are going through rejection, especially if they've experienced it themselves.

If we model healthy relationships for our kids and have ongoing conversations with them about issues like rejection, choosing friends wisely, and working through misunderstandings, they'll learn the value and importance of relationships early in their lives. And we'll raise kids who are living examples of godly qualities like love, forgiveness, empathy, and acceptance.

Conclusion

Striking a Balance

I'm *so* proud of you for hanging with me on this journey. (Tweet me @mandymajors or connect with me on Facebook @authormandymajors so I know you made it to the end. I'd love to hear from you!)

We've covered a lot of territory, haven't we? God has been showing us some amazing things. We've looked at ourselves in the mirror and faced our fears. We recognize the dangers of complacency now, and our guard is up. We're wide awake and learning how to parent more effectively. We've paved a path for open communication in our relationships and worked on becoming a safe place for our kids.

Most important, we've learned the importance of walking with balance in the Spirit. Listening to God. Knowing Him. Letting Him guide our parenting decisions. We've seen how He can turn curses into blessings and completely transform our relationships with our kids.

We have all the tools we need for cyberparenting in this digital world, and we've started using them. But we're not finished yet.

As we wrap up our conversation, I want to camp on the importance of balance. The storms we encounter on this cyberparenting journey have a way of knocking us down and throwing us off balance. One moment we're facing issues, listening to God, walking with balance, and talking openly and honestly with our kids. The next moment we're sliding back into complacency, sweeping things under the rug, going into crazy-mom mode, and swinging to extremes.

No matter how far we've come, we still won't always get this parenting thing right. Trust me, you're going to keep messing up. I still do—all day long. Laugh at yourself from time to time. Remember when I told my daughter that the penis and vagina fit together like a puzzle? If we can see the humor in things, we'll help our kids lighten up too. We all need that because life is way too serious most of the time. It wears us down and makes us feel defeated.

But the beauty of grace is that God doesn't condemn us when we mess up. He knows we struggle. When Satan manipulates us with his lies, God gently brings us back to the truth. He forgives us and sets us back on the right path. He loves us too much to let us drown.

When you lose your balance, instead of beating yourself up, regroup and move on. Don't lie in bed at night obsessing over your failures. Don't let Satan manipulate you into believing that you're a bad mom. Don't buy into his lies. My "No ma'am" friend would be shaking her head right now and waving her index finger in the air.

Our enemy is prowling around looking for the right moment to pounce. He'll do whatever it takes to throw us off balance. Like using our feelings and circumstances against us. We need to be alert!

While I was completing this book, I had an epic mom-fail that knocked me off balance. One morning I was scheduled to speak in front of a couple hundred moms. After I dressed, put on makeup (which is unusual for me), and packed the kids' lunches, we piled in the car and drove to school, saying our prayers on the way (as usual). Everything was going smoothly, and I was feeling like a rock-star mom.

As we pulled up to the elementary school, I noticed kids in comfy flannel pajamas and casually said to my son, "Oh, man, I forgot it was pajama day."

Y'all, he was so mad at me! "How did you forget this, Mom?" he wailed.

I calmly replied, "Honey, it's just pajamas. Calm down. I love you."

He sluggishly got out of the car and walked into school with his head down.

My teen daughter looked at me and said, "Pajama day in elementary school is like *the best day ever.* You messed this up, Mom."

Silence. Then guess what happened?

Satan started messing with my head, and my thoughts went into a downward spiral. He whispered in my ear that I was a bad mom, and if I hadn't been speaking and writing this book, my kid wouldn't be upset. In an instant, I started believing that I should quit everything.

After dropping my daughter off at the middle school, I called my husband and gave him all the details. I started crying (the *one* day I wore makeup) and said, "I wouldn't have missed this if I weren't so busy writing and speaking. I need to quit."

My wise hubby responded with a big dose of truth: "Honey, you missed little details like this and forgot about other things *way before* you started writing or speaking."

First, silence. Then I burst into laughter. Oh my gosh, he was right!

I had plunged from rock-star mom to total failure in 1.2 seconds … OVER PAJAMAS! How did Satan manipulate me into thinking I was a horrible mom? Feelings. That's one of the ways he defeats us and our kids.

After Matt set me straight (I love that man!), I got my feelings under control. Then I went home, grabbed some pajamas for my boy, and dropped them off at the school office with a special apology note for him. I even made it to my speaking event in time and shared this story with the moms.

What would have happened if I hadn't gotten control of my feelings? Would I really have decided to quit everything because of the pajama fail? I'm not sure, but if I had quit, I wouldn't be writing this conclusion. I wouldn't have made it here.

Wow! That really put things in perspective for me.

See how Satan can throw us completely off balance by manipulating our feelings? It's a short trip from feeling like a rock-star mom to feeling like a complete failure. We can't let the Enemy mess with our minds like that. It's exactly what he wants. We need to stay grounded in truth. Balanced and centered.

This brings me to another important point. If we're not careful, we can swing to an extreme and become obsessed with open communication. Don't get me wrong. Open communication is a wonderful gift. An incredible tool in our cyberparenting arsenal. But it works best when we stay balanced.

Throughout this book, we've talked about the importance of continual, on-the-go conversations about the issues that are important to our kids. But that doesn't mean we should talk about issues every waking second of the day. Teachable moments are just that—moments. Not 24/7 teaching marathons. Yes, we want our kids to understand how God's Word relates to their world, but we don't want to beat them over the head with Bible verses. When we get off balance, we can end up driving our kids away from God instead of drawing them to Him.

Open communication is important, but we don't need to talk *all the time* about *every single thing*. That's what happened to me. I became a talking billboard for open communication.

For example, one day my son made a comment about quitting as we were driving down the road. In response, I launched into a five-minute discourse on life lessons, facing it, and doing the hard work. (Remember the arrow?) But he really didn't need all that input. He just needed me to listen in the moment.

Later, when my wise hubby and I were alone, he gently said, "Mandy, not everything has to be a life lesson."

That stung! But he was 100 percent correct. I was letting the pendulum swing into crazy-mom territory.

It all comes down to striking a balance. We know how to do that now. We have a secret weapon: the Holy Spirit. If we listen to Him and follow His lead, He'll keep us centered and on point. He'll let us know when to use a teachable moment, make a joke, show grace, enforce rules, or break out in a dance party. (Our family likes to make up our own raps.)

Keep listening to Him. He's the only parenting expert who has this thing figured out.

James 1:5–8 says,

> If you need wisdom, ask our generous God, and he will give it to you. He will not rebuke you for asking. But when you ask him, be sure that your faith is in God alone. Do not waver, for a person with divided loyalty is as unsettled as a wave of the sea that is blown and

> tossed by the wind. Such people should not expect to receive anything from the Lord. Their loyalty is divided between God and the world, and they are unstable in everything they do.

If we want our kids to be stable, we must be stable. If we want our kids to seek God and listen to Him, we must seek God and listen. If we want our kids to be grounded in love and truth, we must be grounded in love and truth. This is the foundation for open communication.

In the end, this cyberparenting journey is about relationship—our relationships with our kids and with Jesus. He's the only one who can help us strike the balance we need in this crazy, screen-obsessed world.

We can do this, sister! Let's keep the conversation going.

Appendix

Sample Phone Contract

A phone contract has two parts. The first part specifies your tween's rights and responsibilities. It spells out in detail the rules, guidelines, and consequences your tween agrees to abide by. The second part of the contract specifies what you and your spouse commit and promise to do as your part of the agreement. After you and your tween have carefully reviewed both parts and modified any wording that is unclear, sign and date your respective agreements and give a copy to your tween.

Part A—Tween's Agreement

You're getting this phone because we trust you. You have demonstrated to us that you will report inappropriate behavior, will self-regulate so that screens do not take over your life, and will abide by our family technology guidelines.

If at any time you do not abide by these guidelines, your phone may be taken away indefinitely. This is a big privilege that demands personal responsibility from you.

Your phone is not a diary. Do not expect privacy. Technology is public. Anything you type, text, snap, post, etc., can be screenshot and shared with the world. Don't type it if you wouldn't say it in front of us or your school principal.

If at any time your screen becomes an issue with how you communicate with people, it will be taken away. We look people in the eye when we're speaking. Put away the phone and talk with people directly. Invest in people.

You will never give out personal information online to anyone (or through any social-media posts), including your address, school, name, class schedule, phone number, doctor's name, and parents' place of employment.

You will not answer texts, phone calls, DMs, e-mails, or any other types of communication from people you do not know in real life. If you are contacted in any way by someone you don't know, you will report it to us.

You will not search for inappropriate material online, and if you accidentally see inappropriate content, you will inform us immediately. This means any picture or video (with people in a bathing suit or less), any cuss word, profanity, reference to sex, etc. If you question it at all, ask us. That is how we learn together. You will never get in trouble for being honest.

You will not take any picture of yourself or anyone else in a bathing suit or less without our approval. In fact, you will never take a picture of anyone without their consent and approval. There will be no picture taking ever in bathrooms, locker rooms, or dressing rooms, because images can accidentally be caught in mirrors.

None of us will bring our phones/screens to the table when we're eating meals. That is family discussion time. What is said at our family dinner table stays at the table.

If we designate additional times to go screen-free as a family, you will comply and not complain.

Your phone will never be in your bedroom with you unless you're working on a school project with the door open. Your phone will be charged in the mudroom every night at a designated time (this may vary depending on our schedule). You will never go get it once it's there unless you have permission. Turning over your phone at night helps protect your mind and allows you to be well rested for the next day.

As with our current family guidelines, you will not search online from your phone without permission. As always, searches need to be completed in an open area of our house (kitchen, family room, dining room, or study).

You will not download any new apps, books, movies, songs, etc., without permission.

You will keep your security code enabled. You will never give that code to anyone other than us. If you change the code for some reason (such as if your friends accidently find out the code), you will report it to us immediately.

Restrictions are set on your phone to limit content. Even though they're set, inappropriate material can still be seen (especially in apps). You will continue to report all such content to us. Restriction settings, codes, and passwords should never be changed without our permission.

You will not type, text, comment, post, snap, etc., anything online that you would not say directly to someone's face. There is a soul behind that screen. You will not be rude or unkind to others. We are called to love everyone. If you see someone being bullied online, or you are being bullied online, you will report it to us immediately. We'll help you figure out how to deal with online bullies.

When you're on school property, you will stay on the school wifi. There are filters in place to help limit content. Also, you will limit most of your online use to when you are in wifi zones. If you connect online without using wifi and exceed the data limits of our plan, you will be responsible for the overage charges.

If you drop, lose, or damage your phone, we will not provide a replacement. We gave you this phone. If you lose it or fail to take care of it properly, you will need to pay for the next one yourself. If you crack a screen, it is your responsibility to pay for the damages.

Even though your phone has a contact list, you will memorize our phone numbers in the event you don't have your phone (for whatever reason) during an emergency.

We may revise these guidelines at any time. As you get older, you may be given more freedom (as you prove yourself trustworthy), but the freedom has to be earned by your own good decisions.

We pay for your phone. We have access whenever we want. There will be random phone checks.

Failure to abide by these family restrictions will result in the loss of your phone. If you have questions or are unsure of our family guidelines, ask us.

Even though these guidelines are in place, you ultimately answer to God. You are responsible for protecting your own heart and mind. You are responsible for the content you put out to the world. We trust you to do the right thing.

Guard your heart above all else, for it determines the course of your life. (Proverbs 4:23)

My child, listen and be wise: Keep your heart on the right course. (Proverbs 23:19)

I will set no worthless thing before my eyes. (Psalm 101:3, NASB)

____________________________ _______________

Child's Signature Date

Part B—Parents' Agreement

We, in turn, agree to remain calm and never yell when you report inappropriate content to us. For example, if you show us a pornographic picture you saw on Instagram, we will not make you delete Instagram. We will take the appropriate steps to report the photo so it is taken down. You will not lose technology privileges for being honest with us.

The only reason we are implementing guidelines is to keep you safe online. We trust you, or you wouldn't have a phone. But you will be exposed to online strangers, bullies, and inappropriate content in the digital world. We expect you to respond with integrity and honesty. We are with you to help you process and deal with any situation.

We promise to be in your digital world as much as we're involved in your regular, face-to-face world. But we also promise not to intentionally embarrass you online, just as we wouldn't in real life. We promise that we'll continue learning and walking hand in hand with you to figure this out as a family. We are in this together.

____________________________ _______________

Parent's Signature Date

____________________________ _______________

Parent's Signature Date

RECOMMENDED RESOURCES

Books

Gresh, Dannah. *Six Ways to Keep the "Good" in Your Boy: Guiding Your Son from His Tweens to His Teens.* Eugene, OR: Harvest House, 2012.

———. *Six Ways to Keep the "Little" in Your Girl: Guiding Your Daughter from Her Tweens to Her Teens.* Eugene, OR: Harvest House, 2010.

Jenson, Kristen A., and Gail Poyner. *Good Pictures, Bad Pictures: Porn-Proofing Today's Young Kids.* Richland, WA: Glen Cove Press, 2016.

Rothschild, Jennifer. *Me, Myself, and Lies: A Thought Closet Makeover.* Nashville: LifeWay, 2009.

Schaefer, Valorie Lee. *The Care and Keeping of You: The Body Book for Girls.* Middleton, WI: Pleasant Company, 1998.

Smith, Angie. *Seamless: Understanding the Bible as One Complete Story.* Nashville: LifeWay, 2015.

Tobias, Cynthia, and Sue Acuña. *Middle School: The Inside Story.* Carol Stream, IL: Tyndale, 2014.

Organizations and Websites

Common Sense Media— www.commonsensemedia.org; phone: 415-863-0600. Offers a wide range of resources to help parents and educators make wise media choices and effectively navigate the challenges of raising kids in the digital age

FamilyLife—www.familylife.com; phone: 800-FL-TODAY. Committed to helping couples strengthen their marriages and families through Bible-based events, radio broadcasts, and resources.

Fight the New Drug—www.fightthenewdrug.org; phone: 385-313-8629. Uses science-based facts, school presentations, blog articles, and personal stories to increase awareness of pornography's destructive effects. The organization also offers an online program (Fortify) to help people recover from porn addiction.

Focus on the Family—www.focusonthefamily.com; phone: 800-A-FAMILY. Provides a variety of biblically based resources to support and strengthen families. They also offer a help line and counseling referrals.

iMOM—www.imom.com; 813-222-8300. Through its iMom website, Family First offers ideas, insight, and inspiration to help moms grow and flourish in their role as parents.

National Center on Sexual Exploitation—www.endsexualexploitation.org; 202-393-7245. Exposes the connection between pornography, sex trafficking, and other forms of sexual exploitation; educates the public; and fights sexual exploitation through legal and policy channels.

National Suicide Prevention Lifeline—www.suicidepreventionlifeline.org; 800-273-8255. A network of crisis centers that provide 24/7 crisis and suicide-prevention services, resources, and support.

nextTalk—www.nexttalk.org. A nonprofit organization that helps parents learn how to talk openly with their kids about issues they're encountering in their digital world.

Partnership for Drug-Free Kids—www.drugfree.org; 855-DRUGFREE. Connects families with the information and resources they need to help kids overcome substance abuse.

Plugged In—www.pluggedin.com; 800-A-FAMILY. An entertainment guide that provides reviews of movies, TV programs, books, music, video games, and other kinds of entertainment.

Protect Young Minds—www.protectyoungminds.org. Informs, equips, and empowers parents and community leaders to protect kids from pornography and help them heal from sexual exploitation.

Proverbs 31 Ministries—www.proverbs31.org; 877-731-4663. Encourages women to seek a personal relationship with Jesus Christ and grow spiritually through radio messages, Bible studies, conferences, and other resources and events.

NOTES

Chapter 1

1. Jennifer Rothschild, *Me, Myself, and Lies: A Thought Closet Makeover* (Nashville: LifeWay Christian Resources, 2007), 56.

Chapter 2

1. *Merriam-Webster Learner's Dictionary*, s.v. "complacency," www.merriam-webster.com/dictionary/complacency.
2. Casting Crowns, "Slow Fade," *The Altar and the Door*, copyright 2007, My Refuge Music (BMI) (adm. at CapitolCMGPublishing.com) / Be Essential Songs (BMI). International copyright secured. All rights reserved. Used by permission; Be Essential Songs (BMI) / (admin. at EssentialMusicPublishing.com). All rights reserved. Used by permission.
3. Dannah Gresh, *Six Ways to Keep the "Good" in Your Boy: Guiding Your Son from His Tweens to His Teens* (Eugene, OR: Harvest House, 2012), 28.
4. *Merriam-Webster Learner's Dictionary*, s.v. "complacency."

Chapter 3

1. Jennifer Rothschild, *Invisible: How You Feel Is Not Who You Are* (Eugene, OR: Harvest House, 2015), 190.

Chapter 5

1. Kristen A. Jenson and Gail Poyner, *Good Pictures, Bad Pictures: Porn-Proofing Today's Young Kids* (Richland, WA: Glen Cove Press, 2016).

Chapter 6

1. Josh McDowell Ministry and Barna Group, *The Porn Phenomenon: The Explosive Growth of Pornography and How It's Impacting Your Church, Life, and Ministry* (Plano, TX: Josh McDowell Ministry, 2016), cited in Chrissy Gordon, "Key Findings in Landmark Pornography Study Released," Josh McDowell Ministry, January 19, 2016, www.josh.org/key-findings-in-landmark-pornography-study-released/. Used by permission.

Chapter 8

1. Jennifer Rothschild, *Me, Myself, and Lies: A Thought Closet Makeover* (Nashville: LifeWay Christian Resources, 2007), 56.

Chapter 9

1. Pew Research Center, "Teens, Social Media, and Technology Overview 2015," April 9, 2015, www.pewinternet.org/2015/04/09/teens-social-media-technology-2015/.

Chapter 10

1. Chuck Hadad, "Why Some 13-Year-Olds Check Social Media 100 Times a Day," CNN, October 13, 2015, www.cnn.com/2015/10/05/health/being-13-teens-social-media-study/.
2. CNN pilot study, September 2014–October 2015, in *#BeingThirteen: Inside the Secret World of Teens*, CNN Special Report, hosted by Anderson Cooper, aired October 5, 2015. See also Marion K. Underwood and Robert Faris, "#Being Thirteen: Social Media and the Hidden World of Young Adolescents' Peer Culture," accessed November 13, 2016, www.documentcloud.org/documents/2448422-being-13-report.html.
3. Dove Evolution campaign, 2007, cited in Dove Self-Esteem Project, "The Evolution Video: How Images of Beauty Are Manipulated by the Media," June 2, 2013, http://selfesteem.dove.us/Articles/Video/Evolution_video_how_images_of_beauty_are_manipulated_by_the_media.aspx.
4. *Evaluating Information: The Cornerstone of Civic Online Reasoning* (Stanford, CA: Stanford History Education Group, 2016), 10, https://sheg.stanford.edu/upload/V3LessonPlans/Executive%20Summary%2011.21.16.pdf.
5. Sheryl Gay Stolberg and Richard Pérez Peña, "Wildly Popular App Kik Offers Teenagers, and Predators, Anonymity," *New York Times*, February 5, 2016, www.nytimes.com/2016/02/06/us/social-media-apps-anonymous-kik-crime.html?_r=0.

Chapter 11

1. Ravi Somaiya, "Nudes Are Old News at Playboy," *New York Times*, October 12, 2015, www.nytimes.com/2015/10/13/business/media/nudes-are-old-news-at-playboy.html?_r=0. Circulation statistics based on data from the Alliance for Audited Media.
2. Kassia Wosick, quoted in Chris Morris, "Things Are Looking Up in America's Porn Industry," NBC News, January 20, 2015, www.nbcnews.com/business/business-news/things-are-looking-americas-porn-industry-n289431.
3. Josh McDowell Ministry and Barna Group, *The Porn Phenomenon: The Explosive Growth of Pornography and How It's Impacting Your Church, Life, and Ministry* (Plano, TX: Josh McDowell Ministry, 2016), 22,

www.scribd.com/doc/296015049/The-Porn-Phenomenon-Findings. Used by permission.

4. Ana J. Bridges et al., "Aggression and Sexual Behavior in Best-Selling Pornography Videos: A Content Analysis Update," *Violence against Women* 16, no. 10 (October 2010), abstract, www.ncbi.nlm.nih.gov/pubmed/20980228/.
5. Gail Dines, "Is Porn Immoral? It Doesn't Matter: It's a Public Health Crisis," *Washington Post*, April 8, 2016, www.washingtonpost.com/posteverything/wp/2016/04/08/is-porn-immoral-that-doesnt-matter-its-a-public-health-crisis/?utm_term=.953d5ae585da.
6. Todd Weller, "Concurrent Resolution on the Public Health Crisis: 2016 General Session, State of Utah," S.C.R. 9, March 29, 2016, http://le.utah.gov/~2016/bills/static/SCR009.html.
7. *Pornography: A Public Health Crisis; How Pornography Fuels Sex Trafficking, Child Exploitation, and Sexual Violence* (Washington, DC: National Center on Sexual Exploitation, 2015), cover, http://endsexualexploitation.org/publichealth/.
8. Shmuley Boteach and Pamela Anderson, "Take the Pledge: No More Indulging in Porn," Opinion, *Wall Street Journal*, August 31, 2016, www.wsj.com/articles/take-the-pledge-no-more-indulging-porn-1472684658.
9. Advertising copy for Holly Madison, *Down the Rabbit Hole: Curious Adventures and Cautionary Tales of a Former Playboy Bunny* (New York: HarperCollins, 2015), in "Down the Rabbit Hole," Holly Madison, accessed October 10, 2016, http://hollymadison.com/product/down-the-rabbit-hole/.
10. Madison, *Down the Rabbit Hole*, 315.
11. Chris Morris, "Porn's Dirtiest Secret: What Everyone Gets Paid," CNBC, January 20, 2016, www.cnbc.com/2016/01/20/porns-dirtiest-secret-what-everyone-gets-paid.html.
12. Rachel Simmons, "Why More Teen Girls Are Getting Genital Plastic Surgery," *Time*, May 12, 2016, http://time.com/4327126/teen-girls-implants-genital-plastic-surgery/.
13. American Society for Aesthetic Plastic Surgery, "2014 Age Distribution for Cosmetic Procedures—Surgical," in *Cosmetic Surgery National Data Bank Statistics* (New York: ASAPS, 2014), 15, www.surgery.org/sites/default/files/2014-Stats.pdf; American Society for Aesthetic Plastic Surgery, "2015 Age Distribution for Cosmetic Procedures—Surgical," in *Cosmetic Surgery National Data Bank Statistics, 2015* (New York: ASAPS, 2015), 16, www.surgery.org/sites/default/files/ASAPS-Stats2015.pdf.

14. Research cited in Peg Streep, "What Porn Does to Intimacy," *Psychology Today*, July 16, 2014, www.psychologytoday.com/blog/tech-support/201407/what-porn-does-intimacy.
15. Anonymous, "What Porn Taught My Husband to Do During Sex," *Fight the New Drug* (blog), June 24, 2016, http://fightthenewdrug.org/what-porn-taught-my-husband-to-do-during-sex/.
16. Bradford Richardson, "Internet Porn Addicts Behave Like Drug Abusers as Enjoyment Turns into Compulsion," *Washington Times*, August 10, 2016, www.washingtontimes.com/news/2016/aug/10/internet-porn-addicts-behave-like-drug-abusers-as-/.

Chapter 12

1. Benjamin Shain, "Suicide and Suicide Attempts in Adolescents," *Pediatrics* (June/July 2016), http://pediatrics.aappublications.org/content/early/2016/06/24/peds.2016-1420, cited in "With Suicide Now Teens' Second-Leading Cause of Death, Pediatricians Urged to Ask about Its Risks," June 27, 2016, American Academy of Pediatrics, www.aap.org/en-us/about-the-aap/aap-press-room/Pages/With-suicide-Now-Teens%E2%80%99-Second-Leading-Cause-of-Death-Pediatricians-Urged-to-Ask-About-its-Risks.aspx.
2. Melonie Heron, "Deaths: Leading Causes for 2014," *National Vital Statistics Reports* 65, no. 5 (June 2016), www.cdc.gov/nchs/data/nvsr/nvsr65/nvsr65_05.pdf.
3. "Warning Signs of Suicide in Children and Teens—Topic Overview," WebMD, 2015, www.webmd.com/a-to-z-guides/tc/warning-signs-of-suicide-in-children-and-teens-topic-overview.
4. Shain, "Suicide and Suicide Attempts in Adolescents."
5. American Psychological Association, Stress in America survey, August 2013, cited in "American Psychological Association Survey Shows Teen Stress Rivals That of Adults," American Psychological Association, February 11, 2014, www.apa.org/news/press/releases/2014/02/teen-stress.aspx.
6. Kristen Magaldi, "Self-Harm Is on the Rise with Teens, and Needing Attention Has Nothing to Do with It," Medical Daily, June 25, 2015, www.medicaldaily.com/self-harm-rise-teens-and-needing-attention-has-nothing-do-it-339974.
7. Natasha Tracy, "Self-Harm and Suicide: Can Self-Injury Lead to Suicide?," HealthyPlace, August 26, 2016, http://healthyplace.com/abuse/self-injury/self-harm-and-suicide-can-self-injury-lead-to-suicide/.

8. Raychelle Cassada Lohmann, "Understanding Suicide and Self-Harm," *Psychology Today*, October 28, 2012, www.psychologytoday.com/blog/teen-angst/201210/understanding-suicide-and-self-harm.
9. Anat Brunstein Klomek, Andre Sourander, and Madelyn Gould, "The Association of Bullying and Suicide in Childhood to Young Adulthood: A Review of Cross-Sectional and Longitudinal Research Findings," *Canadian Journal of Psychiatry* 55, no. 5 (2010): 282–88, cited in Shain, "Suicide and Suicide Attempts in Adolescents."
10. S. Hinduja and J. W. Patchin, "Bullying, Cyberbullying, and Suicide," *Archives of Suicide Research* 14, no. 3 (2010), cited in David D. Luxton, Jennifer D. June, and Jonathan M. Fairall, "Social Media and Suicide: A Public Health Perspective," *American Journal of Public Health* 102, supp. 2 (May 2012), www.ncbi.nlm.nih.gov/pmc/articles/PMC3477910/.
11. Victor Luckerson, "Can You Go to Jail for Impersonating Someone Online?," *Time*, January 22, 2013, http://business.time.com/2013/01/22/can-you-go-to-jail-for-impersonating-someone-online/.
12. News 4 San Antonio, *Bullying Town Hall*, YouTube, accessed October 10, 2016, www.youtube.com/watch?v=Mh_R3uzs2AQ&feature=youtu.be.
13. I want to thank David Molak's family for granting permission to mention their experience in this chapter.
14. Madalyn Mendoza, "Alamo Heights Student Was a Victim of Bullying before Committing Suicide, Family Says," MySA.com, January 8, 2016, www.mysanantonio.com/news/local/article/Alamo-Heights-High-School-student-was-a-victim-of-6743320.php.
15. Richard Whittaker, "Anti-Bullying Bill Filed for Texas Legislature," *Austin Chronicle*, November 14, 2016, www.austinchronicle.com/daily/news/2016-11-14/anti-bullying-bill-filed-for-texas-legislature/.

Chapter 13

1. Kristen A. Jenson and Gail Poyner, *Good Pictures, Bad Pictures: Porn-Proofing Today's Young Kids* (Richland, WA: Glen Cove Press, 2016), chap. 2.
2. 2016 Monitoring the Future survey, "Drug Facts—High School and Youth Trends," National Institute on Drug Abuse, June 2016, www.drugabuse.gov/publications/drugfacts/high-school-youth-trends.
3. Nora D. Volkow, "Marijuana: Letter from the Director," National Institute on Drug Abuse, August 2016, www.drugabuse.gov/publications/research-reports/marijuana/letter-director.
4. Partnership for Drug-Free Kids, *Marijuana Talk Kit: What You Need to Know to Talk with Your Teen about Marijuana* (New York: Partnership

for Drug-Free Kids, n.d.), 5, www.acpeds.org/wordpress/wp-content/uploads/3.2015-Marijuana_Talk_Kit.pdf.

5. Donald Hagler and Jane Anderson, "Marijuana Use: Detrimental to Youth," American College of Pediatricians (April 2016), www.acpeds.org/marijuana-use-detrimental-to-youth.
6. "Prescription Drugs: What Is Prescription Drug Abuse?," National Institute on Drug Abuse for Teens, December 9, 2016, https://teens.drugabuse.gov/drug-facts/prescription-drugs.
7. Erick Messias et al., "Sadness, Suicide, and Their Association with Video Game and Internet Overuse among Teens: Results from the Youth Risk Behavior Survey 2007 and 2009," *Suicide and Life-Threatening Behavior* 41, no. 3 (June 2011): 307–15, cited in Benjamin Shain, "Suicide and Suicide Attempts in Adolescents," *Pediatrics* (June/July 2016), http://pediatrics.aappublications.org/content/early/2016/06/24/peds.2016-1420.
8. Vicky Rideout, *The Common Sense Census: Media Use by Tweens and Teens*, ed. Seeta Pai (San Francisco: Common Sense Media, 2015), www.commonsensemedia.org/sites/default/files/uploads/research/census_researchreport.pdf.
9. Adapted from Kellyann Petrucci, "Is Your Child Addicted to Electronics," *Huffington Post*, January 11, 2015, www.huffingtonpost.com/kellyann-petrucci/is-your-child-addicted-to_b_6075516.html.
10. Dr. Richard Graham, cited in Victoria Ward, "Toddlers Becoming So Addicted to iPads They Require Therapy," *Telegraph*, April 21, 2013, www.telegraph.co.uk/technology/10008707/Toddlers-becoming-so-addicted-to-iPads-they-require-therapy.html.
11. Caitlyn Gibson, "One Family's Story of a Son Lost to Video-Game Addiction and Their Struggle to Save Him," *Washington Post*, December 7, 2016, www.cleveland.com/entertainment/index.ssf/2016/12/video_games_are_more_addictive.html.
12. Gibson, "Son Lost to Video-Game Addiction."
13. Gibson, "Son Lost to Video-Game Addiction."
14. Kimberly Young, quoted in Gibson, "Son Lost to Video-Game Addiction."
15. Gibson, "Son Lost to Video-Game Addiction."
16. Study cited in Gibson, "Son Lost to Video-Game Addiction."
17. Gibson, "Son Lost to Video-Game Addiction."
18. "ESRB Ratings Guide," Entertainment Software Rating Board, accessed October 10, 2016, www.esrb.org/ratings/ratings_guide.aspx.

Chapter 14

1. Statistics cited in "Past Summary Ledgers: Gun Violence Archive 2015," Gun Violence Archive, accessed December 10, 2016, www.gunviolencearchive.org/past-tolls.
2. "General Methodology: Some Basic Definitions," Gun Violence Archive, accessed December 10, 2016, www.gunviolencearchive.org/methodology.
3. Rukmini Callimachi, "ISIS and the Lonely Young American," *New York Times*, June 27, 2016, www.nytimes.com/2015/06/28/world/americas/isis-online-recruiting-american.html?_r=0.

Chapter 15

1. Cynthia Tobias and Sue Acuña, *Middle School: The Inside Story* (Carol Stream, IL: Tyndale, 2014), 27, 29.
2. Tobias and Acuña, *Middle School*, 29, 30.
3. *Merriam-Webster Online Dictionary*, s.v. "prefrontal cortex," www.merriam-webster.com/dictionary/prefrontal%20cortex.
4. Mariam Arain et al., "Maturation of the Adolescent Brain," *Neuropsychiatric Disease and Treatment* 9 (April 2013): 449–61, www.ncbi.nlm.nih.gov/pmc/articles/PMC3621648/#b5-ndt-9-449.
5. "Understanding the Teen Brain," Stanford Children's Health, accessed December 10, 2016, www.stanfordchildrens.org/en/topic/default?id=understanding-the-teen-brain-1-3051.
6. Arian et al., "Maturation of the Adolescent Brain."
7. Arian et al., "Maturation of the Adolescent Brain."
8. Jay Giedd, National Institute of Mental Health, cited in transcript of *Frontline* documentary *Inside the Teenage Brain*, directed by Sarah Spinks (Spin Free Productions, 2002), www.pbs.org/wgbh/pages/frontline/shows/teenbrain/work/adolescent.html. See also Sara B. Johnson, Robert W. Blum, and Jay N. Giedd, "Adolescent Maturity and the Brain: The Promise and Pitfalls of Neuroscience Research in Adolescent Health Policy," *Journal of Adolescent Health* 45, no. 3 (September 2009): 216–21, www.ncbi.nlm.nih.gov/pmc/articles/PMC2892678/#R7.
9. Melissa Conrad Stöppler, "Puberty," MedicineNet.com, September 1, 2016, www.medicinenet.com/puberty/article.htm.
10. "Early Puberty: Causes and Consequences," WebMD.com, accessed November 18, 2016, www.webmd.com/children/guide/causes-symptoms#1.
11. "Teen Girls: Girls and Puberty," WebMD.com, accessed March 20, 2016, http://teens.webmd.com/girls/facts-about-puberty-girls.

12. "Teen Boys: Guys' FAQ about Puberty," WebMD.com, October 18, 2015, http://teens.webmd.com/boys/puberty-faq-for-guys.
13. "Teen Boys: Guys' FAQ about Puberty."
14. Dannah Gresh, *Six Ways to Keep the "Good" in Your Boy: Guiding Your Son from His Tweens to His Teens* (Eugene, OR: Harvest House, 2012), 147.
15. "Wet Dream FAQ," WebMD.com, December 22, 2015, http://teens.webmd.com/boys/wet-dream-faq?page=2.
16. Kristen A. Jenson and Gail Poyner, *Good Pictures, Bad Pictures: Porn-Proofing Today's Young Kids* (Richland, WA: Glen Cove Press, 2016).

Chapter 16

1. Kurt Smith, "Love Is a Choice More Than a Feeling," *World of Psychology* (blog), PsychCentral, July 20, 2015, https://psychcentral.com/blog/archives/2015/07/20/love-is-a-choice-more-than-a-feeling/.

Chapter 17

1. Dictionary.com, s.v. "masturbation," www.dictionary.com/browse/masturbation.
2. "Your Guide to Masturbation," WebMD, November 2, 2016, www.webmd.com/sex-relationships/guide/masturbation-guide?page=2.
3. Quoted and paraphrased from Dannah Gresh, *Six Ways to Keep the "Good" in Your Boy: Guiding Your Son from His Tweens to His Teens* (Eugene, OR: Harvest House, 2012), 146.

Chapter 18

1. *Merriam-Webster Online Dictionary*, s.v. "sexual orientation," www.merriam-webster.com/dictionary/sexual%20orientation.
2. *Merriam-Webster Online Dictionary*, s.v. "heterosexual," www.merriam-webster.com/dictionary/heterosexual.
3. *Merriam-Webster Online Dictionary*, s.v. "homosexual," www.merriam-webster.com/dictionary/homosexual.
4. *Merriam-Webster Online Dictionary*, s.v. "bisexual," www.merriam-webster.com/dictionary/bisexual.
5. Bella DePaulo, "Asexuals: Who Are They and Why Are They Important?," *Psychology Today*, December 23, 2009, www.psychologytoday.com/blog/living-single/200912/asexuals-who-are-they-and-why-are-they-important.
6. Emanuella Grinberg, "What It Means to Be Pansexual," CNN.com, November 9, 2015, www.cnn.com/2015/11/09/living/pansexual-feat/index.html.

7. Andrea Dresdale, "Miley Cyrus Opens Up about Identifying as Pansexual," ABC News, October 11, 2016, http://abcnews.go.com/Entertainment/miley-cyrus-opens-identifying-pansexual/story?id=42734994.
8. Dave Willis, *The Seven Laws of Love: Essential Principles for Building Stronger Relationships* (Nashville: Nelson Books, 2015), 146.

Chapter 19

1. *Merriam-Webster Online Dictionary*, s.v. "transgender," www.merriam-webster.com/dictionary/transgender.
2. American Psychological Association, "Guidelines for Psychological Practice with Transgender and Gender Nonconforming People," *American Psychologist* 70, no. 9 (December 2015): 834, www.apa.org/practice/guidelines/transgender.pdf.
3. Jessie Szalay, "Chromosomes: Definition and Structure," Live Science, February 19, 2013, www.livescience.com/27248-chromosomes.html.
4. Provisional information on LGBT health and wellness from the American Academy of Pediatrics (2014), in "Explaining Disorders of Sex Development and Intersexuality," HealthyChildren.org, November 21, 2015, www.healthychildren.org/English/health-issues/conditions/genitourinary-tract/Pages/Explaining-Disorders-of-Sex-Development-Intersexuality.aspx.
5. Margaret Schneider et al., *Answers to Your Questions about Individuals with Intersex Conditions* (Washington, DC: American Psychological Association, 2006), www.apa.org/topics/lgbt/intersex.aspx.
6. Consortium on the Management of Disorders of Sex Development, *Clinical Guidelines for the Management of Disorders of Sex Development in Childhood* (Rohnert Park, CA: Intersex Society of North America, 2006), www.dsdguidelines.org/files/clinical.pdf, cited in American College of Pediatricians, "Gender Ideology Harms Children," August 17, 2016, www.acpeds.org/the-college-speaks/position-statements/gender-ideology-harms-children.
7. Crossport Gender Support Group, quoted in Ellen Friedrichs, "What Causes a Transgender Identity?," About.com, February 8, 2016, http://gayteens.about.com/od/transgenderteenissues/f/transgender_causes.htm.
8. Susan Donaldson James, "Intersex Babies: Boy or Girl and Who Decides?," ABC News, March 17, 2011, http://abcnews.go.com/Health/intersex-children-pose-ethical-dilemma-doctors-parents-genital/story?id=13153068.
9. Schneider et al., *Answers to Your Questions*.
10. *Merriam-Webster Online Dictionary*, s.v. "eunuch," www.merriam-webster.com/dictionary/eunuch.

11. J. D. Douglas et al., *The New Bible Dictionary* (Grand Rapids: Eerdmans, 1962), 399.
12. *Understanding Transgender: Frequently Asked Questions about Transgender People* (Washington, DC: National Center for Transgender Equality, 2009), 2, www.transequality.org/sites/default/files/docs/resources/NCTE_UnderstandingTrans.pdf.
13. American Psychiatric Association, *Diagnostic and Statistical Manual of Mental Disorders*, 5th ed. (Arlington, VA: American Psychiatric Association, 2013), 455, cited in American College of Pediatricians, "Gender Ideology Harms Children."
14. "About," *First, Do No Harm: Youth Gender Professionals* (blog), accessed November 22, 2016, https://youthtranscriticalprofessionals.org/about/.
15. Cecilia Dhejne et al., "Long-Term Follow-Up of Transsexual Persons Undergoing Sex Reassignment Surgery: Cohort Study in Sweden," *PLOS One* 6, no. 2 (2011), cited in American College of Pediatricians, "Gender Dysphoria in Children: Summary Points," www.acpeds.org/gender-dysphoria-in-children-summary-points.

Chapter 20

1. Ashlyn Melton, "One Heartbroken Mother's Plea to Other Parents: Ask If There's a Gun in the House," *Today Show*, June 20, 2014, www.today.com/parents/one-heartbroken-mothers-plea-other-parents-ask-if-theres-gun-1D79822434.
2. Crimes Against Children Research Center statistics, cited in "Child Sexual Abuse Statistics," National Center for Victims of Crime, accessed November 22, 2016, https://victimsofcrime.org/media/reporting-on-child-sexual-abuse/child-sexual-abuse-statistics.
3. Gregory Ramey, "Are Sleepovers Safe?," *Get Family Wise with Dr. Ramey* (blog), accessed November 22, 2016, www.childrensdayton.org/cms/resource_library/files/b80f3410eb9da327/are_sleepovers_safe.pdf.

Chapter 21

1. *Urban Dictionary*, s.v. "frenemy," www.urbandictionary.com/define.php?term=frenemy.